Exploring the EVOLVING VIEW of GOD

From Ancient Israel to the Risen Jesus

John Michael Perry

SHEED & WARD

Franklin, Wisconsin

As an apostolate of the Priests of the Sacred Heart, a Catholic religious order, the mission of Sheed & Ward is to publish books of contemporary impact and enduring merit in Catholic Christian thought and action. The books published, however, reflect the opinion of their authors and are not meant to represent the official position of the Priests of the Sacred Heart.

1999

Sheed & Ward
7373 South Lovers Lane Road
Franklin, Wisconsin 53132
1-800-266-5564

Printed in the United States of America

Cover design: Karen Jones

Interior design: GrafixStudio, Inc.

Library of Congress Cataloging-in-Publication Data

Perry, John M., 1929–
Exploring the evolving view of God : from ancient Israel to the risen Jesus / by John Michael Perry.
p. cm.
ISBN 1-58051-067-1 (alk. paper)
1. God—Biblical teaching. 2. God—History of doctrines. I. Title.
BS544 .P44 1999
231' .09—dc21 99-016893
CIP

1 2 3 4 5 / 02 01 00 99

Exploring the EVOLVING VIEW of GOD

Contents

Introduction

1.

Contemporary scholarship informs us that the Bible contains a number of closely related but different ways of understanding God. This should not surprise us if we remember that many inspired authors had a hand in writing the Bible during a span of more than thirteen hundred years. There is, of course, a common denominator in all the varied statements which these authors wrote about God: It is the God of Israel who is continually being written about in changing historical circumstances. Nevertheless, the authors who wrote earlier in ancient Israel's history spoke of God in a manner noticeably less theologically advanced than those who wrote later.

The assertion that the ideas about God in the Bible are somewhat diverse and have undergone an evolution is usually disturbing to those who assume that God has dictated the words which express all these ideas. Such people reason that the words in the Bible should all agree and be totally free of contradiction or error if God has "written" them. But we will see below that there are a number of differing styles and viewpoints as well as historical errors in the Bible. This discovery, however, is no real cause for alarm. All we need to do is make a clarifying distinction about the way God communicated with the priests and prophets who wrote the Bible in God's service.

In the judgment of contemporary biblical scholarship, however, God did not dictate the words in the Bible. Rather, God inspired the priests and prophets to use words already present in their memories. God encouraged them to write for God by communicating the reality of divine Presence to them in an experienceable manner. The inspiring impact of their revelatory encounter with the reality of God enabled the priests and prophets to understand certain things about God and the God-human relationship with stunning new clarity and certainty. These new insights were implicit in God's Self-communication and in the historical circumstances in which God's Self-communication was experienced. In order to express these new insights for themselves and to others, the prophets employed language they had already acquired as social beings.

Many religious people in our time report that they also have experienced God's Presence stirring within them, communicating with them nonverbally through transcendent Love, ineffable Peace, and a Joy which ranges from subtle to ecstatic. This widespread experience suggests that if God presently communicates with humans in nonverbal fashion, then God probably communicated in essentially the same way with the priests and prophets of ancient Israel. The prophets, then, were moved by their nonverbal experience of God's Self-communication to supply the language needed to interpret their revelatory experience for themselves and for others.

Because the explanatory efforts of finite and fallible humans are always culturally conditioned and historically limited, it was inevitable that minor errors about the historical past sometimes occurred. Moreover, the prophets who wrote later in history understandably disagreed with the more limited ideas expressed by those who wrote earlier. Throughout history God is continually revealing the same fundamental reality to humans: the experience of divine Presence and Love. What is continually changing and slowly improving throughout history is our human ability to understand the profound implications of God's repeated Self-communication and the cultural-historical context in which the Bible was written over the centuries.

This contemporary model for God's Self-revelation enables us to explain the historical errors and contradictory statements found in the Bible. For example, the Book of Daniel calls the Persian King Darius a Mede instead of a Persian (Dan 5:31); it also confuses King Jehoiakim of Judah with his son Jehoiakin (Dan 1:1; cp. 2 Kgs 24:1–16). Such errors are inevitable if God has inspired fallible humans to speak for God to the best of their ability. But if God is dictating information to the prophets, the historical errors in the Bible are difficult to explain.

Also, when the law of Moses expresses its understanding of God's justice, it declares that God punishes children for the sins of their parents "to the third and fourth generation" (Ex 20:5). Nevertheless, when the prophet Ezekiel speaks for God centuries later, he insists that God never punishes children for the sins of their parents (Ezek 18:1–20, esp. 20). These contradictory statements are intelligible if they represent inspired interpretations of God's justice spoken in differing historical circumstances. If, however, they are construed as spoken directly by God into the physical or mental "ear" of the prophet, they become intolerable.

At the time when the view of God expressed in Exodus 20:5 was taught, the Israelite concept of justice was still dominated by the ancient practice of blood feud. Those who pursued justice by the standards of blood feud punished a crime by executing not only the guilty person but also every family member who shared the guilty person's tent or dwelling. And because three or four generations usually shared the same tent or dwelling, the justice sought through blood feud was usually collective, not individual. Such collective punishment was believed necessary to prevent retaliation. As long as a collective understanding of justice persisted in ancient Israel, her priests and prophets naturally assumed that God also would exercise collective justice.

Conversely, by the time that Ezekiel the prophet was inspired to speak for God (c. 580 B.C.), blood feud had largely been replaced, at least ideally, by the *law of talion.* The law of talion (*lex talionis*) required strict parity in matters of retribution for crime—an eye for an eye, a tooth for a tooth, and a person for a person (Ex 21:23–25). Ezekiel, therefore, was inspired to teach that God's justice will only punish the offending individual, not the individual's family members.

God had to wait patiently for the historical consciousness of the ancient Israelites to evolve from collective vengeance seeking to individual responsibility. Once a more evolved understanding of justice had arrived, God encouraged Ezekiel (nonverbally) to use it when teaching about divine justice.

The contemporary approach to understanding God's Self-revelation helps us see that God could cause the words in the Bible to be written without dictating them. Instead, God encouraged the authors of the Bible to write on behalf of God and to do the best job they were capable of at their time. God knew that eventually later inspired writers would modify the mistaken assumptions of earlier writers, and that educated readers of the Bible would learn to understand the need for such developments. (More will be said about the contemporary understanding of revelation in the final chapter.)

2.

The task before us will be more successfully accomplished if we consider evolving biblical views of God in the context of universal human striving to understand the mystery of Sacred Reality. We will begin our task in the first chapter by reflecting on the major historical stages of human attempts to visually interpret the reality of God.

Precritical (prephilosophic and prescientific) stages of visual thinking about Sacred Reality are mythological and naively literal in nature. Human efforts to understand God are naively literal as long as they fail to distinguish between "literal" and "figurative" language when explaining Sacred Reality. Such efforts are also mythological if they have not yet learned that invisible causes are not always supernatural in kind.

Briefly examining the major mythological stages of religious thinking will prepare us to understand the mythological ideas sometimes employed by the prophets of ancient Israel. It will also enable us to understand the world view of the nations with whom ancient Israel interacted. Whenever appropriate, the possibly unfamiliar ideas in the first chapter will be related to the concrete history of Israel in the Bible.

Chapters Two though Five will examine the manner in which ancient Israel and her ideas about God came into being during the period of the Judges (c. 1175-1040 B.C.), and continued to develop throughout the monarchy (c. 1040-587 B.C.). The review of Israel's history will be selective and will include only those persons and events deemed essential for comprehending her emergence as a nation, and the evolution of her thinking about God and God's creative purpose for humankind.

It has been assumed traditionally that the ancient Israelites began as a nation of monotheists. That view, however, is probably incorrect. It is much more likely that they were henotheists until very late during the Exile to Babylon in 587 B.C. It was probably not until the fifth decade of the Exile (c. 540 B.C.) that the Israelites began to understand and practice explicit monotheism. (Evidence which justifies these assertions will be presented in the second through the fifth chapters.)

A henotheist believes that there are many gods but that only one of these gods may be lawfully worshiped. (Henotheism is sometimes called monolatry). A monotheist, on the other hand, believes that only one God exists and that only this one God who is truly God should be worshiped. In practice, a henotheist will sometimes sound like a monotheist. But while it is true that a monotheistic tendency is latent in henotheism, it is also true that henotheism is not yet monotheism and must be carefully distinguished from it. (For more on henotheism, see the article by that title in the *Encyclopedia of Religion,* ed. by Mircea Eliade.)

Chapter Six will briefly examine the origin and major steps in the evolution of philosophical reasoning about God. The philosophical tradition of reflecting on the mystery of God with abstract concepts and logical distinctions has contributed greatly to our present ability to deliteralize and more adequately grasp the mythological and legendary language sometimes found in the Bible. Abstract and dialectical (rationally debated) reflection on the mystery of God began with the ancient Greek philosophers and continues to the present. We will also see that for many centuries, biblical ideas about God exercised profound influence on the thinking of Jewish and Christian philosophers.

Contemporary philosophical efforts to clarify the reality of God are best represented by Alfred North Whitehead (who died in 1947). We will briefly consider his dipolar interpretation of God's nature and discover that it is much closer to the biblical view of God than the monopolar interpretation of classical theism. (Classical theism was launched by Philo of Alexandria early in the first century of the Christian era. It is still the view of God preferred by many traditional Jewish and Christian thinkers.)

Chapter Seven will deal with the post-Exilic struggle between the "exclusivism" of the reforming priest-historians (which excluded from God's favor all but Jews who obeyed the law of Moses) and prophetic "universalism." At a time when national crisis had harshly narrowed priestly vision, the prophets of God's universal love were inspired (by their experience of God's love) to dissent vigorously. These prophets remembered that the law of Moses itself states that God's blessing will also be granted to righteous Gentiles from all the nations (see Gen 12:3).

Chapter Eight will explore the dramatic reversal in Israel's understanding of human destiny that arrived with apocalyptic theology. Apocalyptic theology taught that God will soon end the world and restore immortality to the righteous. Before the author of the Book of Daniel was inspired to teach apocalyptic hope to the ancient Jews (c. 165 B.C.), they did not believe that God would bestow Everlasting Life on humans after death. Adam's sin, they believed, had forever deprived us of such hope. The author of Daniel, however, assured faithful Jews that they would be blessed with Life Everlasting when God's reign over creation was fully restored at the end of history.

The Christian claim that God's definitive Self-disclosure was given to ancient Israel through Jesus of Nazareth will be discussed in Chapter Nine. This claim was initially made by Jesus' *Jewish* disciples. The Risen and Spirit-mediating Jesus, they proclaimed, is God's guarantee to Israel (and the nations) that the end-time salvation promised in the Book of Daniel is already being bestowed preliminarily. The Risen and Spirit-mediating Jesus, they announced, is a pledge given in advance by God that all of God's faithful children are empowered by the Gift of God's Spirit to follow Jesus through death into Risen Life.

It might seem odd to the reader to learn that a chapter dealing with the Risen Jesus is included in a book that intends to explore God's gradual Self-revelation to ancient Israel. The Spirit-mediating appearances of the Risen Jesus, however, were revelatory encounters of an *intra-Jewish* kind which definitively concluded God's Self-disclosure to ancient Israel. The Jewish disciples of the Risen Jesus experienced him as God's conclusive endorsement of the end-time salvation promised to Israel in the Book of Daniel. They did not immediately realize that the Good News that God had conclusively revealed to Israel was also meant for the Gentiles. It required time, prayerful reflection on the Scriptures, and God's encouragement for the apostles to come to that realization (see Acts 10). It was not until the period between A.D. 85–100 that a definitive separation occurred between the Christian "Church" and the Jewish "synagogue."

The concluding chapter will provide contemporary answers to questions usually raised by the ideas presented in the first nine chapters.

Readers are urged to open their Bibles and relate the explanations being provided to biblical texts referenced but not quoted. These texts will corroborate and clarify the ideas being presented. Readers who ignore this advice will fail to fully grasp much of what is being explained.

The Scripture quotations in this book are taken from the Revised Standard Version. Whenever they depart from that version they are the author's own translation.

Questions for Review and Discussion

1. How does contemporary biblical scholarship think that God "caused" the words in the Bible to be written?

2. Why should we not be surprised if we sometimes find diverse views about God expressed in the Bible?

3. What is a henotheist?

4. What is a monotheist?

5. Why will a henotheist sometimes sound very much like a monotheist?

Chapter One

A Brief Overview of Efforts to Visualize the Sacred

1.

Human beings have always preferred to reduce any problem they are trying to understand to a visual model. We humans predictably proceed in this fashion because our sense of sight gives us the most accurate and detailed information about the world in which we must survive. Humans at all times and places, therefore, have manifested a profound preference for picture language. When students tell a teacher they cannot "see" what the teacher's statements mean, they are asking for concrete examples or pictures to clarify the teacher's abstract or vague language. Most of us readily understand why "a picture is worth a thousand words."

The philosophers tell us that we are destined to seek and create visual models because of the bidimensional manner in which we experience reality. We begin our encounter with reality in the empirical realm where we perceive things directly and clearly through our five senses. Being human, however, we are not confined to the empirical realm of experience as animals are. Through the power of inference, we also have indirect access to a *transempirical* realm of experience. (The term *transempirical* signifies our indirect or secondary experience arrived at by inference when we reflect on the implications of our empirical or sensory experience.) All creative advances in understanding occur in the transempirical realm. For in this realm our power of intuitive reason enables us to transcend the sensory surface of perceived realities by reflecting indirectly on their "deeper" implications and meanings.

Whenever we engage in reflection we always import abstract ideas already acquired from past experience to facilitate our efforts to "see" or understand the deeper meaning latent in empirical data. This indirect mental probing is called "reflection" because it is somewhat like the way we peer at our reflection in a mirror. The mirror gives us additional access to something we already know—ourselves. But it lets us know ourselves from a perspective not ordinarily accessible. Consequently, we can study ourselves carefully in an indirect light and discover things that we could not know without the reflective power of the mirror.

By analogy, our reason can be thought of as possessing "reflective" power comparable to that of a mirror. This reflective power enables us to "see" empirical data we are trying to understand in the indirect light of our past experiences. Shining the light of insight gained from past experience on present questions is called "inference." To infer means "to bring in" or "to import" past learning to solve or clarify some current problem. Reflectively consulted insights from the past help us to "see" below the surface of our empirical experience in order to "under-stand" its transempirical implications.

For example, if we are walking along a beach and see human footprints in the wet sand, we know that the footprints are effects which imply the recent presence of the human who caused them. When we make such a transempirical recognition, we are guided (unconsciously or consciously) by two fundamental insights called the *law of causality* and the *law of resemblance.* The law of causality is our past experience assuring us that "every effect has a cause." The law of resemblance assures us that "every effect resembles its cause." Most of us have learned from life that these laws are true even when we cannot see the cause in question (because it is either absent or invisible by its nature).

Usually an effect is such that our experience enables us to recognize what its invisible cause is probably like. Lessons we have already learned quickly suggest themselves by association. But sometimes it is difficult to decide about the probable nature of an invisible cause because its effect seems highly dissimilar to any effect we have heretofore learned to under-stand. In such a case there is nothing familiar in our memories that can easily assist us.

We are not, however, totally ignorant of the mysterious cause being considered. To begin with, we know its effect. We might say that we have experienced the effect directly and empirically and its cause indirectly and transempirically. In addition, we are familiar with the law of resemblance which assures us that every effect (albeit dimly) resembles its cause.

Although these initial bits of knowledge are far from fully satisfying, they nevertheless enable us to begin searching for a visual model which will illustrate (in a general and approximating way) the mysterious cause being considered. Such a model helps us satisfy our desire to "see" what the invisible cause is probably like and to better under-stand it. For an approximating model lets us go beneath the surface of some puzzling effect and grasp the nature of its hidden cause in preliminary and tentative fashion. If and when we acquire additional insight into the nature of the invisible cause, we can revise our earlier model in the direction of greater adequacy.

At this stage in our discussion it would be helpful if we used another concrete example to illustrate the abstract ideas being considered. In other words, our mind's "eye" would probably like to "see" more pictures that shed light on the problem before us. Humans who lived when *polytheistic* interpretations of natural forces were in vogue knew nothing about scientific explanations of lightning and thunder. Their experience of these phenomena was undeniably real and even terrifying. But these phenomena were mysterious because their cause could not be directly perceived. Such awe-inspiring mysteries, however, could not be left unsolved. For we humans know that we are responsible for under-standing and avoiding those things in our world which can harm us. Lightning, therefore, had to be explained so that anxious humans could try to influence its cause and either prevent or control its dangerous recurrence.

How, then, did the ancients (including ancient Israel) explain the cause of lightning? Without modern science to explain invisible causes, they had no other choice but to employ the mythological mode of interpretation. A *myth* is a precritical explanation in story form which answers some question for humans. A mythically conceived answer always explains invisible causal power by attributing it (analogically) to supernatural beings.

Ancient mythmakers correctly understood that their attempts to illustrate invisible causes had to be guided by what we now call the laws of causality and resemblance. But they still believed that all invisible causes were supernatural. All that the ancients knew about the cause of lightning was its enormously powerful and destructive effect. They correctly inferred, therefore, that the mysterious cause must be one that possessed enormous destructive power.

Aided by the law of resemblance, the ancients intuitively scanned their memories for a similar effect whose cause they could see. Their intuitive assumption was that if there is something similar about two effects there must also be "something" similar about their causes. They could then use the visible cause as a symbol or model which would tell them "something" about the invisible cause being considered. (They also personified any force they were trying to understand and assumed that it possessed purposeful intelligence like but greater than their own.)

When the ancients consulted their memories for a familiar causal pattern which seemed to approximate the destructive force of lightning, they recalled the destructive power of a wrathful and punitive father (especially as experienced by a small and terrified child). Such a father could easily be associated with an angry and destructive warrior, for he frequently was a warrior. The ancients concluded, then, that the source of lightning was a superhuman being or god whom they thought of as a divine warrior. They surmised that this divine warrior, when angered, could hurl lightning bolts with destructive force just as earthly warriors could hurl spears at their enemies. Thus, lightning became understandable as a supernatural weapon hurled by an angry god to warn or punish mortals.

All ancient peoples of whom we have knowledge believed (at the polytheistic stage of explaining invisible causes) in a superhuman storm god who specialized in producing lightning and thunder (Zeus, Jupiter, Thor, Woden, Hadad, Baal, Marduk). The biblical record indicates that the ancient Israelites also thought of their covenant God, *Yahweh,* as a storm God whose presence and power were manifested by a cloud emitting lightning and thunder. (Yahweh is God's name revealed to Moses in Exodus 3:15.) In the Book of Exodus, Yahweh is specifically described as possessing such attributes when the initial encounter of Israel with her covenant God is described.

The Book of Exodus depicts Yahweh as wrapped in a storm cloud atop Mount Sinai. The lightning that flashes from the cloud is thought of as a display of God's glorious power, and the thunder is said to be God's voice addressing Moses (and the Israelites) in the valley below. Also, the wind howling through the crags of Mount Sinai is understood to be the mournful sound of a ramshorn trumpet blown by an angel to warn the Israelites against treading on the holy mountain while God is in residence at its top:

> On the morning of the third day there were thunders and lightnings, and a thick cloud upon the mountain, and a very loud trumpet blast, so that all the people who were in the camp trembled. Then Moses brought the people out of the camp to meet God; and they took their stand at the foot of the mountain. . . . And as the sound of the trumpet grew louder and louder, Moses spoke, and God answered him in thunder.
> (Ex 19:16–17,19)

Later in Israel's history (c. 600 B.C.) the prophet Habbakuk likened Yahweh to a divine warrior who used lightning bolts as fiery weapons directed against Israel's enemies:

> You stripped the sheath from your bow and put the arrow to the string. . . . The sun and moon stood still in their habitation at the light of your arrows as they sped, at the flash of your glittering spear. You bestrode the earth in fury, you trampled the nations in anger.
> (Hab 3:9a, 11–12)

2.

Guided by their intuitive awareness of the laws of causality and resemblance, humans everywhere in history have concluded that there is a Sacred or Supernatural dimension which manifests itself to us through the powerful and mysterious phenomena we encounter in our world. The Sacred Power inhabiting this dimension is judged to be vastly superior to the power possessed by frail and mortal humans. Sacred Power is everlasting and totally secure. It is not threatened by nonbeing as fragile humans are. (Average life expectancy in the early Stone Age was eighteen years.)

The Numinous Beings who inhabit the Sacred Realm are not subject to the destructive forces periodically unleashed in our world (numinous = supernatural and awe-inspiring). Rather, these Sacred Beings are judged to be the ambivalent source of destructive power as well as the Sacred Order on which all life in our world depends: night and day, the seasons, the annual renewal of vegetation, the mysterious process of human birth and death. Sacred Power is thought to determine whatever well-being humans may hope for as well as the woes that periodically befall us. (For more on the dimension of the Sacred see *The Sacred and the Profane,* by Mircea Eliade.)

When perplexing forces in nature caused unusual phenomena to occur (storms, floods, droughts, earthquakes), these phenomena were explained as manifestations of a Mysterious Reality beyond the realm of perceivable and transitory beings. It was, of course, natural that humans should try to name, understand, and influence this Sacred Reality, for it seemed evident that their survival depended on Its dispensations.

Our distant forebears were essentially right when they concluded that a dimension of Sacred Power must be inferred as the Ultimate Cause of all the mysterious phenomena which occur in our world. These precritical thinkers, however, had not yet learned to distinguish between invisible causal power which is truly Supernatural or Ultimate, and invisible forces which are merely aspects of nature. The failure to make this distinction is the basic error of mythological thinkers.

It is important to recognize that the mythological explanations of the ancients are not completely mistaken. Myths are not pure nonsense or diabolical attempts to lead humans away from biblical monotheism. As we proceed, it will become clear that the Bible itself uses mythical models or analogies to teach about monotheism. When we make an honest effort to understand the historically limited presuppositions of mythical thinkers, we soon realize that they are sincerely striving after truth and attempting to be logical. Our present stage of explaining invisible causal powers is indebted to and has built upon the creative efforts of ancient mythmakers.

3.

The process by which humans creatively imagine and name the Sacred Power which manifests itself in the world has undergone a number of fascinating changes in the course of history. Mircea Eliade, the renowned twentieth-century historian of religions, advises us in the introduction to his *Patterns in Comparative Religion* that these changes do not come about or evolve in a monolithically uniform or synchronous manner. Such changes always depend on a constellation of factors peculiar to a specific culture at a particular time and place. They never happen in the same way or at the same time, they always overlap with earlier paradigms, and they sometimes skip stages found elsewhere because of extraneous influences.

Throughout most of the early Stone Age (from human beginnings until c. 35,000 B.C.) there was probably a varied amalgam of *animism, totemism,* and *ancestor worship.* Ancestor worship was very likely encouraged by the appearance of deceased family members in dreams. Archaic thinkers were not able to distinguish clearly between waking and dreaming states. Their nighttime experiences probably convinced them that the spirits of the dead were still nearby and able to exercise either benevolent or malign influence over the living. It seemed imperative, therefore, to employ rituals which would encourage ancestral spirits to act beneficently and prevent them from causing harm.

Deceased ancestors were frequently believed to have power to cause fertility or to inflict disease and death. But they were not ordinarily thought of as Sacred Beings. Moreover, one did not have to decide what visual form to give them because they already possessed a form when they appeared in dreams or were remembered. It seems fitting, therefore, to omit ancestral spirits from the remainder of our discussion.

Before we consider the major paradigms created to interpret the reality of Sacred Power, it would be beneficial to reflect briefly on the way naive psychological projection entered into such interpretations. The evidence provided by cultural anthropology indicates that very early humans, since they had learned very little about advanced ways of understanding their world, were extremely childlike in many respects, even as adults. They unconsciously projected their own inner ability to think and freely decide onto every significant bodily being which they encountered. Since they experienced rational consciousness within their own bodies, they seem initially to have concluded that all bodily beings enjoyed inner consciousness like or superior to their own. For these early humans, the entire universe was alive and personal.

An analogy from contemporary experience might prove helpful. Very young children in our society still have not mastered the distinction between animate and inanimate beings or reasoning and nonreasoning beings. Consequently, they unwittingly project their own conscious life onto all other bodily beings. They commonly think, for example, that a household pet can fully comprehend all the words they speak to it.

And if, through poor coordination, they accidentally strike a hand against a piece of furniture (which, after all, usually has "legs" and frequently "arms" and "backs"), they conclude that the inanimate object has lashed out at them (as siblings or playmates sometimes do). It is not uncommon to observe a child striking or scolding a piece of furniture in response to an assumed affront. In such a case the inexperienced child is unconsciously projecting his or her own inner life onto inanimate objects. For untold millennia adult humans related to nonreasoning and inanimate beings in essentially the same way as the children in our example. It was such naive projecting that led to the very early interpretations of Sacred Power, called "animism" or "totemism."

Animistic thinkers usually assume that all physical objects possess consciousness essentially like their own. More importantly, they believe that certain large, impressive and, above all, permanent beings in their world—a mountain, the forest, a river, the ocean, certain large rocks, the sun, moon, and stars and, above all, the earth itself—are filled with the Superior Power of permanence and are, therefore, sacred or everlasting beings. Which of such beings are invested with numinous power depends on a society's geographical location and historical experiences.

Because of increased experience and slowly developing technical skills, the numinous awe originally engendered by the mysterious permanence of certain beings eventually began to wane. Other interpretations of the Sacred then began to suggest themselves. Societies with more advanced insights gradually realized that seemingly "permanent" physical beings were actually devoid of consciousness and were not truly superior to "conscious" beings. In such societies, therefore, large and permanent physical realities were no longer the preferred models for visualizing Sacred Reality.

Long-held beliefs, however, are abandoned very slowly. Even after the ancient Greeks had decided to visualize Sacred Reality in the form of superhuman gods and goddesses, they still retained vestiges of their much earlier animistic thinking. Homer tells us in the *Iliad* (c. 850 B.C.?) that when Achilles angered the Sacred River Xanthus, the River rose up like a tidal wave and wrathfully pursued Achilles across the plain of Troy.

There are still a few places in the world where mountains, especially if they are volcanically active, are venerated as Sacred Beings or gods. The Pygmy people who dwell in the forests of equatorial Africa are responding animistically when they assure anthropologists that their Mother and Father the Forest provide them with all they need for a secure existence. The seemingly permanent and always-providing forest is still a viable animistic symbol for Sacred Reality in the limited experience of these relatively isolated humans. This example illustrates that a geographically remote environment sufficiently endowed with life's necessities and relatively devoid of menacing predators will encourage the perpetuation of a very early mode of interpretation of Sacred Power like animism.

4.

Totemism, broadly understood, is the belief that supernatural animals have given birth to all animal species on earth, including humans. The Sacred Totems also watch over and provide for the living beings which they have engendered. Totemistic interpretations of Sacred Power presuppose that humans do not yet have an awareness of their mental superiority to animals.

Initially, humans probably judged that many animal species were superior to them. For (one on one), the great cave bear, a large feline, or a huge crocodile seemed much better equipped by nature for hunting and killing than a human. Large predators are protected by a tough hide or a thick coat of hair. They are always armed with sharp instruments of destruction (claws, fangs, horns, hooves), and are usually stronger and faster than a thin-skinned, hairless, and barefooted human. Humans obviously lack the physical advantages possessed by many animals.

It would have seemed to very early humans (those from human beginnings until c. 35,000 B.C.) that they were among the underdeveloped and underequipped runts of the animal kingdom. For that reason they created totemistic myths which explained that the Sacred Totems who had originally given birth to humans observed their plight and took pity on them: The Totems taught humans how to make weapons to compensate for their physical disadvantage when competing with other predators for food.

During the extensive period when all humans were hunters and gatherers (from human beginnings until c. 8,000 B.C.), many of them had to compete with (and escape from) fierce animals. Humans, quite understandably, admired and envied the physical prowess of various animals. They also believed that these animals possessed rational intelligence like or superior to that of humans. During this period, the most powerful beings in the experience of humans would have been physically superior animals. It was for that reason, then, that they visualized Sacred Power in the form of supernatural animals. Humans always choose as their preferred model for representing Sacred Power that being which currently seems most powerful.

But humans who were not seriously menaced by large predators focused on the mysterious beings in their world which they thought of as possessing the power of permanence (mountains, oceans, forests, rivers, earth, sun, moon). These permanent beings seemed far more powerful and impressive than the relatively nonthreatening animal species of that region. Certain of these mysterious permanent beings, therefore, were experienced as *Numinous* (Supernatural and Mysterious) and were judged animistically to be the primary manifestations of Sacred Power.

Frequently, both animistic and totemistic interpretations of Sacred Reality coexisted in early societies. The circumstances already mentioned would have determined which of the two interpretations became primary in a particular geographical region. Some Australian aborigines, for example, believe that their world received its familiar form when a Supernatural Crocodile flew over the land thrashing its powerful tail. Wherever its tail struck the earth a valley was cleft and surrounding mountains were raised. When this Sacred Crocodile had completed its mythical journey, it flew into (and remained present in) a massive rock which rests on a valley floor. This rock is considered Sacred by the aborigines; they bury their dead in a large hollow at its base. Such a creation myth combines both totemistic and animistic views of Sacred Power. But the earth-forming activity of the powerful Crocodile Totem would seem to be primary and its subsequent residence in a huge Sacred Rock is secondary.

5.

Archeological discoveries and carbon dating technology have demonstrated that somewhere between 35,000 and 25,000 B.C. a major shift took place in human efforts to visualize Sacred Reality: Humans began to create small (therefore portable) figurines which depicted Mother Earth as a Super-human Female. One of the best known of these sacred figurines is called the "Venus of Willendorf," named for the town in Austria near its discovery. The limestone figurine has been dated to c. 25,000 B.C. and is eleven centimeters tall.

The Venus of Willendorf bears little resemblance to her classical Greek descendants, for she has an extremely obese and rotund body. She is depicted as the Sacred Source of the Power which providentially sustains all living beings. It is manifestly "She" who presides over the mystery of fecundity in the world. And the huge pendulous breasts being proffered by her arms suggest that all living beings are nourished by her inexhaustible maternity.

Moreover, the Willendorf figurine has a large, round head strangely devoid of features. We know from contemporaneous cave paintings and carvings that the artists of that period could render the likeness of animals with canny accuracy and detail. The figurine's creator, therefore, did not intend to represent a *human* female.

The surreal head of the Numinous female figure is probably intended to convey that the Great Mother of all living beings is, in reality, a faceless mystery. We all know the great round surface of her body, for we all live on her sustaining surface within the great circle of the horizon. We also know, however, that even though we are supported and nourished by Mother Earth, we never see her mysterious face, for she is larger by far than all the forms of life which she mysteriously sustains.

Many similar figurines have been found from Europe to Siberia. Some of them are not as corpulent as the Willendorf Venus, but they all share her symbolically exaggerated female anatomy and represent the same Great Mother. These sacred figurines were probably used ritually to invoke Mother Earth's help during the dangers of childbirth and to obtain fertility both for humans and the animal herds on which communities of hunter-gatherers depended.

At Laussel in France, a relief carving of the Great Mother holding a curved animal horn (thought to be a "horn of plenty") was found in a daylit cave whose dark inner chambers contain paintings of animals hunted by humans. The Great Mother was probably associated with the animals painted in the cave because she was believed to be the Sacred Source of all living beings and their fertility. As such, her assistance at the hunt was likely sought through a ritual in which the cave paintings of animal herds played an essential role. Through some form of "suggestive magic" ritually enacted in the cave, a community of hunters probably signified to Mother Earth their hope that she would provide the game they required for continued existence. To these hunters, a cavern deep within the Earth would have suggested Mother Earth's life-spawning womb.

At that stage in evolving human consciousness, developing human technology and hunting strategies had begun to suggest to humans that they were, in fact, not inferior but far superior to all the animals in the world. It was then that human imagination was especially engaged by the astonishing ability of women to give birth and nourishment to offspring. Women were perceived as the most powerful members of the most powerful species of living beings.

To fully appreciate the awe aroused in archaic societies by the child-bearing power of women, we must recall that at the "matriarchal" stage of human consciousness humans did not yet understand biological reproduction. They assumed that women became pregnant with no assistance from men. Everyone believed that women conceived, gave birth to, and nursed their offspring by means of female magic. Female magic, they concluded, was a mysterious gift of power that Mother Earth conferred on women. Precisely how this power was activated was variously explained by different societies.

Not until the beginning of the late Stone Age (between 9,000 and 8,000 B.C.) did humans discover (through their early efforts at animal husbandry and agriculture) that a male contributes a "seed" (Latin = semen) which fertilizes a female's "egg" (Latin = ovum) when conception takes place. Prior to that discovery, the Great Mother did not require a divine consort to fertilize her before she could bestow the gift of life. She was usually regarded as a Virgin-

Mother who caused the mysteries of regeneration and fecundity solely by her own Sacred Power.

It seemed appropriate, therefore, to envision the Sacred Reality which imparts life to all living beings as a Supernatural Woman who is the Great Mother of all the living. For many millennia human communities had animistically personified and worshiped the immense and sustaining reality of the Earth as Sacred Mother. But now the incipiently polytheistic step was taken of explicitly likening the Earth's Sacred Maternity to that of a superhuman Mother.

Polytheism is the stage of explaining Sacred Power which assumes that such power is possessed and dispensed by many gods and goddesses in superhuman form. When speaking of the earliest stage of polytheism, we must distinguish between its pre-agricultural phase (before c. 8,000 B.C.) when the Great Mother bestowed fertility without need of a fecundator, and its agricultural phase (after c. 8,000 B.C.) when she required the cooperation of a divine husband. (For more on the Great Mother and her symbolism see Erick Neumann's *The Great Mother* and *The Origins and History of Consciousness.*)

6.

As indicated above, the developments of agriculture and animal husbandry brought another major shift in the way humans visualized Sacred Power. When humans surmised that males were contributing to the fertility of females, their belief in the myth of female magic receded, and the myths that explained the earth's fertility had to be revised. Mother Earth, they now concluded, must unite in Sacred Marriage with Father Sky in order to become fruitful.

(Egypt provides an interesting exception to the general rule that the earth is viewed as maternal and the sky as paternal. In Egypt the mother goddess, Nut, was identified with the Sky, and her husband, Geb, was the Earth who lay beneath her. The Egyptians believed that the vast "stream" of stars in the "Milky Way" was a stream of divine milk flowing from Nut's maternal breasts.)

Eventually, Father Sky and Mother Earth produced a family of divine offspring who personified the various forces of nature involved in the annual cycle. It was then that the fertility of fields, flocks, and wives (all of great concern to farmers) became the special province of a god and goddess who specialized in causing fertility.

The goddess of fertility was no longer identified with Mother Earth. Instead, she was usually a daughter of Mother Earth's successor, the mother goddess—the divine mother who had ultimately given birth to all the gods. The fertility god, on the other hand, was usually a storm god and the son or grandson of the supreme god in a people's pantheon. (The supreme god was ordinarily the sky god who became increasingly less important after the discovery of agriculture and its dependence on rain which fell from storm clouds).

To explain the yearly renewal of vegetation, the priests of agricultural societies created the myth of the annually renewed Sacred Marriage between the god and goddess of fertility. Because this popular myth had a pronounced impact on the behavior of the ancient Israelites when they entered the land of Canaan, we will consider the Canaanite version. Israel's pre-Exilic priests and prophets (those prior to the Exile in 587 B.C.) had to do battle continually with this myth. We will see that a general knowledge of the Canaanite fertility myth sheds essential light on many biblical stories and prophetic denunciations of Israelite farmers.

The Canaanite myth of fertility explained that the seasonal rains began to fall in late autumn and continued until spring because the storm god Baal (known as Hadad in Syria and Adad in Mesopotamia) was renewing his Sacred Marriage with his divine consort, the fertility goddess. Depending on the region, Baal's consort was called Astarte or Anath. We shall see in a later chapter that in addition, the Israelites possibly paired Asherah, the consort of the god El, with Baal.

The Canaanite literature discovered at ancient Ugarit in nearby Phoenicia does not envision Asherah as a fertility goddess. Instead, she is regarded as the mother of the gods and the wife of El, the chief god in the Canaanite pantheon. Archeological evidence suggests, however, that in the land of Canaan she may also have been worshiped as a fertility goddess. (For more information, see the article "Asherah" in the *Anchor Bible Dictionary*.)

According to Canaanite myth, Baal came annually as the Storm Clouds of the rainy season and poured his fertilizing seed (in the form of rain) into the receptive womb of the fertility goddess. (Baal was also symbolized as a roaring and fertilizing bull: storm clouds = thunder = roaring bull = fertilizing power). It was this sacred union between Baal and his variously named consort that produced the renewal of vegetation in the spring and its fruition in the summer.

The Canaanites regularly offered gifts of sacrificial food to the fertility gods to win their favor. In addition, the Canaanites engaged in a ritual practice detested by the priests and prophets of Israel—sacred prostitution.

Sacred prostitution (an oxymoron by present moral standards) involved a ritual act of sexual intercourse with a *hierodule* (sacred slave) who served at one of the sanctuaries of the fertility gods. Such sacred slaves might be people captured in war, older children purchased from parents suffering extreme economic hardship, or adults who sold their service at fertility shrines to escape from a life of poverty. The law of Moses was responding to this practice when it strictly prohibited cult prostitution:

> There shall be no cult prostitutes of the daughters of Israel, neither shall there be a cult prostitute of the sons of Israel. You shall not bring the hire of a female prostitute or the wages of a male prostitute into the house of Yahweh your God in payment for any vow. For both of these are an abomination to Yahweh your God.
> (Deut 23:17)

The practice of ritual intercourse was intended as a form of "suggestive" magic. It was meant to gain the attention and favor of the god Baal and suggest that he renew his sacred union with the fertility goddess. By such means, the worshiper believed, one could arouse and influence Baal with magical efficacy and cause the power of fertility to flow into one's fields and flocks.

The Canaanite practice of consorting with a sacred prostitute at the time of planting, harvesting, or shearing underlies the unusual story in the Book of Genesis about Jacob's son Judah and Judah's widowed daughter-in-law Tamar. The language of the Hebrew account indicates that Tamar disguised herself as a "sacred" or cult prostitute when she sought to circumvent Judah's refusal to provide her with a husband and an opportunity to bear children (Gen 38:6–26).

7.

The proliferation of gods and goddesses in superhuman form after the discovery of agriculture eventually led to the creation of eerie images for some of the gods. By 3,000 B.C. many hybrid images of gods and goddesses had begun to appear which combined supernatural-human and supernatural-animal attributes.

Some of these gods were depicted with a superhuman body and the head of a supernatural animal. Others were given a superhuman head and the body of a supernatural animal. Sometimes a god's body was entirely that of a supernatural animal (lingering totemism) or was a composite of various animal parts.

Examples of this mode of visualizing Sacred Beings can be found almost everywhere in the ancient world. The region, however, where a wealth of such images was created and preserved is Egypt. Ancient Egypt's geographic isolation, extraordinarily static culture, ample supply of stone for temples and tombs, and exceptionally dry climate all contributed to the abundance and remarkable preservation of its images of the gods.

H. Frankfort has observed in his *Ancient Egyptian Religion,* that the Egyptians seem to have given animal characteristics to their gods for several reasons. To begin with, animals could engender a special kind of numinous awe because of their strange "otherness." This otherness could readily suggest the uncanniness of Sacred Reality.

In addition, animals could more easily call to mind the time-transcending permanence of Sacred Beings than humans. For each human is experienced as highly individual and more unlike than like others. But a mysterious sameness and continuity characterize the members of an animal species. Animals, therefore, could visually connote the enduring Sacred Power which keeps the world from chaos by insuring its fundamental order and stability.

Conversely, once the stylized superhuman images for the gods began to be established as artistic conventions, it became difficult to distinguish one god from another. For example, since the goddess Isis and her sister Nephthys were depicted with highly similar superhuman images, their distinct identities had to be indicated by placing specifying symbols or hieroglyphs atop the head of each. The gods could be more easily identified when a physical trait of an animal associated with a particular god (more frequently the animal's head) was joined to that god's *hieratic* (sacred and stylized) form.

8.

After ancient Israel embraced the law of Moses, she officially rejected the use of any kind of physical image to represent her covenant God, Yahweh:

> You shall not make for yourself a graven image, or any likeness of anything that is in heaven above, or that is in the earth beneath, or that is in the water under the earth. (Ex 20:4)

We, nevertheless, find several supernatural beings in the service of Israel's God who possessed both human and animal characteristics—the *cherubim* and *seraphim.* Israel learned of these composite beings from neighboring peoples who regarded them as lesser deities.

Throughout the Ancient Near East, the cherubim were thought of as minor gods who guarded sacred places and objects for the major gods. In post-Mosaic Israel, however, the cherubim were demoted to angelic status and regarded as supernatural creatures who served Yahweh. The oldest of the two creation stories in Genesis tells us that Yahweh posted two cherubim to guard the entrance to the Garden of Eden after Adam was expelled:

> He drove out the man; and at the east of the Garden of Eden he placed the cherubim, and a flaming sword which turned every way, to guard the way to the tree of life. (Gen 3:24)

Cherubim could be variously depicted, but those which decorated Solomon's temple and guarded the ark of the Covenant were probably given a superhuman head, a supernatural lion's body, and the wings of a supernatural eagle. The same is true of the smaller images of the cherubim attached to the top of the golden lid (the mercy seat) of the ark of the Covenant (Ex 25:18–22):

> And you shall make two cherubim of gold; of hammered work you shall make them, on the two ends of the mercy seat. . . . The cherubim shall spread out their wings above, overshadowing the mercy seat with their wings, their faces one to another. (Ex 25:18, 20a)

The two cherubim faced each other and extended their wings before themselves to provide a throne for God's invisible presence to rest upon (Ps 80:1; 99:1; Is 37:16; Ez 9:3):

> Yahweh reigns; let the peoples tremble! He sits enthroned upon the cherubim; let the earth quake. (Ps 99:1)

In addition, King Solomon commissioned two large gilded statues of cherubim (each fifteen feet in height and width) for the Holy of Holies in Yahweh's Jerusalem temple. They were stationed in the innermost sanctuary so that the ark could be placed beneath their protective wings:

1 Kgs 6:27–28

> He put the cherubim in the innermost part of the house; and the wings of the cherubim were spread out so that a wing of one touched the one wall, and the wing of the other cherub touched the other wall; their other wings touched each other in the middle of the house. And he overlaid the cherubim with gold.

2 Chr 5:7–8

> So the priests brought the ark of the covenant of Yahweh to its place, in the inner sanctuary of the house, in the most holy place, underneath the wings of the cherubim. For the cherubim spread out their wings over the place of the ark, so that the cherubim made a covering above the ark.

Solomon also decorated the walls of the Holy of Holies (the inner chamber) and the walls and doors of the holy place (the outer chamber) with carved images of cherubim, palm trees, and opened flowers. (The cherubim were symbols of protection and warning; the palm trees and flowers were ritually "suggestive" symbols of the desired blessing of fertility):

1 Kgs 6:29

> He carved the walls of the house round about with carved figures of cherubim and palm trees and open flowers, in the inner and outer rooms.

1 Kgs 6:32

> He covered the two doors of olivewood with carvings of cherubim, palm trees, and open flowers; he overlaid them with gold and spread gold upon the cherubim and upon the palm trees.

The seraphim, on the other hand, were angelic beings with six wings. They are described in the Book of Isaiah as posted above God's throne and warning those who approach it of God's inviolable holiness. Their familiar words of warning have been appropriated for worship by many branches of the Christian family:

> In the year that King Uzziah died I saw Yahweh sitting on a throne, high and lifted up; and his train filled the temple. Above him stood the seraphim; each had six wings: with two he covered his face, with two he covered his feet, and with two he flew. And one called to another and said: "Holy, holy, holy is Yahweh of hosts; the whole earth is full of his glory." (Is 6:1–3)

When we are told in the description of the seraphim that with two of their wings they covered their "feet," we should probably read "genitals" instead of feet. After the Exile the priests who edited the Scriptures for regular use at the Sabbath service prudishly changed the word for genitals to feet in Isaiah's description of the seraphim. Isaiah, however, because of the strict ban in Israel on the ritual nudity, which was part of Canaanite worship, very likely assumed that the angelic beings who served in God's presence took care that their genitals not be exposed:

Ex 20:26

> And you shall not go up by steps to my altar that your nakedness be not exposed on it.

Ex 28:42–43

> And you shall make for them [the priests] linen breeches to cover their naked flesh; from the loins to the thighs they shall reach; and they shall be upon Aaron and upon his sons when they come near the altar to minister in the holy place; lest they bring guilt upon themselves and die.

9.

Finally, evolving human consciousness reached the measure of reflective insight that enabled the Israelite prophet called Second Isaiah (c. 540 B.C.)to grasp the necessary oneness and omnipresence of Sacred Reality: There is only one God who is everywhere in the universe. There can be only one God, he intuitively discerned, for God is the Absolute Being.

(Philosophical reasoning confirms Second Isaiah's intuitive recognition that there can be only one Absolute Being. It is logically impossible to assume the existence of a number of Absolute beings, for they would all be relative to each other, and none of them, therefore, would be Absolute. We—and they—would still require, as our Ultimate Ground, an Absolute Being who is eternally able to protect all relative and contingent beings from the threat of absolute nothingness.) Our recognition of God's absolute and eternal power to be (and to prevent absolute nonbeing) enables us to understand why there is something instead of nothing.

Because all images are finite and relative, it is impossible to create an image of Absolute Being. And so God was visualized by Second Isaiah as an All-powerful, All-knowing, and Eternal King who rules over the nations from the "higher" perspective and "universal" embrace of heaven or the sky. The sky is the only elevated thing in our empirical experience that seems to be unlimited or infinite. It is an appropriate symbol, therefore, for suggesting the transcendence and omnipresence of God in the universe.

There is, of course, nothing intrinsically male about God. Absolute Being necessarily transcends sexual distinctions based on finite reproductive organs. But the ancient teachers who developed and taught monotheism lived in patriarchal societies where men almost always exercised political and economic power to the exclusion of women.

Males began behaving in a patriarchal fashion for several reasons: (1) They were no longer awed by female magic. (2) They had to defend with physical force the land which they now owned and cultivated. (3) They failed to appreciate that women are programmed biologically to accomplish the different but equally important tasks of bearing and nurturing the children who continue the human species. (4) They failed to recognize that although women do not have the same physical strength as male warrior-protectors, they nevertheless are mentally equal to men, have the same intrinsic dignity and rights as men, and should be treated accordingly.

From earliest childhood, males in a patriarchal society were unconsciously conditioned by unquestioned social attitudes to perceive themselves as the superior protectors of "weaker" females. In such a society, God was predictably likened to an omnipotent warrior king because the king was the most powerful person in that society. We have already observed that humans always choose the most powerful being in their historical experience as their preferred symbol for Sacred Reality.

It is illuminating to recall, however, that in matriarchal societies, which still believed in female magic, the most powerful person was the current matriarch. In such societies God was not imagined as the Almighty Father who is King of heaven and earth, but as the Great Mother who is Queen of earth and heaven (the Egyptian goddess Nut). There is, therefore, something relative and provisional, not absolute and fixed, about the symbols which humans choose to illustrate their evolving insight into the mysterious reality of God.

We can readily grasp why developing human insight learns to prefer one set of symbols over another for illustrating its current interpretation of Sacred Reality. Religious symbols are called forth by developing historical consciousness, and they will wane and finally be replaced when the conditions which shaped that stage of consciousness ceases to pertain. All religious symbols are historically conditioned, and none of them can claim an absolute or exclusive right to mediate our human understanding of the mystery of God. Such symbols, by their very nature, are subject to revision when increasing knowledge indicates that a more adequate illustration is called for.

Surprisingly, God's exclusive oneness was grasped and taught almost simultaneously by two teachers widely separated by culture and geography. The first was an anonymous Israelite prophet who taught about God with the aid of mythological images or symbols. He likened the one God to an imperial king who rules with sovereign power over all the nations.

This first monotheistic prophet in ancient Israel is called Second Isaiah, or Deutero Isaiah, by biblical scholars, because he was the "second" prophet to contribute to the writings found in the Book of Isaiah (chs. 40–56). Second Isaiah probably considered himself to be a disciple of the prophet Isaiah (who taught more than a century and a half before him). It was very likely for that reason that he (or others) joined his writings to those of Isaiah. We will see in chapter five that by 540 B.C. Second Isaiah had begun teaching monotheism to the Israelites who were captives in Babylon.

The second monotheistic teacher was the ancient Greek philosopher Xenophanes. He taught about God's oneness in 536 B.C. However, he taught not with concrete mythological images but with abstract ideas which he used insightfully to criticize the literal acceptance of traditional myths. The innovative ideas of Second Isaiah and Xenophanes are so important that we will return to each of these teachers in later chapters to consider the historical circumstances that contributed to their discovery of monotheism.

We someties read or hear that Egyptian pharaoh Akhenaten (also called Ikhnaton) was the first monotheist. A number of scholars advanced that interpretation in the first half of the twentieth century (see James H. Breasted's *The Dawn of Conscience*). Sigmund Freud took up their view and popularized it in his widely read but seriously flawed book, *Moses and Monotheism.* Recent Egyptologists, however, have concluded that Akhenaten was probably a henotheist who spoke hyperbolically about his exclusive devotion to the god Aten and acted correspondingly for essentially political reasons (see "Akhenaten" in the *Encyclopedia of Religion,* ed. by Mircea Eliade.) Recall that a henotheist is someone who worships one god exclusively but believes that other gods exist. Henotheists, in certain instances, will sound very much like monotheists. Their statements must be carefully weighed against other elements in their practices and historical context before one can reasonably decide the difference.

Akhenaten tried to break the power of the priests of Amun (the ascendant god in Egypt at the beginning of Akhenaten's reign) by vigorously advocating exclusive worship of the sun god Aten. The priests of Amun (who administered the many gifts dedicated to that god) had acquired ownership over one third of Egypt. It was probably to counteract their encroaching influence that Akhenaten vigorously prohibited the worship of Amun (and all the other gods, because their temples and gifts were also administered by the high priest of Amun) and championed sole devotion to Aten. After Akhenaten's death, his henotheistic reform was repudiated as heretical by his successors. (For a clearer picture of the political motivation underlying Akhenaten's unusual religious reform, see the chapter on "Aten" in Barbara Watterson's *The God's of Ancient Egypt.*)

Questions for Review and Discussion

1. Why do we humans always try to reduce any problem we are trying to solve to a "visual model"?

2. What is it about the structure of our minds that requires us to create visual models or symbols?

3. What two "laws" or insights help us to correctly interpret the implications of a footprint in the sand?

4. What is an analogy? What is it about the structure of our minds that requires us to employ analogies?

5. By what analogical process did polytheists explain lightning and thunder?

6. What two insights or laws did polytheists correctly employ when they explained invisible causal power?

7. The basic mistake of mythological thinkers was their failure to make what important distinction about invisible causes?

8. How is animism defined in this chapter?

9. How is totemism defined in this chapter?

10. How does polytheism differ from animism and totemism?

11. What naive projection is unconsciously involved in animistic and totemistic interpretations of reality?

12. What significant change in their historical experience led humans to move beyond animism and totemism to the earliest or incipient form of polytheism?

13. What did archaic societies mean by "female magic"?

14. What distinguishes pre-agricultural from agricultural views of the Great Mother's fecundity?

15. Who were the first two teachers in the ancient world to teach exclusive monotheism? In what basic way did their teaching about God's oneness differ?

16. How does a henotheist differ from a monotheist, and why can a henotheist easily sound like a monotheist in practice?

Chapter Two

The Origin of the Twelve Tribes and their Henotheism

1.

A critical reading of the Bible indicates that ancient Israel's understanding of God was not initially monotheistic. The religious ideas of the twelve tribes who became the nation Israel underwent a complex development. This development began with polytheism and journeyed with great difficulty through henotheism before finally arriving, during the Exile, at exclusive monotheism. We will review the major stages of the journey that led to Israel's ambiguous and turbulent embrace of henotheism in this chapter. We will also review some of the evidence indicating that pre-Exilic Israel was not yet monotheistic.

In general, we will be following the critical analysis of ancient Israel's origin provided by Martin Noth (*History of Israel*). Some of Noth's views, such as the *amphyctionic* structure of the tribes of Israel, have been rejected by the majority of scholars. The basic outline of his analysis, however, still seems to the author of this book to be an essentially reliable interpretation of the biblical data. (For a brief overview of other opinions about the origin of ancient Israel, see "Israel, History of," in the *Anchor Bible Dictionary.* When recounting the history of Israel's pre-Exilic view of God, we will be guided primarily, but not exclusively, by Mark S. Smith's *The Early History of God: Yahweh and the Deities in Ancient Israel.*)

If the reader assumes that God has dictated every word in the Bible and that every word therein is "literally" true, then he or she will probably be disturbed by some of the explanations of biblical history presented in this and the following chapters. The author apologizes in advance for any pain or alarm the reader might feel. And yet, the author knows from experience that usually there is no significant growth in understanding the ancient religious history in the Bible without the patient acceptance of the "pain" that sometimes accompanies serious study and realistic adjustment. It is difficult to unlearn what we have already learned. Jesus himself forewarns us of the difficulty of adjusting to new ideas:

> No one having drunk old wine will immediately like the new; he will say, "The old is better." (Lk 5:39)

If, however, we truly wish to deepen our understanding of God's definitive Self-disclosure to humankind at the conclusion of biblical history, we will be willing to make the required effort and to endure the temporary pain. The pangs of such adjustment are like the pain of childbirth; what begins in sorrow ends in great joy:

> When a woman is giving birth she has sorrow, because her hour has come; but when she has delivered her child, she no longer remembers her anguish, for joy that a child has come into the world. (Jn 16:21)

The reader is encouraged, therefore, to endure the pain of adjustment, for it will contribute to new insights into the marvelous process by which God finally brought the Good News of salvation into our world. We must always remember that God was continually working through the dedicated Israelite priests and prophets who were inspired by their experience of God to write the Jewish Scriptures: "For salvation is from the Jews" (Jn 4:22b). God encouraged the priests and prophets to provide gradually improving insights into the mystery of God and God's saving purpose in history. It was God, therefore, who indirectly and ultimately "wielded the pen" when the words of sacred Scripture were written.

Because God works through our freedom without violating it, God had to wait patiently throughout ancient Israel's long history for the right religiously concerned—persons capable of grasping the best ideas at the opportune time. God then encouraged those individuals (by an inspiring nonverbal communication of divine Presence and Love) to speak or act for God in their changing circumstances. Their inspired efforts were instrumental in moving Israel's understanding of God forward. It was God, therefore, who (indirectly) called ancient Israel into being though the complex process which contemporary scholarship has uncovered in the Jewish Scriptures. And it was God who encouraged Israel to continue on her difficult journey from polytheism through henotheism to monotheism.

God's inspiring and encouraging activity in the hearts of Israel's priests and prophets was remote preparation for the full attainment of God's revelatory purpose in history. Until Israel had learned to comprehend God's oneness and omnipresence in the universe, she was not yet ready to understand God's definitive and universal offer of love, forgiveness, and the sublime privilege of participating forever in God's creative Discovery and Joy. God "spoke" this definitive offer to Israel and to humankind through the Risen and Spirit-mediating Jesus:

Heb 1:1–2

> In many and various ways God spoke of old to our forefathers by the prophets; but in these last days he has spoken to us through a Son.

Acts 13:32–33a

> We bring you the Good New that what God promised to our forefathers, this he has fulfilled to us their children by raising Jesus.

Jn 20:19, 22

> On the evening of that day, the first day of the week . . . Jesus came and stood among them and said to them, "Peace be with you." . . . And when he had said this he breathed on them, and said to them, "Receive the Holy Spirit."

Rom 5:5b

God's love has been poured into our hearts through the Holy Spirit which has been given to us.

Cor 1:21–22

But it is God who . . . has . . . given his Spirit in our hearts as a guarantee.

Extraordinary encouragement (which resulted in extraordinary insight) was lavished on ancient Israel for the sake of all humankind. God knew that Israel's time and place in history could best serve God's purpose for all nations. Israel's own prophets eventually understood and expressed something of this realization:

Gen 12:2a, 3b

I will make of you a great nation . . . and by you all the nations of the earth shall be blessed.

Is 42:5a, 6

Thus says God, . . . "I am Yahweh, I have called you in righteousness, I have taken you by the hand and kept you; I have given you as a covenant to the people, a light to the nations."

Is 49:1, 3, 5a, 6

Listen to me, O coastlands, and hearken, you people from afar. Yahweh called me from the womb, from the body of my mother he named my name. . . . And now Yahweh says . . . "I will give you as a light to the nations, that my salvation may reach to the end of the earth."

2.

Israel's priest-historians remembered that their patriarchal ancestors had been polytheists:

> Your fathers lived of old beyond the Euphrates, Terah, the father of Abraham and Nahor; and they served other gods. (Jos 24:2)

The Book of Genesis tells us that Israel's God, Yahweh, befriended Abraham and promised him two major gifts in return for faithful and exclusive worship. First, God promised him a multitude of descendants:

> **Gen 12:1–2**
> Now Yahweh said to Abram, "Go from your country and your kindred and your father's house to the land that I will show you. And I will make of you a great nation and I will bless you."

> **Gen 22:17**
> I will indeed bless you and will multiply your descendants as the stars of heaven and as the sand which is on the seashore.

Second, God promised to give the land of Canaan to Abraham's descendants as an everlasting inheritance:

> **Gen 17:7–8**
> And I will establish my covenant between me and you and your descendants after you throughout their generations for an everlasting covenant, to be God to you and your descendants after you. And I will give to you and your descendants after you the land of your sojournings, the land of Canaan, for an everlasting possession, and I will be their God.

> **Gen 15:6**
> And he [Abraham] believed Yahweh, and he [God] reckoned it to him [Abraham] as righteousness.

Moreover, the Book of Genesis states that God repeated the promise of divine blessing to Abraham's son Isaac:

> And Yahweh appeared to him [Isaac] . . . and said, "I am the God of Abraham your father; fear not, for I am with you and will bless you and multiply your descendants for my servant Abraham's sake." (Gen 26:24)

Isaac, in turn, assumed that God would also bestow this promise on his son Jacob:

> May God Almighty bless you and make you fruitful and multiply you, that you may become a company of peoples. May he give the blessing of Abraham to you and to your descendants with you, that you may take possession of the land of your sojournings which God gave to Abraham. (Gen 28:3–4)

The Bible assures us that Isaac's faith and trust were confirmed: the God of Abraham and Isaac appeared to Jacob in a revelatory dream while Jacob slept at night near ancient Bethel. God repeated to Jacob the promise of innumerable progeny. Moreover, God assured Jacob that his many descendants would inherit the land of Canaan as a divine favor:

> I am Yahweh, the God of Abraham your father and the God of Isaac; the land on which you lie I will give to you and to your descendants; and your descendants shall be like the dust of the earth. (Gen 28:13–14a)

Contemporary scholarship concludes, however, that Israel's memories of Abraham, Isaac, and Jacob have been embellished with promises that are, in reality, *vaticinia post eventum* (predictions made after the fact). That is, after the twelve tribes of Israel had come into being and had succeeded under David's kingship in conquering the entire land of Canaan, her priest-historians concluded that Israel's covenant God, Yahweh, must have not only bestowed but also foreintended this highly favorable historical development.

Guided by folk norms then current, the priest-historians retrojected Israel's good fortune onto their memories of the Patriarchs. Israel's covenant God, the priests surmised, surely must have informed their righteous ancestors of the blessing of land which their many descendants would eventually obtain with God's help. After all, God communicated with Moses at Mount Sinai; why, therefore, would God not have communicated with Israel's righteous ancestors? For if matters had been otherwise, the priests concluded, their ancestors would not have been favored with such numerous offspring, and the twelve tribes would not have been able to conquer the promised land. Surely such a boon was foreintended and foreannounced to the righteous ancestors who had been so blessed.

Our contemporary faith experience assures us that it was God who inspired Israel's priest-historians to interpret the history of their patriarchal ancestors retrojectively in a sacred and promise-filled fashion. God did so not only to help them meet the need for religious meaning in their lives but also (on a deeper level and at a later time) to help us learn to find positive religious meaning in our lives. God wanted Israel's priests to write a sacred history that would eventually help all religiously concerned humans understand that God's mysterious Presence and Love are at work in all of our personal histories.

The Bible vividly reminds us that God's Providence watches over our lives continually with experienceable Love and will enable us to arrive finally at the sublime goal of Eternal Life and Joy for which we were created:

> Behold I am with you and will keep you wherever you go, and will bring you back to this land; for I will not leave you until I have done that which I have spoken to you. (Gen 28:15)

We, too, are called by God to undertake with faith and trust a mysterious journey like that of Abraham and his descendants. Our faith-filled journey through life and death will finally bring us to the true promised land of Eternal Life and Joy. We will then have entered into our promised inheritance in God's Reign which triumphs everlastingly over tragedy, injustice, and death.

The implications of our self-transcending design already suggest that we have a sublime and death-transcending destiny. Why else would "recycled stardust" aspire to immortality and permanent participation in the infinity and eternity of our Ultimate Ground and Source? It is profoundly significant that we have been programmed to think about everlasting *permanence* even though nothing in our universe is permanent. In other words, our design implies the purpose of our Designer. Furthermore, at critical times in our lives, God bestows on us a reassuring foretaste of divine Presence which communicates Love, Peace, and Joy (God's Holy Spirit). God confers the divine Self-gift on us to confirm the correctness of our anticipation of unending friendship with our Creator beyond death.

The abiding reality of God's Presence and Love in our lives, however, is subtle and transempirical; the implications of God's Self-gift can only be grasped clearly with the aid of concrete "personal" signs. These personal signs predispose us to recognize life's deeper implications. The nature of human reality is such that these predisposing signs must initially and primarily be familial. It is the responsible and tender love of parents for their children which helps most of us to eventually realize that "God is love" (1 Jn 4:8b).

It was fitting, therefore, for God to inspire the writing of a sacred history which begins with the hopes, joys, and sorrows of a family consisting of grandparents, parents, and children (Abraham and Sara, Isaac and Rebecca, Jacob and his wives and children). For only through parents (and grandparents) can God begin to reveal to children the mystery of divine Love and its implicit promise of sublime fulfillment to come. God begins loving us indirectly through each other, and unless we have experienced genuine love from others, especially parents, we will not be prepared to experience and understand God's directly communicated but subtle Love for us.

Biblical history reminds us over and over that Abraham and Sara, Isaac and Rebecca, and Jacob and his wives and children had to believe and trust in God's "promise" of blessings for themselves and their children which would be fully attained only in the mysterious future. We, too, guided by the deeper and divinely intended significance of their stories, are encouraged to believe and trust in the "promise" of sublime blessings to come. The attainability of these blessings is already implied by our self-transcending design and is confirmed by our experience of God's Self-communication as Love.

The ancient Israelites were not yet able to fully understand the promise of blessing implicit in their experience of God's Self-communication. They still assumed that the sin of our first parents required all humans to be punished forever after death in Sheol, the subterranean prison where the souls of the dead were consigned. Accordingly, they believed that God was promising them (nonverbally) a secure future in this world.

Christians, however, have been taught by Jesus that the future blessing which God's Self-gift implies is not fully attained in this world. We know that our faith in God's Self-gift (the Holy Spirit) will enable us to defeat death and to be gathered finally into the arms of God's Love in the true promised land of God's Eternal Life (which means unending participation in God's Creative Discovery and Joy). The Risen Jesus and the "foretaste" of God's Love (the Spirit) are God's guarantee that our "future hope" has a secure basis in God's creative purpose. The full disclosure of this Good News is the divinely intended outcome of the history of ancient Israel.

3.

At this point it would be wise to reflect briefly on the "folk" mentality typical of ancient Israel's priest-historians: The folk mentality characterizes the thinking of people who are still essentially preliterate. With acquired instinct, folk historians adapt their message to the needs of their preliterate communities and the requirements of oral transmission. For economy's sake, therefore, they preserve only the bare essentials of a remembered event. They also use *hyperbole* (artistic exaggeration) to insure that their listeners will truly "hear" the most important parts of a narrative.

Furthermore, folk historians will freely expand (and, on occasion, will even create) a narrative in order to defend or clarify an important memory or belief cherished by their community. They also draw on traditional ideas (including mythological assumptions about invisible causal power) to interpret remembered events. Since such strategies and assumptions are part of their community's tradition, folk historians reach for them spontaneously when attempting to explain the meaning of significant happenings, present and past. When Israel's priest-historians eventually learned to write, they recorded their memories of her history. Their memories, however, included their interpretations of that history.

Obviously, the legendary history shaped by folk historians differs from contemporary history in a number of ways. Folk historians basically remember real persons and events. But they weave into their memories of these persons and events folk interpretations and teaching devices designed to meet the peculiar needs of their precritical communities. It is frequently difficult, therefore, for nonspecialists to distinguish ancient Israel's genuine historical memories from her folk interpretations of such memories.

The reader should understand that not all biblical scholars agree about how to interpret the ancient and legendary history found in the Bible. Opinions range from the literalism of the far right to the unbridled skepticism of the extreme left. There is usually, however, a moderate consensus about most matters. It is the moderating views of the center which will be presented in this work.

4.

The next problem we must briefly examine is the complicated and somewhat ambiguous process by which the ancient league of twelve Israelite tribes was formed. Understanding the major steps in this process sheds important light on the fierce struggles that occurred before the Exile (587 B.C.) as the priests and prophets of Yahweh strove to establish exclusive worship of Yahweh among the twelve tribes.

Biblical and archeological evidence suggests that the six "Leah" tribes (Reuben, Simeon, Levi, Judah, Issachar, and Zebulun) had probably settled in the land of Canaan (c. 1700-1650 B.C.), well before the advent of the tribes who entered the land under Joshua (c. 1200-1175 B.C.). Prior to entering Canaan, the Leah tribes had probably banded together to form a six-tribe league called "Israel." Not long after the Leah tribes had arrived in Canaan, the "Zilpah" tribes (Gad and Asher) followed (c. 1600-1550 B.C.), and probably sometime after them (c. 1500-1450 B.C.) came the "Bilhah" tribes (Dan and Naphtali).

The Egyptian Pharaoh Merneptah probably encountered members of the six-tribe league called Israel (c. 1220 B.C.) during his military campaign in Canaan. A victory *stele* (inscribed stone monument) celebrating this campaign mentions "Israel" among the peoples he claims to have then vanquished (see *Pritchard's Ancient Near Eastern Texts,* 378). Many biblical historians believe, however, that when Merneptah encountered this people called Israel, the "Rachel" tribes (Joseph and Benjamin), and the tribe of Levi had not yet been led by Joshua into Canaan.

When the Leah tribes began to occupy the central highlands of Canaan, the highlands were still wooded and largely unoccupied by Canaanites. The Canaanites preferred the coastal plain and the regions with broad fertile valleys. Some of the Leah tribes, therefore, probably experienced very little conflict with the Canaanites. Simeon and Levi, however, were not so fortunate. They apparently were challenged by Canaanites and suffered serious defeat at their hands. These two tribes, accordingly, did not succeed in establishing themselves in the central highlands.

Simeon and Levi probably ran afoul of the Canaanites while trying to seize territory in the region of Shechem (Gen 34:25–30). Because the surviving Simeonites were greatly reduced in number, they sought permanent refuge within the large tribe of Judah (Josh 19:9). The rebuffed Levites, however, apparently met and joined the still seminomadic "Rachel" tribes (Joseph and Benjamin) who probably sojourned in the region south of Beersheba. (Abraham, Isaac, and Jacob, the ancestors of the Rachel tribes, were remembered as having encamped near Beersheba.)

The Levites who had joined the Rachel tribes eventually journeyed with them into Egypt to escape from famine (caused by either drought or the turmoil of warfare). In reality, therefore, it was probably only the Rachel tribes (Joseph and Benjamin) and the Levites who had joined them, who escaped from Egypt with Moses and entered into covenant with Yahweh at Mount Horeb/Sinai. (Both names are assigned to the mountain where Moses received the law from Yahweh.)

Eventually the Levites became the priestly tribe in Israel because of their privileged relation to Moses, who was from their tribe (see Ex 2:1–10; 6:1, 16, 18, 20). Moses and other Levites—Hophni, Phineas, Merari, and perhaps Aaron—had Egyptian names which confirm that Levites had probably traveled with the Rachel tribes to Egypt.

The memory of Simeon's and Levi's membership in the original six-tribe alliance called "Israel" was preserved even after these two tribes had become too small or discouraged to occupy and defend territory of their own. Their traditional rank in the sacred league was also kept when the six-tribe league was later expanded to twelve tribes (Gen 35:23–26; 49:1–27; Ex 1:2–3; Deut 27:12–13).

Only after the tribe of Levi had become the priestly tribe dwelling among all the other tribes was Levi omitted from the later tribal lists (see Num 1:2–50, esp. 47–50; 26:3–50). The large tribe of Joseph was then divided into the two half tribes of Ephraim and Manasseh to preserve the sacred number "twelve" (Num 1:32–35; 26:28–37; see the story in Ex 48:1–20 created by the priest-historians as "justification" for this later change in the twelve-tribe league's original composition).

It was probably more than four centuries later (c. 1200-1175 B.C.) before the long-settled Leah tribes finally encountered the most recently arrived "Rachel" tribes led by Joshua. There are a number of telltale clues in the Bible which indicate that the Leah tribes then invited the Rachel tribes (and the neighboring Zilpah and Bilhah tribes) to unite with them in a sacred league of "twelve" tribes. This twelve-tribe alliance promised its members greater security. And since the original tribal league called "Israel" had long been established, the new twelve-tribe league formed at the time of Joshua retained that traditional name.

The early Israelites and neighboring peoples who shared their general ethnic heritage (the Ammonites, Moabites, Ishmaelites, Edomites, and Midianites) customarily gathered themselves at the tribal stage into leagues of twelve (Gen 17:20; 22:20–24; 25:13–16; 35:22–26; 36:10–14; 49:28; Num 1:4–16). In theory, the major purpose of such an alliance was defense, but in practice it required a crisis of major proportions to induce the tribes not directly affected to assist those being menaced by outsiders.

Whenever possible, a league of twelve tribes was preferred to six because of practicality and sacred custom. To begin with, a larger league was judged to be a greater deterrent to aggression. Moreover, shared responsibilities involving a commonly venerated central sanctuary could be more easily apportioned by observing the reliable regularity of the twelve lunar months in the solar year:

Is 66:23

> "From new moon to new moon . . . all flesh shall come before me to worship," says Yahweh.

Ex 40:2–2, 17

> Yahweh said to Moses, "On the first day of the first month [new moon] you shall erect the tabernacle of the tent of meeting. And you shall put in it the ark of the testimony, and you shall screen the ark with a veil" . . . And in the first month in the second year, on the first day of the month [new moon], the tabernacle was erected.

Each "new moon" waxes and wanes by exact halves every seven days. After a twenty-eight-day cycle, the old moon disappears in the darkness of its own shadow for three days and then reappears as the "new moon." It was probably the four exactly demarcated periods of seven days from new moon to old moon which originally determined the time of Sabbath observance. Dependence on the moon for periodic fulfillment of ritual obligations explains the importance assigned to the new moon festival in ancient Israel. (For more information, see "New Moon" in *The Interpreter's Dictionary of the Bible.*)

The moon was the only reliable means of computing extended periods of time in archaic societies. For thousands of years the moon was the great gauge of temporal change because it waxed and waned with predictable regularity in the night sky. Adhering to the mysterious pattern of twelve lunar months in each solar year enabled a tribal league to live in harmony with the sacred forces governing the annual cycle. A league of six tribes conformed to this sacred pattern by assigning biannually to each tribe its turn at maintaining the league's central sanctuary.

The later practice of observing the Sabbath every seven days irrespective of the lunar month's seven-day quarters was probably adopted after the Exile. Because the post-Exilic priests became scrupulous about Sabbath observance, the new method of simply counting every seventh day as the Sabbath would have seemed safer than searching uncertainly for the state of the moon during a series of cloudy nights.

(We still regulate our social affairs by dividing twelve months [moons] into seven-day weeks. And most of our clocks have faces that are "round," "white," and divided by "twelve" numbers in conscious imitation of the moon and its dependable regularity. There is something archetypal about the design of such clocks: They mechanically reflect the predictable rhythm of the moon in the night sky. We still say that it is "quarter past" the hour and "quarter till" the new hour with an eye to the lunar month's four quarters.)

5.

Membership in the expanded twelve-tribe league of "Israel" was only possible for the three tribes led by Joshua, however, if the other nine tribes agreed to observe the Mosaic covenant and worship Yahweh exclusively as the Rachel tribes and Levi did. The other tribes probably agreed to Joshua's conditions because he had fully informed them of Yahweh's spectacular victories over the powerful gods of Egypt. Joshua very likely urged that it would be to the advantage of all if Yahweh were worshiped exclusively by the other members of the tribal alliance.

We find in the Book of Joshua a (relocated and modified) story that probably remembers the solemn occasion when Joshua invited the converting tribes to accept the Mosaic covenant and obey its demand for exclusive worship of Yahweh:

Jos 24:1–2, 14–16

> Then Joshua gathered all the tribes . . . to Shechem. . . . And Joshua said to all the people. . . . "Fear Yahweh, and serve him in sincerity and faithfulness; put away the gods which your fathers served beyond the River . . . and serve Yahweh. And if you be unwilling to serve Yahweh, choose this day whom you will serve, whether the gods your fathers served in the region beyond the River, or the gods of the Amorites [Canaanites] in whose land you dwell; but as for me and my house, we will serve Yahweh." Then the people answered, "Far be it from us that we should forsake Yahweh to serve other gods"

Jos 24:22a, 23–24

> Joshua said to the people . . . "Then put away the foreign gods which are among you, and incline your hearts to Yahweh, the God of Israel." And the people said to Joshua, "We will serve Yahweh as our God, and his voice we will obey."

It is highly unlikely that the tribes who had just completed the Exodus journey and entered Canaan with Joshua would have needed to be told to put away "the gods your fathers served in the region beyond the River" or "the gods of the Amorites [Canaanites] in whose land you dwell." Such demands are far more intelligible if Joshua was addressing the nine tribes who had not participated in the Exodus event and had not agreed at Sinai to worship Yahweh exclusively.

It is likely, however, that the tribes who converted to the exclusive worship of Yahweh also required a concession from the tribes led by Joshua. The tribes led by Joshua were probably required to accept the practice of circumcision so that tribal loyalty and intermarriage with the tribes long established in the land would be possible. The Syrians and Canaanites already practiced circumcision when the six-tribe alliance of Israel and the Zilpah and Bilhah tribes entered the land. Because all of these tribes (except Levi) had settled in Canaan and assimilated Canaanite culture, they probably also had learned to practice circumcision at the time of marriage (see Gen 34:13–17; Ex 4:24–26).

The interpretation just suggested is supported by the unusual account in Josh 5:2–3 which relates that Joshua circumcised the tribes whom he had recently led from the wilderness into the land of Canaan: (The tribes in this account were called "Israelites" by one of the later priest-historians who created a unified account of Israel's origin after the twelve-tribe league had been formed.)

> At that time Yahweh said to Joshua, "Make flint knives and circumcise the people of Israel again the second time." So Joshua made flint knives and circumcised the people of Israel at Gibeath-haaraloth [the hill of the foreskins]. (Jos 5:2–3)

In reality, the men who were circumcised at the time of Joshua probably belonged to the three recently arrived tribes who had never adopted the custom of circumcision. The words "the second time" were added to the tradition by a later priest-historian who wished to create the impression that these tribes had already been circumcised at the time of Moses. The Old Greek version of the Book of Joshua remembered that Joshua circumcised men who had come out of Egypt (5:4) and not merely the children who were born in the wilderness. It also recalls that the flint knives used for their circumcision were buried along with Joshua in his tomb (Jos 24:30).

The earliest Israelite law codes did not enjoin circumcision, probably because the custom was already traditional at the time of marriage (see Ex 4:24–26) in the land of Canaan/Israel. (The word for father-in-law in Hebrew, a dialect of Canaanite, basically means "circumcisor," and the word for son-in-law and bridegroom also means "circumcised man.") It was only during the Exile to Babylon (587 B.C.) that circumcision was conferred eight days after birth and made a sacred sign of loyalty to Israel's covenant God. Because the Babylonians did not practice circumcision, it distinguished Israelites from Babylonians and was intended to discourage assimilation and loss of faith in Yahweh.

The priest-historian who later wrote the Book of Joshua offered a different explanation for the circumcision of the adult males recounted in Joshua 5:2–3. He did so (without truly explaining their state of uncircumcision) in order to conform to the unified post-Joshua tradition that all twelve tribes in the newly formed league called Israel had sojourned in Egypt, escaped with Moses, and had been taught by Moses to practice circumcision:

> **Jos 5:4**
>
> And this is the reason why Joshua circumcised them: all the males of the people who came out of Egypt, all the men of war, had died on the way in the wilderness after they had come out of Egypt.

> **Jos 5:7–8**
>
> So it was their children whom he [God] raised up in their stead, that Joshua circumcised; for they were uncircumcised, because they had not been circumcised on the way. When the circumcising of all the nation was done, they remained in their places in the camp till they were healed.

(For more on the history of circumcision, see the article "Circumcision" in the *Anchor Bible Dictionary*.)

6.

It seems likely that only the Rachel tribes were descended from "Abraham, Isaac, and Jacob." The six Leah tribes traced their descent from an ancestor named "Israel." This ancestral memory of the Leah tribes was preserved by the priest-historian called the "Yahwist," who recorded tribal traditions from the perspective of Judah—the largest and most powerful of the Leah tribes.

The Rachel tribes, to the contrary, remembered their tribal ancestor as "Jacob," the descendant of Abraham and Isaac. This memory of the Rachel tribes was preserved by the priest-historian called the "Elohist," who passed on the traditions of the tribe of Joseph—the largest and most powerful of the Rachel tribes.

After Joshua negotiated the agreement of the "twelve-tribe" league to serve Yahweh, Yahweh became the covenant God who was to be worshiped exclusively by the members of the league. From that time forward, the ark of the Covenant, regarded as

Yahweh's throne (Num 10:35–36; Jer 3:16–17), was enshrined in Israel's central sanctuary. The first central sanctuary of the twelve-tribe alliance was probably located at Shechem (Jos 24:1), which had very likely been the central sanctuary of the former six-tribe league.

Soon after the twelve-tribe league was formed, the Levitical priests who zealously guarded Yahweh's ark expanded a tradition about the patriarch "Jacob" in order to identify him with "Israel," the ancestor of the Leah tribes whose name had been retained by the twelve-tribe alliance:

> The same night he arose and took his two wives, his two maids, and his eleven children [Benjamin, according to the story created by the Levitical priests, had not yet been born], and crossed the ford of the Jabbok. . . . And Jacob was left alone; and a man wrestled with him until daybreak. When the man saw that he did not prevail against Jacob . . . he said, "Let me go, for the day is breaking." But Jacob said, "I will not let you go, unless you bless me."
>
> And he said to him, "What is your name?" And he said, "Jacob." And he said, "Your name shall no more be called Jacob, but Israel, for you have striven with God and with men and have prevailed." (Gen 32:22, 24–25a, 26–28)

This strange tale relates that while Jacob was returning to the land of Canaan from his sojourn with his uncle, Laban, God tested Jacob's faith in the promise of blessing which Jacob had earlier received from God at Bethel (Gen 28:13–17). God tested Jacob near the ford of the Jabbok River through a mysterious angelic emissary sent at night. After successfully wrestling with the angel, Jacob was given a new name, "Israel," as a sign of God's continued favor. Jacob, the patriarchal ancestor of the Rachel tribes, was thereby identified with Israel, the patriarchal ancestor of the Leah tribes. The recently united tribes, therefore, could now regard themselves as one people descended from a common ancestor.

After the Exile, the "Priestly Author" (who acted as final editor of the five books attributed to Moses: Genesis, Exodus, Leviticus,

Numbers, and Deuteronomy) decided that it was not sufficient for Jacob to receive his "new" name Israel from a mere angel. Accordingly, he expanded the tradition of Jacob's two names by relating that God later appeared to Jacob and confirmed the new name bestowed earlier by the angel:

> God appeared to Jacob again, when he came from Paddan-aram, and blessed him. And God said to him, "Your name is Jacob; no longer shall your name be called Jacob, but Israel shall be your name." So his name was called Israel. And God said to him, "I am God Almighty [El shaddai] . . . a nation and a company of nations shall come from you." (Gen 35:9–11)

For the same unifying and henotheizing reasons, the priests of Yahweh created the other narratives which assigned four wives (Rachel, Leah, Zilpah, and Bilhah; Gen 29:1–30:22) and twelve sons (Reuben, Simeon, Levi, Judah, Issachar, Zebulun, Dan, Naphtali, Gad, Asher, Joseph, and Benjamin; Gen 29:31–30:24; 35:16–20) to Jacob/Israel. In actuality, Jacob probably had only one wife, Rachel, and only "Joseph" and "Benjamin" were their descendants. Leah, Zilpah, and Bilhah were probably matriarchal ancestors of the tribes said to be descended from them in the modified biblical stories created by the Levitical priests.

This Priestly revision of the history of the Patriarchs and Matriarchs of the various "Israelite" tribes made it possible for the Leah, Zilpah, and Bilhah tribes to be taught that they, too, were descended from Abraham, Isaac, and Jacob. They also, therefore, were the privileged recipients of the blessings promised by Yahweh to the descendants of the Patriarchs in return for faith, trust, and exclusive worship.

These newly created narratives also recounted that all "twelve" of the sons born to Jacob of his four wives had gone down with him into Egypt. Furthermore, the theologically motivated narratives related that the descendants of those twelve sons became the "twelve tribes" who were led out of Egypt by Moses and agreed to worship Yahweh exclusively at Sinai/Horeb. This unified history of the twelve tribes affirmed that they had all entered the promised land together under Joshua as Yahweh's Chosen People.

7.

Ancient Israel's priest-historians ordinarily taught that the Patriarchs had worshiped Yahweh exclusively just as their descendants were later commanded to do by the law of Moses:

> I am Yahweh your God, who brought you out of the land of Egypt, out of the house of bondage. You shall have no other gods before me. (Ex 20:2–3)

Yet, despite the Bible's priestly attributions of patriarchal devotion to Yahweh, one of Israel's priest-historians preserved the discrepant memory (ultimately derived from one of the Rachel tribes) that the Patriarchs had not actually addressed their God as Yahweh. The priest-historian who preserved this memory did so while attempting to join the tradition of the Patriarchs to Israel's later Mosaic covenant with Yahweh:

> And God said to Moses, "I am Yahweh. I appeared to Abraham, to Isaac, and to Jacob, as God Almighty [El Shaddai], but by my name Yahweh, I did not make myself known to them. I also established my covenant with them, to give them the land of Canaan, the land in which they dwelt as sojourners." (Ex 6:2–4)

Because this memory runs contrary to the usual "theological" (not "historical") view that the Patriarchs had worshiped Yahweh, we may safely infer that it is probably reliable. It follows, therefore, that the Patriarchs and their families probably did not worship Yahweh exclusively as their covenant God. Not until centuries later (c. 1250 B.C.) did Moses teach the Rachel tribes, and the Levites who had allied with them, to worship "Yahweh" exclusively.

Moses probably learned to name God "Yahweh" after he fled from Egypt to the land of Midian (Ex 2:15). While residing in Midian, Moses married Zipporah (Ex 2:21), the daughter of Jethro, "the priest of Midian" (Ex 2:18; 3:1). It is not likely that Moses' Midianite sojourn and marriage were theological inventions. For enmity eventually developed between Midian, on one side, and Moses (Num 22:4–7; 31:1–7; Jos 13:21) and Israel (Judg 6:1–6) on the other.

Moses was probably told by his father-in-law, Jethro (a local authority in religious matters), that in the past "Hebrews" had sometimes visited a nearby holy mountain to worship the god who dwelt on its summit. This mountain was likely located in Midian or some neighboring region where the Midianites ranged. At the present time it is impossible to locate the holy mountain with any degree of certainty. The mountain was named Horeb (Ex 3:1) by the early priest-historian known as the Elohist (because he always called God "Elohim"), but it was named Sinai (Ex 19:11) by the early priest-historian known as the Yahwist (because he always called God "Yahweh").

The holy mountain (as remembered by the Yahwist) was volcanically active, and its seismic phenomena were understood mythologically as manifestations of Yahweh:

> And Mount Sinai was wrapped in smoke, because Yahweh descended upon it in fire; and the smoke of it went up like the smoke of a kiln, and the whole mountain quaked greatly. (Ex 19:18)

Seminomadic tribes would have periodically visited this holy mountain to invoke the favor of the storm god who was believed to reside at its top. It was probably Jethro who told Moses that the god was called "Yahweh." Such a connection would account for the honor paid Jethro when he came to the same mountain to meet Moses and the Hebrew tribes after they had escaped from Egypt (Ex 18:5–12):

> And Jethro said, "Blessed be Yahweh, who has delivered you out of the hand of the Egyptians and out of the hand of Pharaoh. Now I know that Yahweh is greater than all gods, because he delivered the people from under the hand of the Egyptians."
>
> And Jethro, Moses' father-in-law, offered a burnt offering and sacrifices to God; and Aaron came with all the elders . . . to eat bread with Moses' father-in-law before God. (Ex 18:10–12)

Perhaps a backdrop like the one suggested above is what led Moses to interpret his encounter with God at the holy mountain as an encounter with the God of his "Hebrew" kinsmen still in Egypt.

It is fair to infer that Moses, while tending his father-in-law's flocks near the mountain, experienced God's Self-communication with revelatory intensity. His revelatory encounter was possibly triggered by a startling experience of "St. Elmo's fire" (an unusual atmospheric phenomenon caused by electric charges contacting an object and producing a fiery but harmless display) enveloping a bush or small tree on a lower slope of the mountain. Although natural, such a rare and elusive phenomenon would have been construed mythologically by Moses and would have suggested the presence of the fire-displaying Numen thought to dwell atop the mountain.

Moses would then have assumed that it was "Yahweh," the God whom he had been told dwelt at the top of the mountain, who had mysteriously (nonverbally) communicated with him. (The priest-historians later assumed and supplied the "theological" dialog between Yahweh and Moses which we find in Ex 3:4–4:23.) Yahweh had laid hold of his being, Moses probably concluded, to encourage him to return to Egypt and seek the release of his Hebrew kinsmen—a project whose feasibility Moses had very likely been brooding over for some time.

When Moses later succeeded in securing the release of the Hebrews, he probably decided that he should bring them back to the holy mountain in the hope that they would experience the numinous Presence of Yahweh as he had. This assumption would explain why Moses hastened to lead the Hebrews to the mountain of revelation. (Moses' Hebrew kinsmen would not yet have thought of themselves as "Israelites"; see Ex 1:15–22; 2:6–7, 11–13.)

Upon arrival, Moses and the Hebrew escapees encamped in the valley below the mountain and waited for Yahweh's revelatory manifestation. Some days after they encamped (according to the Elohist), a storm arose and a storm cloud gathered at the top of the mountain. We have already noted in the first chapter that (1) the cloud would have been perceived as a sign of Yahweh's numinous Presence, (2) the lightning would have been seen as a manifestation of Yahweh's glorious power, and (3) the thunder would have been heard as Yahweh's awe-inspiring voice:

> On the morning of the third day there were thunders and lightnings, and a thick cloud upon the mountain, and a very loud trumpet blast, so that all the people who

> were in the camp trembled. Then Moses brought the people out of the camp to meet God; and they took their stand at the foot of the mountain. . . . And as the sound of the trumpet grew louder and louder, Moses spoke, and God answered him in thunder .
> (Ex 19:16–17, 19)

After prayerful reflection, Moses probably concluded that since Yahweh had accomplished their deliverance from Egypt and had come to meet them at the holy mountain, Yahweh desired them to enter into a covenant (a sacred agreement): Yahweh wanted them to agree to serve Yahweh exclusively as their covenant God. If they so agreed and served Yahweh righteously, then Yahweh would surely continue to bless and protect them—for a "promise" of intended blessing was implicit in Moses' extraordinary experience of God's gracious Self-communication.

In order that his fellow Hebrews might clearly comprehend their covenant obligations, Moses created a practical law code consisting (originally) of ten brief commandments. These "ten" commandments were designed to be memorized and recalled easily with the aid of "ten" fingers. Over the centuries (especially during the Exile and shortly thereafter, c. 587-500 B.C.), Yahweh's priests created an appropriate narrative that related the solemn origin of the commandments. They also added (or substituted) a number of clarifying words, phrases, and sentences to the original form of the commandments. It is impossible to determine precisely their original form, but it was probably close to the following (easily memorizable) reconstruction:

1. You shall not have other gods before Yahweh.
2. You shall not make a graven image of Yahweh.
3. You shall not take Yahweh's name in vain.
4. You shall not fail to keep the Sabbath.
5. You shall not fail to honor your father and mother.
6. You shall not commit murder.
7. You shall not commit adultery.
8. You shall not steal.
9. You shall not bear false witness.
10. You shall not covet what belongs to your neighbor.

It should be noted that none of the moral standards expressed in the Ten Commandments originated with Moses. Similar moral norms had already been taught in Ancient Near Eastern law codes many centuries before Moses (most notably the Code of Hammurabi, c. 1750 B.C.). Even the henotheistic demand of the first commandment had already been legislated c. 1370 B.C. by Akhenaten, the "heretical" Pharaoh. (Perhaps Moses, while in Egypt, had heard of and was influenced by Akhenaten's attempt at henotheistic reform.)

One of ancient Israel's early priest-historians (the "Yahwist") remembered that originally the Ten Commandments had constituted the substance of the Mosaic covenant with Yahweh:

> And Yahweh said to Moses, "Write these words; in accordance with these words I have made a covenant with you and with Israel." And he was there with Yahweh forty days and forty nights; he neither ate bread nor drank water. And he wrote upon the tables the words of the covenant, the Ten Commandments.
> (Ex 34:27–28)

Over the course of many centuries, the priests continued to expand Moses' original law code by adding later legislation and their theologically unified history of God's covenant people. All of these additions were attributed in folk fashion to Moses so that the authority of his original law code would accrue to them. By the time the law of Moses had essentially reached its final form (c. 500 B.C.), it had become five books: Genesis, Exodus, Leviticus, Numbers, and Deuteronomy. (It is possible that it was not Moses but Israel's priest-historians who introduced the word "covenant" to describe the sacred agreement which Moses mediated between Yahweh and the Hebrews at Horeb/Sinai.)

8.

There is other telltale evidence in the Old Testament that suggests that the Patriarchs had not yet learned to practice henotheism (the exclusive worship of one god while still believing that other gods exist). For example, Jacob's wife, Rachel, stole her father Laban's household gods (idols) and took them with her when she and Jacob departed permanently from her father's camp. (She very likely would not have done so if she and Jacob had truly been henotheists or monotheists.) Laban pursued them and angrily demanded the return of his household gods:

Gen 31:31a, 32

> Jacob answered Laban. . . . "Anyone with whom you find your gods shall not live." . . . Now Jacob did know that Rachel had stolen them.

Gen 31:34, 35b

> Rachel had taken the household gods and put them in the camel's saddle, and sat upon them. Laban felt all about the tent, but did not find them. . . . He searched but did not find the household gods.

At a later stage in the story of Jacob we again learn about the images of foreign gods who are worshiped by members of Jacob's own family:

> So Jacob said to his household and all who were with him, "Put away the foreign gods that are among you, and purify yourselves. . . . then let us arise and go to Bethel that I may make there an altar to the God who answered me in the day of my distress and has gone with me wherever I have gone." So they gave to Jacob all the foreign gods that they had . . . and Jacob hid them under the oak which was near Shechem. (Gen 35:2–4)

An early priest-historian in Israel modified the memory of patriarchal polytheism in order to present Jacob as an exemplary henotheist who worshiped God at Bethel. (We will return to the sanctuary at Bethel below.)

9.

After the twelve-tribe league was formed, the Levitical priests who guarded the ark of Yahweh at the central sanctuary worked assiduously to propagate their unified view of Israel's sacred history. They did so in the hope of encouraging the long-settled tribes who had recently been polytheists to obey the Mosaic covenant law by which the newly formed alliance was theoretically bound. The overarching concern of the priests who guarded Yahweh's ark was always the successful attainment of exclusive worship of Yahweh (as required by the first and most important of the ten Mosaic commandments).

These henotheizing priests of Yahweh were usually the descendants of the Levites who had participated in the covenant at Sinai with the Rachel tribes. We may reasonably assume that God regularly encouraged the henotheizing zeal of the Levitical priests who guarded Yahweh's ark, because ancient Israel, against enormous odds, eventually became the first nation to understand and practice exclusive monotheism. Ordinarily, smaller, less powerful, and technically less developed nations acculturate to larger, more powerful, and more technically advanced nations. In the case of Israel, however, this expected outcome did not occur; the opposite eventually occurred.

It was relatively easy for tribal leaders to agree to the exclusive worship of Yahweh at the central sanctuary. However, it was quite another matter to insure that individual Israelites would locally abide by such an agreement. There are many indications in the Bible that the priests who guarded Yahweh's ark had good reason to be anxious about local practices among the twelve tribes.

We already observed that the Leah tribes (and also the Zilpah and Bilhah tribes) had settled in the land of Canaan well before the arrival of Joshua, the Rachel tribes, and the Levites. During that earlier period, the settled tribes lived near and traded with Canaanite neighbors. The biblical and archeological evidence suggests that the tribes who had settled in the land earlier had assimilated much of Canaanite culture, including the religion and language of Canaan. (We have already noted above that biblical Hebrew is a Canaanite dialect; see 2 Kgs 18:26, 28; Is 36:11, 13; 2 Chr 32:18; Neh 13:24.)

There are many indications that the tribes who settled earlier in Canaan identified the chief of their ancestral gods with "El," the chief god of the Canaanite pantheon. Accordingly, they learned to worship El at that god's traditional sanctuaries—Beth-El, Penu-El, El-Khadr—and used various of El's local titles—El Shaddai, El Elyon, El Berith, El Olam. It is not surprising, therefore, that many of the early Israelites bore the name of the god El as a sacred component of their names: Isra-el, Ishma-el, Othni-el, Jei-el, Eli-el,

El-iezer, El-kanah, El-ishana, El-easah—a practice obviously meant to honor their god (or chief god).

At that stage in their history, the tribes who settled early probably also worshiped the goddess Asherah as the consort of El. It had long been customary for an El sanctuary to include a stone pillar which symbolized El's phallic power as the male divinity who was father of the gods. Such a sanctuary would also have included either a living tree or a stylized tree carved from wood which symbolized the life-engendering power which enabled Asherah to be the mother of the gods (Gen 12:6–7; Jos 24:26; Judg 9:6; Ezek 6:13). The stylized tree at an El sanctuary was called *the* asherah. This suggests that a cult object symbolizing her life-bestowing power was being spoken of and not the goddess herself.

When the long-settled tribes later promised Joshua that they would worship Yahweh exclusively, many of them identified their traditional god El with Yahweh, the covenant God of their newly formed twelve-tribe league. Those who made this identification believed that the name El could be used interchangeably with the name Yahweh. Using El's name as a synonym for Yahweh presented little difficulty for these early Israelites because the proper noun El was the same as the common Hebrew (Canaanite) noun for any male god (el).

Once this identification was made, the Israelites decided that Yahweh could be worshiped at the long-established and venerable sanctuaries of El in the land of Canaan. (We find no priestly or prophetic protests against the worship of El in the Bible, whereas protests against the worship of Baal, Astarte, and Asherah are frequent.) The Israelites also seem to have decided that the traditional sacred pillar and sacred tree placed in El shrines could remain as symbols of Yahweh's life-bestowing power. (The textual evidence which invites this inference will appear below.)

These traditional cult objects were probably not considered incompatible with Yahweh worship by most Israelites both before and throughout the monarchy:

Judg 9:6

> And all the citizens of Shechem came together . . . and they went and made Abimilech king, by the oak of the pillar at Shechem.

Hos 3:4

For the children of Israel shall dwell many days without king or prince, without sacrifice or pillar.

Jer 2:26–27

As a thief is shamed when caught, so the house of Israel shall be shamed: they, their kings, their princes, their priests, and their prophets, who say to a tree, "You are my father," and to a stone, "You gave me birth."

In order to "justify" the use of such pillars at Yahweh shrines, some of the priests in early Israel very likely created the stories in which the patriarch Jacob used a stone pillar to worship Yahweh:

Gen 28:13, 18

And behold, Yahweh . . . said, "I am Yahweh, the God of Abraham your father and the God of Isaac; the land on which you lie I will give to you and to your descendants" . . . . So Jacob rose early in the morning, and he took the stone which he had put under his head and set it up for a pillar and poured oil on top of it.

Gen 35:14

And Jacob set up a pillar in the place where he [God] had spoken with him, a pillar of stone; and he poured out a drink offering on it, and poured oil on it.

Before King Josiah's reform (c. 620 B.C.), the same tolerant attitude toward cultic pillar and tree probably also characterized most Israelites in the southern kingdom (Judah), even many in Jerusalem:

2 Kgs 23:6

And he [King Josiah] brought out the asherah from the house of Yahweh, outside Jerusalem, to the book Kidron, and beat it to dust and cast the dust on the graves of the common people.

The very fact that the reforming priests and prophets who wrote after Josiah's reform outlawed or objected to such pillars and stylized trees indicates that they were probably still widely used in sanctuaries away from Jerusalem, and sometimes even there (depending on the will of the reigning king):

Deut 16:21–22

You shall not plant any tree as an asherah beside the altar of Yahweh your God which you shall make. And you shall not set up a pillar, which Yahweh your God hates.

Jer 3:9

She [Israel] polluted the land, committing adultery with stone and tree.

The conversion of El sanctuaries to the worship of Yahweh probably seemed acceptable to the early priests of Yahweh (many of whom were not Levites) because Abraham, Isaac, and Jacob were also remembered as having worshiped their God "El Shaddai" at El sanctuaries when they sojourned in Canaan:

Gen 17:1

Yahweh appeared to Abram and said to him, "I am God Almighty" [El shaddai]; walk before me blameless. And I will make my covenant between me and you, and will multiply you exceedingly."

Gen 21:33

Abraham planted a tamarisk tree in Beer-sheba, and called there on the name of . . . God Eternal [El olam].

Gen 28:1, 3

Then Isaac called Jacob and blessed him. . . . "May God Almighty [El shaddai] bless you and make you fruitful and multiply you, and may you become a company of peoples.

Gen 35:11

God appeared to Jacob again, when he came from Paddan-aram, and blessed him . . . . And God said to him, "I am God Almighty [El shaddai]. . . . The land which I gave to Abraham and Isaac I will give . . . to your descendants after you." . . . So Jacob called the

> name of the place where God had spoken with him, Beth-el [House of El].

> **Ex 6:2**
>
> And God said to Moses, "I am Yahweh. I appeared to Abraham, to Isaac, and to Jacob as God almighty [El Shaddai].

Such patriarchal traditions were either created or adapted by the Yahwistic priests of early Israel in order to "justify" the right of the Patriarchs' descendants to worship at former El sanctuaries (where a stone pillar and an asherah were always found).

We encounter such a justification story when we are told that Jacob stopped to rest at "Beth-el" while fleeing from Esau to his uncle, Laban. The story recounts that while sleeping near the well-known shrine of El at Beth-el (House of El), Jacob had a revelatory dream which confirmed that this sanctuary was indeed the "house of El and the gateway to heaven" (two of the traditional epithets of the ancient shrine at Beth-el). It was fitting and lawful, therefore, for Jacob's descendants to worship their covenant God, Yahweh, at this ancient El shrine after it had been converted to a Yahweh shrine:

> Jacob left Beersheba and went toward Haran. And he came to a certain place, and stayed there that night, because the sun had set. Taking one of the stones of that place, he put it under his head and lay down in that place to sleep.
>
> And he dreamed that there was a ladder set up on earth, and the top of it reached to heaven; and behold, the angels of God were ascending and descending on it! And behold, Yahweh stood above it and said, "I am Yahweh, the God of Abraham your father, and the God of Isaac; the land on which you lie I will give to you and to your descendants." . . .
>
> "Behold I am with you and will keep you wherever you go, for I will not leave you until I have done that of which I have spoken to you." Then Jacob awoke from his sleep and said, "Surely Yahweh is in this place and I

> did not know it." And he was afraid and said, How awesome is this place! This is none other than the house of God [El], and this is the gate of heaven."
> (Gen 28:10–17)

A similar justification story involving the patriarch Abraham was created by the Yahwistic priests who guarded the sacred ark in Jerusalem after David had transported it there. The priests who introduced this story (possibly with David's encouragement) made a conscious effort to identify Yahweh with the god "El elyon" (El most high) who had been worshiped in pre-Davidic Jerusalem. The story relates that invading kings had carried off Abraham's nephew, Lot, with other captives from the region. Abraham pursued the invaders, freed their captives, and repossessed the goods which the invaders had plundered. Upon his successful return, he and his hungry companions were met with a gift of food by Melchi-zedek, the priest-king of Salem (Salem = Jeru-salem):

> And Melchi-zedek king of Salem brought out bread and wine; he was priest of God Most High [El elyon]. And he blessed him [Abraham] and said,
>
> "Blessed be Abram by God Most High
>   [El elyon], maker of heaven and earth;
> And blessed be God Most High
>   [El elyon], who has delivered
> your enemies into your hand!"
>
> And Abram gave him a tenth of everything. And the king of Sodom said to Abram, "Give me the persons, but take the goods for yourself." But Abram said to the king of Sodom, "I have sworn to *Yahweh, God Most High* [El elyon], maker of heaven and earth, that I would not take . . . anything that is yours."
> (Gen 14:18–23)

This story was probably created and recited by Yahweh's priests to legitimize their decision that Yahweh could be worshiped in Jerusalem after David had taken it from the Jebusites (Canaanites). More importantly, however, the story also seems to have justified the paying of tithes (offerings meant to support God's priests) to the priest Zadok. Zadok unexpectedly appears alongside Abiathar as a priest of Yahweh after David took Jerusalem (2 Sam 8:17; 1 Kgs 1:7–8).

There is scholarly disagreement about the identity of Zadok. Probably a majority would hold that he was a Jebusite priest who had served El elyon in Jerusalem before David took the city. The author of this book, however, favors a minority view that Zadok was the last priest-king of Jebusite Jerusalem. Confronted by David's military superiority, Zadok agreed (1) to surrender the city to David by means of a secret password ("The blind and the lame shall not come into the house;" 2 Sam 5:8–9), and (2) to convert to the worship of Yahweh in exchange for the privilege of serving as a priest of Yahweh in David's Jerusalem.

That agreement would have provided Zadok with an honorable means of livelihood in exchange for his peaceful surrender of the city to David. Such an arrangement would have seemed feasible to David, for the custom of preferring a Levite as a priest had not yet hardened into law (see Judg 17:1–13). David also appointed some of his own sons to serve as priests at Yahweh's sanctuary in Jerusalem (2 Sam 8:18).

The Yahwistic priests justified David's concession to Zadok by creating a sacred story relating that Abraham, while sojourning in Canaan, had worshiped El elyon the god of ancient Salem. (They probably assumed in folk fashion that their story was likely to be true because they remembered that the Patriarchs had worshiped the god El; Ex 6:2–3). Moreover, they related that Abraham had paid tithes to Melchi-zedek the priest-king of El elyon in Salem. Surely, therefore, it was permissible for Abraham's descendants to worship in the same place, to accept the priestly ministrations of Zadok, Melchi-zedek's priestly descendant, and also to offer Yahweh's tithes to Zadok. Furthermore, when David became the new priest-king of Jerusalem (see Ps 110:1–4), he too was entitled to partake of the tithes offered to Yahweh in Jerusalem. (For a brief review of other interpretations of Zadok's identity, see "Zadok" in the *Anchor Bible Dictionary*.)

10.

When the Israelites who had formerly worshiped El began to identify El with Yahweh, some of them might have assumed that El's consort, Asherah, could also be worshiped as Yahweh's consort. Whether or not such worship actually occurred is debated by scholars. There is no clear and unambiguous evidence that the Israelites ever worshiped Asherah in that manner even though the Bible indicates that the cult object called "the asherah" was commonly placed at the side of Yahweh's altar:

Jos 24:26

> And Joshua wrote these words in the Scroll of the Law of God; and he took a great stone, and he set it up there under the oak in the sanctuary of Yahweh.

Judg 9:6

> And all the citizens of Shechem came together . . . and they went and made Abimelech king, by the oak of the pillar at Shechem.

Some scholars think "the asherah" was an idolatrous image of the goddess Asherah. Many others, however, believe that it was either a living or a stylized tree which had become a traditional sacred fixture at Yahweh shrines because there had always been such a tree beside the altar of an El shrine. (There can be little doubt that the asherah at an El shrine was originally intended as a symbol of the goddess Asherah, El's consort.)

When El shrines were converted by Israelites into Yahweh shrines (after the agreement brokered by Joshua), the asherah was probably allowed by custom to remain at the side of Yahweh's altar. However, it would then have been understood as a symbol of the blessings of life and fertility which Yahweh would bestow on his worshipers (without need of a divine consort). The prophet Hosea, when speaking in the person of Israel's God (in the northern kingdom, c. 730 B.C.), clearly assumed that such "tree" symbolism was not idolatrous and would be understood when applied to Yahweh:

> O Ephraim, what have I to do with idols? It is I [Yahweh] who answer and look after you. I am like an evergreen cypress, from me comes your fruit. (Hos 14:8)

About a century and a half later, Jeremiah the prophet (who prophesied in the Southern Kingdom shortly before the Exile to

Babylon in 587 B.C.) was aware that prayers spoken to Yahweh were being addressed to the pillar and tree still present in many Yahweh shrines:

> As a thief is shamed when caught, so the house of Israel shall be shamed: they, their kings, their princes, their priests, and their prophets, who say to a tree, "You are my father," and to a stone, "You gave me birth."
> (Jer 2:26–27)

It is noteworthy that the tree referred to just above by Jeremiah pointed to the presence of Yahweh and not Asherah for Israelite worshipers. Nevertheless, Jeremiah had learned to share the scorn of the Jerusalem priests for the ritual invocation of such a cultic tree; he, too, regarded such an ambiguous practice as an intolerable violation of the second commandment.

Whatever the Israelites may have *originally* thought about "the asherah," eventually (early in the first half of the monarchy) the priests of Yahweh in Jerusalem began to fiercely oppose its presence near Yahweh's altar:

> You shall not plant any wooden object as an asherah beside the altar of Yahweh your God. (Deut 16:21)

The Jerusalem priests possibly began waging war against the asherah because some of the remaining Canaanites or earliest Israelites had never ceased worshiping the goddess Asherah, and her cult continued in the land. We learn, for example, in the First Book of Kings that Maacah, the queen mother of King Asa of Judah, might have been a devotee of the goddess Asherah:

> And Asa . . . removed Maacah his mother from being queen mother because she had an abominable wooden pole made for Asherah; and Asa cut down her wooden pole and burned it at the brook Kidron.
> (1 Kgs 15:11a, 13)

The Hebrew text, however, is ambiguous and can be interpreted in two ways: (1) Maacah commissioned and placed in the Jerusalem temple a carved image of the goddess Asherah, or (2) she placed in the temple a carved wooden pole which was a version of the traditional cult object called "the asherah." If the latter was the case, it might be that Maacah was the first to introduce the traditional asherah into the Jerusalem temple as a symbol of Yahweh's fertile power. (There is no mention of an asherah in the detailed description of Solomon's temple and its sacred furnishings in 1 Kgs 6–7.)

The continuation of the cult of Asherah, if such there was, would, certainly have alarmed the henotheistic priests of Yahweh. They would understandably have been hostile toward the traditional cult object which shared Ashera's name. But it is equally possible that the novel intrusion of "the asherah" into the Jerusalem temple (the central sanctuary where Yahweh's sacred ark was kept) was enough to trigger the hostile response of the Jerusalem priests. A custom they had perhaps tolerated at Yahweh's shrines away from Jerusalem might have been judged as intolerable when it began to compete with Yahweh's *ark*.

Whatever the cult object placed in the temple by Maacah may have been, there is no doubt that the Yahwistic priests in Jerusalem viewed it as an unacceptable intrusion. From that time on, for whatever reason, the Jerusalem priests and the prophets who concurred with them railed against it as a threat to Yahweh's lawful worship:

> Yahweh said to me in the days of King Josiah, "Have you seen what she did, that faithless one, Israel, how . . . she polluted the land, committing adultery [unlawful worship] with stone and tree." (Jer 3:6, 9)

Nevertheless, the asherah continued to be venerated by many Israelites until the Exile to Babylon in 587 B.C. (see 1 Kgs 14:15; 16:33; 2 Kgs 13:6; 17:16; 21:3; 23:6–7; Deut 16:21). The tenacious refusal of so many Israelites to repudiate the asherah possibly indicates that the goddess Asherah was still being worshiped in the land.

But their refusal more likely indicates that veneration of the ashera" had been judged compatible with Yahwism well before it eventually incurred the undying enmity of the Levitical priests who served Yahweh in Jerusalem. It probably remained a source of contention throughout the remainder of the monarchy because of honestly differing interpretations of lawful Yahweh worship.

Shortly after the reign of the reforming King Josiah (c. 600 B.C.) and during the Exile in Babylonia (587-538 B.C.), the reforming

Jerusalem priests served as Judah's historians. These priest-historians wrote the collection of books known as the Deuteronomic History (Joshua, Judges, 1 and 2 Samuel, 1 and 2 Kings). When writing this history, they consistently imposed their hostile view of the asherah on Israel's pre-Exilic history.

11.

It was the cult of the fertility god, Baal, that proved to be the greatest threat to the exclusive worship of Yahweh before the Exile. Not only El but also Baal had been worshiped by many of the tribes who settled in Canaan before the formation of the twelve-tribe league. The cult of the rain-producing god Baal had strong appeal to farmers in a thirsty land.

A critical reading of Israel's pre-Exilic history indicates that after the twelve tribes agreed to worship Yahweh as their covenant God, some of the Israelites assigned various Baal attributes and titles to Yahweh. In the early monarchy, we find Israelites who very probably are worshipers of Yahweh, who either have the title Baal (= Lord, Master) as a component of their own names or who have given such names to their children.

For example, one of the "mighty" warriors who joined David when he fled from King Saul was a kinsman of Saul named Beal-iah (= Yahweh is Baal or Lord; 1 Chr 12:5). And David himself had a son named Beel-iada (= the Lord knows; 1 Chr 14:7). Saul also had a son (Esh-baal = man of the Lord; 1 Chr 8:33; 9:39) and grandson (Meri-baal = either "man of the Lord" or "loved by the Lord"; Chr 9:40) whose names contained the title Baal. Since David and Saul were loyal worshipers of Yahweh, it seems likely that the title Baal in the names of their children was meant to honor Yahweh. It is fair to conclude that the title had earlier been borrowed from the worship of Baal and given to Yahweh as a fitting honorific.

However, when the reforming priest-historians from Judah wrote the books of Samuel and Kings, they changed the names of David's and Saul's sons (noted just above in the citations from Chronicles) in order to remove from them the ambiguous and hateful word Baal: Beel-iada (= the Lord knows) became El-iada (= God knows; 2 Sam 5:16); Esh-baal (= man of the Lord) became Ish-bosheth (= man of shame; 2 Sam 2:10).

In addition, the reforming prophet Hosea indicated disapprovingly that many Israelites in the northern kingdom addressed Yahweh with the ambiguous title Baal:

> And in that day, says Yahweh, you will call me "My husband," and no longer will you call me "My Baal." For I will remove the names of the Baals from her mouth, and they shall be mentioned by name no more.
> (Hos 2:16–17)

It is altogether possible that after the refugees from the northern kingdom carried Hosea's words south to Judah, it was his words which encouraged Judah's reforming priests to remove the title Baal from the names discussed above.

12.

The pre-Exilic history of Israel indicates that a minority of Israelite farmers continued to worship Baal locally even after Yahweh had "officially" become the exclusive covenant God of the twelve-tribe league. Evidence for this conclusion is provided in the Book of Judges by the story of Gideon's conversion to Yahweh's exclusive worship. The story relates that Gideon was moved by a revelatory "experience" of Yahweh to champion Yahweh's cause while living in a farming community in which most, even his own family, seem to have been devoted to Baal:

> That night Yahweh said to him, "Take your father's bull, the second bull seven years old, and pull down the altar of Baal which your father has [and cut down the asherah that is beside it]; and build an altar to Yahweh your God on top of the stronghold here, with stones laid in due order; then take the second bull, and offer it as a burnt offering [with the wood of the asherah which you shall cut down]."
>
> So Gideon took ten men of his servants, and did as Yahweh had told him; but because he was too afraid of his family and the men of the town to do it by day, he did it by night. (Judg 6:25–27)

The references to the asherah which are bracketed in the account of Gideon's dramatic conversion were probably added to the original story at a later date. It seems likely that the reforming priest-historians who wrote the Book of Judges introduced the asherah into the Gideon tradition in order to lend support to their emphatic view that the asherah was an unlawful cult object.

Because the asherah is sometimes mentioned in connection with the worship of Baal, the impression is easily given that Asherah was worshiped by Israelites as Baal's consort. That, however, was probably not the case. We have already noted earlier in this chapter that Asherah was the consort of El. It seems very likely that Astarte was the fertility goddess usually worshiped as Baal's consort during the period of the twelve-tribe league and the monarchy (Judg 2:13; 10:6; 1 Sam 7:3–4; 12:10; 31:10; 2 Kgs 23:13).

The customary pairing of Baal and Astarte would explain why the priest-historians of Yahweh regularly went out of their way to dishonor Astarte's name by combining it with the word "bosheth," which means shame (Astarte + bosheth = Ashtoreth, sing., Ashtaroth, pl.). The priests would not have gone regularly to the trouble to dishonor Astarte in this manner if they had not perceived her as a serious threat to Yahweh's exclusive worship in Israel. (In the citation that follows, "Ashtaroth" is the plural form for unlawful images of Astarte, just as "Baals" is the plural form for unlawful images of Baal.)

> Then Samuel said to all the house of Israel, "If you are returning to Yahweh with all your heart, then put away the foreign gods and the Ashtaroth from among you, and direct your heart to Yahweh, and serve him only, and he will deliver you out of the hand of the Philistines."
>
> So Israel put away the Baals and the Ashtaroth, and they served Yahweh only. (1 Sam 7:3–4)

To be sure, 1 Kings 18:19 speaks of "the four hundred and fifty prophets of Baal, and the four hundred prophets of Asherah, who eat at Jezebel's table." This pairing seems to imply that Asherah was worshiped in the northern kingdom as Baal's consort. Many biblical scholars think, however, that the mention of Asherah's prophets is a later addition to the story. For after her prophets are mentioned, they play no further role in the story. The priests of Baal, on the other hand, are adverted to again and again. It seems very likely, therefore, that an earlier version of the story featured only the prophets of Baal as the adversaries of Elijah. The addition was probably made by the priest-historians in Jerusalem after King Josiah's reform (c. 621 B.C.) attempted to eliminate the traditional asherah from Israelite worship (2 Kgs 23:1–22).

The Phoenician (Canaanite) princess Jezebel certainly encouraged the worship of Baal, the chief god of Sidon, when she became the wife of King Ahab of Israel. But since there is no evidence whatsoever that Asherah was ever worshiped at Sidon, Jezebel probably did not foster Asherah's cult at Ahab's court, as we are told in 1 Kings 18:19. It is far more likely that the reference to Asherah's many prophets is a secondary addition intended as polemic against the continued presence of the suspect asherah in Israelite worship of Yahweh. The original story of Elijah's zealous struggle against Baal worship was probably expanded by Yahweh's priests to invite an equally zealous battle against the hated asherah.

By now it should be evident to the reader that the early Israelite tribes (from Joshua to the inception of the monarchy) were not yet monotheists. On the contrary, in the next chapter we shall see that even their commitment to henotheism remained fragile and tenuous until the collapse of the monarchy and the Exile to Babylon in 587 B.C. Indeed, if God had not regularly conferred the encouraging experience of divine Presence and Love on Israel's Yahwistic priests and prophets, they would probably not have persevered in their struggle against polytheism and would not have been able to grasp and foster monotheism as soon as they did.

Questions for Review and Discussion

1. Why do folk historians "oversimplify" and "hyperbolize" their narratives?

2. When do folk historians think it is permissible and even necessary to "create" a narrative?

3. Which of the "twelve tribes" were probably the first to

settle in the central highlands of Canaan? On what indirect evidence is this conclusion based?

4. Which of the "twelve tribes" were probably the last to settle in the central highlands of Canaan? On what indirect evidence is this conclusion based?

5. Who probably negotiated the henotheistic agreement that led to the formation of the "twelve-tribe" league called Israel? Why did he have to negotiate that agreement?

6. Which of the "Leah" tribes were unable to successfully seize and defend territory of their own in Canaan? What subsequent fate befell these tribes? On what indirect evidence is this conclusion based?

7. Which of the Israelite tribes were probably descended from Abraham, Isaac, and Jacob? Which were probably descended from Israel? What indirect evidence supports your answers?

8. What was probably the actual reason for Joshua requiring so many adult Israelite males to receive circumcision? Where do we read about this event?

9. Why did some seminomadic tribes in the Ancient Near East organize themselves into leagues of "twelve" or "six" tribes?

10. Where and how did Moses probably learn to call God "Yahweh"? Explain your answer.

11. What were the two possible reasons the priests of Yahweh eventually decided to wage war against "the asherah"? What did an asherah probably look like?

12. Why did some Israelite farmers continue to worship the god Baal even after their tribal leaders swore exclusive allegiance to Yahweh at Shechem?

Chapter Three

Israel's Henotheistic Faith during the First Half of the Monarchy

1.

Before we begin to deal with the primary subject of this chapter, we need to reflect briefly on the important distinction between *exegesis* and *eisegesis:* These terms refer to opposite ways of interpreting a biblical text. Exegesis is the approach that attempts to take out of the text the essential meaning which its author truly intended. Eisegesis, to the contrary, unwittingly reads into the text a foreign meaning which its author did not intend. Responsible scholarship reminds us that we should always strive to practice exegesis and avoid eisegesis.

Arming ourselves with this critical distinction will help us avoid the unwitting error of retrojecting ancient Israel's later discovery of monotheism into earlier henotheistic statements made by her prophets and priest-historians. Consider, for example, the well known language of the first Mosaic commandment:

> I am Yahweh, your God, who brought
> you out of the land of Egypt, out of

> that house of bondage. You shall have no other gods besides me. (Ex 20:2–3)

Because ancient Israel discovered and embraced monotheism near the end of her captivity in Babylon (c. 540 B.C.), subsequent tradition has assumed that the much earlier Mosaic commandment (c. 1250 B.C.) is also monotheistic in nature. Yet contemporary scholarship reminds us that if we take the commandment's language at face value and refrain from reading monotheistic assumptions into it, its intent appears to be henotheistic. For the commandment does not admonish us to avoid worshiping "false gods" or "dumb idols" that are "not gods." After the Exile, however, all of these negative expressions were used by Israel's priests and prophets to teach and defend her newly discovered monotheism.

What the first commandment actually required of Israel was abstinence from the worship of "other" gods, the gods of other nations. If we read no preconceived notions into the word "other," we should conclude that the commandment's author probably believed that "other" gods truly existed, but they were not to be worshiped along with or instead of Yahweh. It is understandable that ancient Israel interpreted the first commandment monotheistically when she later embraced monotheism. Moses, however, probably meant to teach Israel that she should practice henotheistic devotion to Yahweh.

The same problem confronts us when some of the pre-Exilic psalms assert that Yahweh is the greatest of the gods. If we take the words of these psalms as we find them, they imply that their authors were henotheists, not monotheists:

Ps 84:7

> The God of gods will be seen in Zion.

Ps 86:8

> There is none like you among the gods, O Yahweh.

Ps 89:6–7

> Who among the heavenly beings is like Yahweh, a God feared in the council of the holy ones, great and terrifying above all that are round about him?

Ps 96:4

> For Yahweh is a great God, and a great King among all the gods.

Ps 136:2

> Give thanks to the God of gods, for his steadfast love endures forever.

Ps 138:1

> O Yahweh . . . before the gods I sing your praise.

There are several other psalms that contain similar henotheistic language but also admonish against the folly of worshiping dumb idols. Clearly, their idol-ridiculing language is monotheistic. But that language was probably supplied by a priest-editor after the Exile when Israel had begun to practice monotheism. In the psalm verses cited below, the later additions are bracketed:

Ps 96:4–5

> For great is Yahweh, and greatly to be praised; he is to be feared above all gods. [For all the gods of the peoples are idols; but Yahweh made the heavens.]

Ps 97:6–7, 9

> The heavens proclaim his righteousness; and all the peoples behold his glory. [All worshipers of images are put to shame, who make their boast in worthless idols;] all gods bow down before him . . . For you, O Yahweh . . . are exalted above all gods.

Ps 135:5, 15–18

> For I know that Yahweh is great, and that our Lord is above all gods . . . [The idols of the nations are silver and gold, the work of human hands. They have mouths but speak not, they have eyes, but see not, they have ears, but hear not, nor is there any breath in their mouths. Like them be those who make them!]

We may reasonably assume that the diatribe against idols found in Psalm 135:15-18 was added later to prevent the possible misconstrual of its henotheistic language in v. 5 (and similar language present in other psalms). This diatribe seems to be a later refinement of the post-Exilic ridicule of idols expressed in Is 44:9–20.

2.

In addition to the evidence in the psalms, there are several stories in the Bible which imply that the priest-historians who recorded them still thought henotheistically about the gods of Israel's neighbors. One such story from the period of the Judges recalls that the Philistines defeated the Israelites and captured Yahweh's ark in a battle near the town of Ebenezer in the central highlands:

> So the Philistines fought, and Israel was defeated, and they fled, every man to his home . . . And the ark of God was captured. (1 Sam 4:10a, 11b)

The Philistines then took the ark to the city of Ashdod and placed it at the side of the idol of Dagon, their god. They brought the ark as a gift for Dagon in thanksgiving for their stunning victory over Israel. Placing the ark as a trophy alongside Dagon's idol was also meant to emphasize the humiliating defeat inflicted on Yahweh by Dagon:

> Then the Philistines took the ark of God and brought it into the house of Dagon and set it up beside Dagon. (1 Sam 5:2)

However, shortly after Yahweh's ark was placed in Dagon's temple, a plague broke out in Ashdod (the mention of "tumors" in the text below indicates the "swelling" suffered by the victims of the plague):

> The hand of Yahweh was heavy upon the people of Ashdod, and he terrified and afflicted them with tumors, both Ashdod and its territory. And when the men of Ashdod saw how things were, they said, "The ark of the God of Israel must not remain with us; for his hand is heavy upon us and upon Dagon our god." (1 Sam 5:6–7)

We learn later in the story that along with the plague, the Philistines experienced an inundation of rats (1 Sam 6:5). The rats probably arrived on the ships of the seafaring Philistines and brought plague-bearing fleas with them. The connection between bubonic plague and rats, of course, was not then understood. The plague, therefore, was explained mythologically.

Because the plague had begun soon after the arrival of Yahweh's ark, the Philistines concluded by association that the plague and the accompanying infestation of rats had been inflicted on them by Israel's angry God. Accordingly, they determined to send Yahweh's ark back to Israel accompanied by an appeasing gift from each of the five Philistine city-states. The gifts were symbolic expressions of sympathetic magic: They were meant to win Yahweh's sympathy and to signify to Yahweh the afflictions from which the Philistines hoped to be freed:

> And they said, "What is the guilt offering that we should return to him?" They answered, "Five golden tumors, and five golden rats. . . . You must make images of your tumors and images of your rats that ravage the land, and give glory to the God of Israel." (1 Sam 6:4a, 5)

After Yahweh's priests jubilantly received the returned ark, they created a story which explained why the plague had erupted and why the Philistines had been forced to return Yahweh's ark. They then placed their story before the remembered account of the plague and the ark's return as a preparatory indication of why both events had occurred:

> The Philistines took the ark of God and brought it into the house of Dagon and set it up beside Dagon. And when the people of Ashdod rose early the next day, behold, Dagon had fallen face downward upon the ground before the ark of Yahweh. [All gods bow down before him; Ps 97:7] So they took Dagon and put him back in his place.
>
> But when they arose early on the next morning, behold, Dagon had fallen face downward on the ground before the ark of Yahweh, and the head of Dagon and both his hands were lying cut off. (1 Sam 5:2–4a)

Manifestly, this story was designed to illustrate that Yahweh was mightier than Dagon and, consequently, Dagon was "powerless" to prevent Yahweh from punishing the Philistines with plague and rats. It was for that reason, therefore, that the plague had erupted and that the Philistines had been compelled to return Yahweh's ark.

A critical reading of the entire story being considered indicates that the capture of the ark (an embarrassing memory for Israel) and the outbreak of plague (a common enough occurrence among ancient seafaring merchants) were probably events that happened in close proximity as described. The patently mythical story of Yahweh's shaming of Dagon, however, was a later creation of Yahweh's priests intended to explain why the plague occurred and the ark was returned.

It seems evident that the priests who created the story of Dagon's abject submission to Yahweh actually believed that Dagon was a god but that Yahweh was greater by far than Dagon. For that reason, therefore, Dagon was depicted as lying prostrate before Yahweh's ark on two successive mornings, offering his obeisance to Yahweh's invisible presence. In other words, the priests who created this story were probably henotheists not monotheists.

Another story, one from the period of the monarchy, invites a henotheistic reading even more obvious than the story of the ark's capture and return: We read in the Second Book of Kings that the king of Israel and the king of Judah joined forces to wage war against the king of Moab. The besieged king of Moab, in desperation, sacrificed his eldest son to the god Chemosh on the wall of the city. The king's public sacrifice of his son was a ritual form of sympathetic magic calculated to (1) win powerful support from Chemosh the god of the Moabites and (2) discourage those besieging the city (an ancient form of psychological warfare):

> Then he took his eldest son who was to reign in his stead, and offered him for a burnt offering on the wall. And there came a great wrath upon Israel; and they withdrew from him and returned to their own land. (2 Kgs 3:27)

The departure of the frightened Israelites who had almost won a victory over Moab indicates that they believed Chemosh would surely fight "wrathfully" for the king of Moab. Accordingly, we must conclude that the Israelites (and the priest-historian who reported their behavior) were still henotheists. They believed that the god Chemosh was terrifyingly real and would do fierce battle for so devoted a worshiper as the king of Moab.

It was not, however, only foreign kings who sometimes burned their children as sacrifices. We read in the Second Book of Kings that two kings of Judah also engaged in that hideous practice:

> **2 Kgs 16:2–3a**
>
> Ahaz was twenty years old when he began to reign, and he reigned sixteen years in Jerusalem. And he did not do what was right in the eyes of Yahweh his God as his father David had done. . . . He even burned his son as an offering.

> **2 Kgs 21:1a, 6a**
>
> Manasseh was twelve years old when he began to reign, and he reigned fifty-five years in Jerusalem. And he did what was evil in the sight of Yahweh. . . . And he burned his son as an offering.

In the next chapter we will consider further the practice of child sacrifice. We will then learn more about what might have motivated these two kings of Judah when they engaged in such a religious ritual.

3.

Because the Israelite tribes were so endangered by Philistine aggression, they reluctantly decided c. 1040 B.C. to surrender their tribal autonomy in favor of monarchy. Only a king with supreme authority, they realized, could draft, equip, and train an army able to guarantee Israel's security. Saul, the son of Kish, was Israel's first king (1 Sam 10:1), but his fledgling dynasty was ill-fated (1 Sam 28:15–19; 31:1–7). After the collapse of the house of Saul (2 Sam 4:1–12), the twelve tribes chose David, the son of Jesse, to be their king and to lead them in battle against the threatening Philistines (2 Sam 5:1–3).

After David defeated the Philistines conclusively (2 Sam 8:1), he also compelled the Canaanites who remained unconquered in the land to submit to his authority (2 Sam 24:2, 7; 1 Kgs 9:20–21).

It was King David, therefore, and not Joshua (Jos 11:16–23; Judg 1:1) who completed the conquest of the land of Canaan. A gifted military leader, David went on to subjugate most of the nations that bordered Israel (Phoenicia was the only exception), and he required them to pay annual tribute (2 Sam 8:2–14). Consequently, during the last half of David's reign (c. 1000-960 B.C.) Israel enjoyed previously unknown prestige and prosperity. Even the Pharaoh of Egypt, for reasons of political security, was willing to give his daughter in marriage to David's son Solomon (1 Kgs 3:1).

The priests of Yahweh saw David's spectacular success as a sign of Yahweh's blessing on Israel for the sake of their righteous ancestors, Abraham, Isaac, and Jacob/Israel. The priests also celebrated David's stellar rise to power (Num 24:17) by creating a theology of universal Davidic kingship. They began to teach that through the everlasting dynasty which God had promised David through Nathan the prophet (2 Sam 7:11–15), God's Kingly Reign would eventually be extended over all nations. And when all nations finally submitted to God's Reign and obeyed God's law, the Golden Age would arrive.

When the Golden Age finally arrived, the prophets taught, God would bestow unprecedented prosperity and longevity on Israel and the nations over which she ruled (Is 11:6–9). This divine blessing would be mediated through the Davidic dynasty which would enforce God's law universally (Ps 72:8–11). There would then be universal justice and peace on earth (Is 2:2–4). Echoes of this lofty theology of kingship are heard in Psalm 2 which the priests wrote to celebrate the anointing of David's heirs on the day of their succession. The anointed Son of David (God's Messiah) who represents God's Kingly Reign on earth is the one speaking throughout the psalm:

> Why do the nations conspire, and the peoples plot in vain? The kings of the earth . . . take council together against Yahweh and his anointed [representative] saying, "Let us burst their bonds asunder and cast their cords from us."
>
> He who sits in heaven laughs; Yahweh has them in derision. Then he will speak to them in his wrath, and terrify them in his fury, saying, "I have set my king on Zion, my holy hill."

> I will tell of the decree of Yahweh: He said to me, "You are my son, today I have begotten you. Ask of me, and I will make the nations your heritage, and the ends of the earth your possession. You shall break them with a rod of iron, and dash them in pieces like a potters vessel." (Ps 2:1–8)

Anticipation of the Golden Age to be ushered in by a worthy Davidic heir is also expressed in the following psalm:

Ps 72:1–3

> Give the king your justice, O God, and your righteousness to the royal son! May he judge your people with righteousness and your poor with justice. Let the mountains bring forth prosperity for the people, and the hills in righteousness.

Ps 72:5–6

> May he live while the sun endures, and as long as the moon, throughout all generations! May he be like rain that falls on the mown grass, like showers that water the earth. In his days may righteousness flourish, and peace abound, till the moon be no more!

High hopes, therefore, were attached by the priests of Yahweh to David's dynasty. Subsequent history, however, proved their historical expectations to have been overly optimistic. They did not have to wait long to discover that the picture they had painted of the Davidic dynasty's historical future was far too sanguine. Solomon, David's successor, soon convinced the priests that he did not truly share his father's henotheistic devotion to Yahweh.

(We should note that the prophetic promise that David's sons would reign forever as representatives of God's Kingly Reign was not fulfilled historically, [within history]. Yet, transhistorically, the promise has been marvelously fulfilled in Jesus, the Great Son of David. For the Risen Jesus will reign forever at God's "right hand" [Ps 110:1] as victorious Lord of life and death. Since the Risen Jesus defeated death and despair by the power of his faith and trust in God, he is now God's assurance to all humankind that tragedy and death can be defeated forever through faith and trust in God's goodness.)

After Solomon succeeded his father, David, as king of Israel (1 Kgs 1:28–40), he proceeded to build a splendid temple for Israel's covenant God. When the temple was completed, the ark of Yahweh (which David had brought to Jerusalem; 2 Sam 6:12–17) was solemnly enshrined in its innermost chamber, the Holy of Holies (1 Kgs 8:1–11). The Jerusalem temple then became the new central sanctuary of the twelve tribes.

The priests of Yahweh were, of course, pleased by King Solomon's munificence. At the same time, however, they were deeply troubled by his willingness to tolerate the polytheism of his foreign wives. Solomon allowed these wives to worship the gods of their own nations ("other gods"). Moreover, he built sanctuaries for that purpose on the Mount of Olives within sight of Yahweh's temple:

> Then Solomon built a high place for Chemosh the abomination of Moab, and for Molech the abomination of the Ammonites, on the mountain east of Jerusalem. And he did so for all his foreign wives, who burned incense and offered sacrifice to their gods. And Yahweh was angry with Solomon, because his heart had turned away from Yahweh, the God of Israel. (1 Kgs 11:7–9a)

Understandably, the henotheistic priests of Yahweh were alarmed by Solomon's worldly behavior: He was publicly violating the first and most important of Yahweh's commandments for the sake of his foreign policy. (He probably did not wish to offend the royal daughters of foreign kings.) He was also, the priests realized, giving encouragement to those farmers in the land who were already worshiping or inclined to worship the fertility gods Baal and Astarte. If this state of affairs continued, they feared, Yahweh's wrath would descend upon Israel and all that David had achieved for the nation would be lost. Anxiety over Solomon's scandalous behavior prompted the priests to devise an ingenious strategy.

There are indications that Solomon had commissioned the priest-historians in Jerusalem to write a history of the nation, and especially of the monarchy. He wanted the history for his royal archives, but he also wanted the priests to circulate this history so that portions of it could be read regularly to the people. For Solomon knew that there were factions in the land who believed that the house of David had no right to rule over all of Israel (2 Sam 20:1–22). Some still believed that only God should be King over Israel (1 Sam 8:4–20). Others contended that a descendant or kinsman of Saul should rightfully be king (2 Sam 16:1–3, 5–8; 1 Kgs 2:8–9). And most importantly, Solomon's older brother Adonijah, encouraged by custom and powerful allies, thought that he should be king in Solomon's stead (1 Kgs 1:5–53).

The priests decided, therefore, that they should prudently, guardedly, and indirectly remind King Solomon of the folly of his behavior by placing a veiled warning at the beginning of the history he had commissioned. To accomplish their purpose, they agreed that one of them should revise a traditional creation story and make it the introduction to the history requested by Solomon. (The priest who carried out this task is called the "Yahwist," because he consistently used God's personal name, "Yahweh," when speaking of Israel's God.)

This traditional creation story related that the first man was tested by God. The test consisted of the man being tempted by a cunning serpent to disobey God. The man foolishly succumbed to the serpent's suggestion and ate the forbidden fruit. He thereby lost the privilege (for himself and for all other humans) of eating the fruit of the tree of life which conferred immortality. He and all other humans, therefore, became subject to suffering and death.

In this version of the story, which antedated the Yahwist's revision, the woman was not created until after the man's fall and expulsion from the garden. She, therefore, played no role in his temptation. That is why she is conspicuously absent in the unedited passages in the earlier version where God (1) warns only the man about the deadly consequences of eating the forbidden fruit (Gen 2:16–17), (2) rebukes only the man for disobeying God (3:22–23), and (3) drives only the man from the garden (3:24):

Gen 2:16–17

> And Yahweh God took the man and put him in the Garden of Eden to till it and keep it. And Yahweh God commanded the man saying, "You may freely eat of every tree of the garden; but of the tree of the knowledge of good and evil you shall not eat, for in the day that you eat of it dying you shall die."

Gen 3:22–24

> Then Yahweh God said, "Behold, the man has become like one of us, knowing good and evil; and now he may attempt to put forth his hand and take and eat the fruit of the tree of life and try to live forever"—therefore Yahweh God sent him forth from the Garden of Eden, to till the ground from which he was taken. He drove out the man; and at the east of the Garden of Eden he placed the cherubim, and a flaming sword which turned every way, to guard the way to the tree of life.

These two passages differ noticeably from the material placed between them later by the Yahwist; there the man and his wife are always mentioned together when both are involved in the unfolding action (Gen 2:21–24; 3:6–21).

The Yahwist decided to modify the original story so that the foolish man is tempted to disobey God not by the wily serpent but by the coaxing of his wife (Gen 3:6b). This change in the story was meant to provide Solomon with a striking parallel to what was currently happening between himself and his foreign wives. The Yahwist, to achieve his aim, moved the creation of the man's wife from after to before the Fall (Gen 2:18–24) so that she could be the one who yielded initially to the serpent's enticement (Gen 3:1–6a), and could become, in turn, the one who directly tempted her husband to disobey God (Gen 3:6b). In the Yahwist's revision, the disobedient man is rebuked by God with words intended primarily for Solomon's ears:

> And to the man he said, "Because you have listened to the voice of your wife, and have eaten of the tree of which I commanded you, 'You shall not eat of it,' cursed is the ground because of you." (Gen 3:17a)

(The story revised by the Yahwist [Gen 2:4b–3:24] is the oldest of the two creation accounts in the Book of Genesis. The more recent of the two stories [Gen 1:1–24a] was written and placed before the older story [c. 500 B.C.] by the final editor of Genesis called the "Priestly Author." We will consider the Priestly Author's creation story in a later chapter.)

Everything indicates that King Solomon ignored the guarded admonition of the henotheizing priests of Yahweh. He probably continued undeterred with his expedient foreign policy until his death. The priests of Yahweh interpreted the revolt of the ten northern tribes against the house of David shortly after Solomon's death as divine punishment for Solomon's violation of the first commandment:

> Therefore Yahweh said to Solomon, "Since . . . you have not kept my covenant and my statutes which I have commanded you, I will surely tear the kingdom from you . . . Yet for the sake of David your father I will not do it in your days, but I will tear it out of the hand of your son. However, I will not tear away all of the kingdom; but I will give one tribe [Judah] to your son, for the sake of . . . Jerusalem which I have chosen."
> (1 Kgs 11:11–13)

Open revolt against the house of David occurred when Rehoboam, Solomon's son, refused to change his father's foolish policy of inflicting heavy taxation and forced labor upon the ten northern tribes while exempting his own tribe, Judah:

> All the assembly of Israel came and said to Rehoboam, "Your father made our yoke heavy. Now therefore lighten the hard service of your father and his heavy yoke upon us, and we will serve you." . . . And the king answered them harshly . . . saying, "My father made your yoke heavy, but I will add to your yoke; my father chastised you with whips, but I will chastise you with scorpions." So the king did not hearken to the people.
> (1 Kgs 12:3–4, 13–15a)

Consequently, the ten northern tribes declared their independence:

> And when all Israel saw that the king did not hearken to them, the people answered the king, "What portion have we in David? We have no inheritance in the son of Jesse. To your tents, O Israel! Look now to your own house, David." So Israel departed to their tents. (1 Kgs 12:16)

After the ten northern tribes declared their independence in 922 B.C., they chose Jeroboam, the son of Nebat, to be their king (1 Kgs 12:20). And since most of the tribes who had belonged to the twelve-tribe alliance of Israel had broken away from the house of David, they called themselves the kingdom of "Israel." It was only the tribe of Judah in the south (which included the greatly diminished tribe of Simeon) that remained loyal to the house of David (who had belonged to the tribe of Judah). After the schism, therefore, the southern territory governed by David's heirs was known as the kingdom of "Judah."

4.

When Jeroboam, the son of Nebat, began to reign over the northern kingdom (Israel), he did so with a measure of political anxiety. For since Yahweh's ark still remained in Jerusalem, where the central sanctuary had been located during the reigns of David and Solomon, he feared that many of the Israelites in his newly formed kingdom might continue to travel there to worship. If they did, he feared their allegiance to the house of David might revive and his own authority would be subverted:

> And Jeroboam said in his heart, "Now the kingdom will turn back to the house of David; if this people go up to offer sacrifices in the house of Yahweh at Jerusalem, then the heart of this people will turn again to their lord, to Rehoboam king of Judah, and they will kill me and return to Rehoboam king of Judah."
> (1 Kgs 12:26–27)

King Jeroboam, therefore, established two royal sanctuaries in the territory of Israel, one in the northern city of Dan and the other at Bethel near the southern border with Judah. These sanctuaries, he hoped, would rival the royal sanctuary in Jerusalem. He strategically located the southern sanctuary at Bethel (eleven miles north of Jerusalem) because it offered two advantages.

First, Bethel had long been the home of a venerable sanctuary at or near which the Patriarchs were believed to have worshiped (Gen 12:8; 13:2–4; 31:13; 35:1, 3, 6; 35:11–15). Moreover, during the period of the Judges, Bethel had served for a time as Israel's central sanctuary (Judg 20:18–20). It was probably at that time that the priests of Yahweh embellished the Jacob tradition by assuring the Israelites that God had appeared to Jacob in a dream at Bethel to renew the promises made to Abraham and Isaac (Gen 28:10–22). Bethel, therefore, was a divinely favored location for Israel's central sanctuary.

Second, any Israelite pilgrims from the central highlands who might be traveling south to Jerusalem would have to pass by Bethel. Jeroboam obviously hoped that the lure of his royal sanctuary would dissuade them from traveling farther.

Jeroboam established his second royal sanctuary in the northern city of Dan. The city of Dan also possessed a sanctuary which was greatly revered because it was maintained by a family of Levitical priests who were descendants of Moses himself:

> And Jonathan the son of Gershom, son of Moses, and his sons were priests to the tribe of the Danites until the day of the captivity of the land [by the Assyrians]. (Judg 18:30b)

The Jerusalem temple had power to attract pilgrims, Jeroboam realized, not only because of its architectural splendor but also because it was the home of Yahweh's celebrated ark. And on top of the gold-covered ark stood two gold-covered cherubim which provided Yahweh's invisible presence with a visible resting place. Accordingly, to enhance the appeal of his rival sanctuaries, Jeroboam commissioned two carved statues of bulls overlaid with gold. He then placed one of these golden bulls or "calves" in each of his sanctuaries as pedestals on which Yahweh's invisible Presence could rest. Such impressive signs of Yahweh's Presence, Jeroboam recognized, would greatly increase the attractiveness of his two royal sanctuaries:

> So the king took counsel, and made two calves [young bulls] of gold. And he said to the people, "You have gone up to Jerusalem long enough." (1 Kgs 12:28a)

The "calves" mentioned in the passage cited above should be understood as "small bulls." For, in reality, the images commissioned by Jeroboam were meant to signify bulls not calves. But because it would have been too costly to cover the images with gold if they were as large as actual bulls, the artisan commissioned by Jeroboam reduced their size. The finished bulls, therefore, were much nearer the size of calves and that is why the (disapproving) priest-historian in Judah named them as he did. A bull was probably chosen as Yahweh's pedestal for several reasons: (1) Canaanite culture traditionally spoke of the gods El and Baal as bulls; relatedly, images of male deities standing on the backs of bulls have been found at pre-Israelite levels of habitation in Palestine (see Pritchard's *The Ancient Near East in Pictures,* pp. 170, 179–81). More significantly, (2) we learned earlier that after the agreement between the twelve tribes brokered by Joshua, the long-settled tribes replaced the god El with Yahweh and also assigned many of El's (and Baal's) traits to Yahweh. It was then that Yahweh began to be associated with bull symbolism.

Yahweh is several times spoken of in the Hebrew Scriptures as the "mighty one" of Israel (Gen 49:26; Ps 132:2; Is 49:26; 60:16). But the Hebrew word translated as "mighty one" could also have meant "bull." There are good reasons for thinking that originally the texts in question referred figuratively to Yahweh as the "bull" of Israel (the powerful God who bestowed the blessing of fertility on Israel's fields and flocks). However, the priests of Yahweh in Jerusalem who disapproved of Jeroboam's golden bulls later decided to change the word "bull" in these texts to "mighty one."

(All that the later priest-transmitters of this word had to do to change its meaning from "bull" to "mighty one" was read an alternate vowel sound into the Hebrew consonants of the word bull [br]. Before the "masoretic text" was produced between the seventh and tenth centuries of the Christian era, there were no written vowel points in biblical Hebrew. A written text then consisted only of consonants. A fluent reader knew from context how to supply the required vowel sounds. The later monotheistic Jewish scholars (called masoretes) who supplied the text with vowel points only had to assign different vowel points to the consonants of the word "bull" to render it as "mighty one," in agreement with later monotheistic tradition. This later tradition was very guarded and strict in its use of language for God.)

The majority of biblical scholars are convinced that Jeroboam did not intend his golden bulls to be understood as images of Yahweh. Instead, he meant them as cultic pedestals which would help worshipers "locate" Yahweh's invisible presence. Also, the second commandment was probably still understood as forbidding graven images of Yahweh (and, implicitly, of other gods) not carved images in general. Otherwise, the cherubim placed on top of Yahweh's ark (and the huge cherubim which overshadowed the ark in Solomon's temple) would also have been forbidden, which they clearly were not. (It is noteworthy, however, that after King Josiah's reform [c. 621 B.C.] the priest-historians of Judah, also known as the Deuteronomic Historians, avoided mentioning the cherubim on top of Yahweh's ark.)

Moreover, it is significant that neither Elijah the prophet (1 Kgs 18–19) nor King Jehu (2 Kgs 9–10), both of whom fought vigorously against Baal worship in the northern kingdom, ever spoke against or tried to remove Jeroboam's golden bulls. It was probably only after Solomon's temple had been destroyed and the ark and its cherubim had very likely been carried away by the Babylonians (c. 587 B.C.), that one of the priest-historians (probably the Priestly Author) expanded the commandment banning images of Yahweh to include "all" graven (carved) images having to do with worship:

> You shall not make for yourself a graven image, or any likeness of anything that is in heaven above, or that is in the earth beneath, or that is in the water under the earth; you shall not bow down to them or serve them; for I Yahweh your God am a jealous God. (Ex 20:4–5a)

Nevertheless, the priest-historian in Jerusalem who wrote about Jeroboam's reign looked back with harsh disapproval at the memory of his golden bulls (probably after King Josiah's reform in 621 B.C.; see 2 Kgs 23:1–20). Jeroboam's golden bulls were judged in hindsight as abhorrent symbols of the apostasy which had led to the northern kingdom's destruction by Assyria in 721 B.C. Consequently, the reforming priest-historian who wrote the books of Kings never tired of condemning what he considered Jeroboam's heinous sin.

Even during the earlier reform (c. 700 B.C.) of King Hezekiah of Judah, the Jerusalem priests probably associated the golden bulls at Bethel and Dan with the worship of Baal, which had been mightily encouraged in the northern kingdom by Jezebel, the Phoenician wife of King Ahab:

> In the thirty-eighth year of Asa king of Judah, Ahab the son of Omri began to reign over Israel. . . . And Ahab the son of Omri did evil in the sight of Yahweh more than all that were before him. And as if it had been a light thing for him to walk in the sins of Jeroboam the son of Nebat, he took for wife Jezebel the daughter of Eth-baal king of the Sidonians, and went and served Baal and worshiped him. He erected an altar for Baal in the house of Baal which he built in Samaria.
> (1 Kgs 16:29–32)

To defame the memory of Jeroboam's golden bulls, the reforming priest-historians deliberately (but mistakenly) suggested that Jeroboam had meant the bulls to be worshiped as images of Yahweh in violation of the second commandment. They further implied that the worship of those images soon led to the worship of other gods and the violation of the first commandment:

> So the king [Jeroboam] took counsel and made two calves [small bulls] of gold. And he said to the people, "You have gone up to Jerusalem long enough. Behold your gods, O Israel, who brought you up out of the land of Egypt." And he set one in Bethel and the other he set in Dan. And this thing became a sin, for the people went to the one at Bethel and to the other as far as Dan.
> (1 Kgs 12:28–30)

We find a peculiar story in Ex 32:1–14, 21–24 which was probably created and inserted there by the same priest-historian who disapprovingly recounted the story of Jeroboam's golden bulls in 1 Kings 12:26–30. The story he inserted in the Book of Exodus relates that the Israelites, fearful because Moses had stayed so long on Mount Sinai, demanded that Aaron make them "gods" to call upon. To our astonishment, the story relates that Aaron willingly complied with their polytheistic demand and produced a golden calf (small bull) for them to worship:

Ex 32:1–2

> When the people saw that Moses delayed to come down from the mountain, the people gathered themselves

> together to Aaron, and said to him, "Up, make us gods who shall go before us; as for this Moses, the man who brought us out of the land of Egypt, we do not know what has become of him."
>
> And Aaron said to them, "Take off the rings of gold which are in the ears of your wives, your sons, and your daughters, and bring them to me."
>
> Ex 32:4–6
>
> And he received the gold at their hand, and fashioned it with a graving tool, and made a molten calf [small bull]; and they said, "These are your gods, O Israel, who brought you up out of the land of Egypt!"
>
> When Aaron saw this, he built an altar before it; and Aaron made a proclamation and said, "Tomorrow shall be a feast to Yahweh." And they rose up early on the morrow, and offered burnt offerings and brought peace offerings; and the people sat down to eat and drink and rose up to play.

We should not fail to notice that when Aaron presents the people with the golden bull, their response is almost identical to the words attributed to King Jeroboam when he introduced Israel to his golden bulls ("Behold your gods, O Israel, who brought you up out of the land of Egypt"; 1 Kgs 12:28b). Manifestly, the idolatrous golden bull made by Aaron is meant to recall the golden bulls made by Jeroboam, and the idolatrous cooperation of Aaron is meant to suggest the wicked complicity of the Aaronic priests at Bethel (as later understood by the reforming priests in Jerusalem).

The idolatrous festival, as described by the reforming priest-historian at Jerusalem, suggests the erotic revelry which accompanied the forbidden worship of fertility gods (Baal and Astarte). But even more so, it is meant to recall the "unlawful" festival celebrated by Jeroboam when he inaugurated his rival royal sanctuary at Bethel. His festival was calculated to compete with a similar festival celebrated annually in Jerusalem:

> And Jeroboam appointed a feast on the fifteenth day of the eighth month like the feast that was in Judah, and

> he offered sacrifices upon the altar; so he did in Bethel, sacrificing to the calves [small bulls] that he had made. (1 Kgs 12:32)

In the Exodus story, when God wrathfully informed Moses of the apostasy occurring in the valley below, Moses returned quickly to the Israelites and was greeted by the sounds of their idolatrous feast:

Ex 32:15a, 19

> And Moses turned, and went down from the mountain with the two tables of the testimony in his hands. . . . And as soon as he came near the camp and saw the calf [small bull] and the dancing, Moses' anger burned hot, and he threw the tables out of his hands and broke them at the foot of the mountain.

Ex 32:21–24

> And Moses said to Aaron, "What did this people do to you that you have brought this great sin upon them?" And Aaron said, "Let not the anger of my lord burn hot; you know the people, that they are set on evil. For they said to me, 'Make us gods, who shall go before us; as for this Moses, the man who brought us up out of the land of Egypt, we do not know what has become of him.' And I said to them, 'Let any who have gold take it off;' so they gave it to me, and I threw it into the fire, and there came out this calf [small bull]."

Moses' disapproving anger and the disingenuous language of Aaron's response were meant by the priest-historian as a blistering commentary on the behavior of the Aaronic priests at Bethel who claimed to be faithful servants of Yahweh.

We are also told in the First Book of Kings that Jeroboam appointed priests who were not Levites to minister at his royal sanctuary in Bethel:

> He also made houses [temples] on high places, and appointed priests from among all the people who were not of the Levites. . . . And he placed in Bethel the

> priests of the high places that he had made.
> (1 Kgs 12:31, 32b)

This information, however, was very likely added to the story of Bethel's golden bull in the early post-Exilic period to exculpate the Aaronic priests who had served at Bethel. The exonerating addition was made by one of the Aaronic priests from Jerusalem (probably the Priestly Author who served as final editor of the Pentateuch). The Aaronites from Jerusalem had to defend their right to serve as priests after they had been discredited for a time by the reforming "Zadokite" priests from Jerusalem. (For example, additions made to the Book of Ezekiel by Zadokite priests during the Exile taught that only the Zadokites should be allowed to minister to God in the restored Jerusalem temple—for only the priests descended from Zadok, they contended, had not defiled themselves by idolatrous worship; see Ezek 44:15; 48:11.)

If, however, Jeroboam had truly appointed priests who were not Levites to serve in the royal shrine at Bethel, he would probably have done the same at Dan. We know, however, that he did not. The priests at Dan who were descended from Moses continued to serve there until Dan and its surrounding territory were seized by Assyria in 732 B.C. (Judg 18:30).

5.

The priest-historian who wrote (c. 600 B.C.) after King Josiah's reform (c. 620 B.C.) also wished to discredit the memory of King Jeroboam's other royal sanctuary at Dan. (We already noted above that the priests who presided at Dan were highly esteemed because they were descended from Moses.) Accordingly, just as this priest-historian created the story in Exodus 32:1–24 which indirectly condemned the Aaronic priests and golden bull at Bethel, he likewise reshaped a story in the Book of Judges to imply that the royal sanctuary at Dan and its Mushite priests were equally tainted by idolatry and sacrilege (Mushite = descended from Moses).

(The reforming priest-historian had an opportunity to revise the story in Judges when he acted as the book's reforming-editor. As such, he is also known as the "first Deuteronomic Historian," the historian who wrote (c. 600 B.C.) shortly after the death of King Josiah. His work was completed during the Exile (c. 570 B.C.) by a later reforming-priest from Jerusalem known as the "second Deuteronomic Historian.")

To achieve his aim, the first Deuteronomic Historian probably added idolatrous details to a story written down earlier by a priest who had served King Solomon (c. 950 B.C.). The original story had been recorded by Solomon's historian for two reasons: (1) He wished to exemplify the rampant lawlessness in Israel before the monarchy was established as a divinely approved source of law and order (Judg 17:6; 18:1), and (2) he was also an Aaronite priest eager to discredit the Mushites who served at the sanctuary in Dan. Aaronites and Mushites were engaged in a power struggle for control of Yahweh's ark during Solomon's reign.

The long and ugly story expanded by the first Deuteronomic Historian is filled with theft, the making and worship of idols, priestly betrayal, and violence. Some of these negative elements were present in the original story. But we shall see below that the Deuteronomic Historian probably augmented the original story's unsavory details for theological reasons.

There can be no reasonable doubt that he meant his expansion of the story to reflect shamefully on the priests and sanctuary at Dan where Jeroboam had placed the second of his two golden bulls. And while it is certainly possible that all of the events in the story occurred essentially as recounted, it is far more likely that the Deuteronomic Historian added Micah's "two" idolatrous images (and the sordid account of their origin) to an earlier story:

Judg 17:1–2

There was a man of the hill country of Ephraim whose name was Micah. And he said to his mother, "The eleven hundred pieces of silver which were taken from you, about which you uttered a curse, and also spoke it in my ear, behold the silver is with me; I took it." And his mother said, "Blessed be my son by Yahweh."

Judg 17:4

So when he restored the money to his mother, his mother took two hundred pieces of silver and gave it to the silversmith, who made it into a graven image and a molten image; and it was in the house of Micah.

Judg 17:5–6

And the man Micah had a shrine, and he made an ephod and teraphim, and installed one of his sons who became his priest. In those days there was no king in Israel; every man did what was right in his own eyes.

Judg 17:7–8, 10–11, 12

Now there was a young man of Bethlehem in Judah . . . who was a Levite. . . . He came to the hill country of Ephraim to the house of Micah. . . . And Micah said to him, "Stay with me, and be to me a father and a priest, and I will give you ten pieces of silver a year, and a suit of apparel, and your living. And the Levite was content to dwell with the man . . . and became to him like one of his sons . . . Then Micah said, "Now I know that Yahweh will prosper me, because I have a Levite as a priest."

(The precise nature of the ephod and teraphim is unclear. An *ephod* was a sacred garment of some kind worn by a priest in a cultic (frequently oracular) context. And *teraphim* were religious objects widely prized by Israelites until they were banned by King Josiah's reform. They seem to have been sacred images of some kind, possibly of ancestors, used for divination.)

The inconsistent references to the cult paraphernalia in the story suggest that in its earlier form, Micah made only an ephod and teraphim to place in his shrine (Judg 17:5). Accordingly, the original story probably moved directly from verse one to verse five, and the reader should observe that if all references to the two forbidden images and their tainted origin are excised, the story flows more smoothly, makes better sense, and is historically more probable.

At the time of King Josiah's reform (c. 621 B.C.), teraphim were officially outlawed (2 Kgs 23:24). And there can be no doubt that the reforming-priest who revised the story about Micah regarded Micah's teraphim and ephod as sacrilegious. His negative view, however, represents a later stage in Israel's religious understanding.

Throughout the period of the Judges (c. 1175-1040 B.C.) and even during most of the monarchy (c. 1040-621 B.C.), an ephod and teraphim would have been sacred objects that Israelites in general could lawfully possess and use by custom. (The exclusive right of Levites to serve as priests of Yahweh and their imposition of restrictive cultic laws had not yet developed. King David, for example, wore the priestly ephod when he brought Yahweh's ark to Jerusalem. (David served Yahweh in a priestly capacity on that occasion; he also appointed some of his sons (non-Levites) as priests after the ark arrived in Jerusalem; see 2 Sam 8:18b):

> So David went and brought up the ark of God from the house of Obed-edom to the city of David with rejoicing; and when those who bore the ark of Yahweh had gone six paces, he sacrificed an ox and a fatling. And David danced before Yahweh with all his might; and David was girded with a linen ephod. (2 Sam 6:12b-14)

David also kept teraphim in his home at Hebron before he fled from King Saul:

> That night Saul sent messengers to David's house . . . that he might kill him in the morning. But Michal, David's wife . . . let David down through the window; and he fled away and escaped. Michal took the teraphim and laid them on the bed and put a pillow of goat's hair at its head, and covered them with clothes. (1 Sam 19:11–13)

The language which describes Micah's two idolatrous images in the expanded story is vexingly ambiguous (Judg 17:4) and inconsistent. At times it speaks of only one image (Judg 18:20, 30), but at other times of two (Judg 18:17–18). Because Micah and his mother are purportedly Yahwists, the story implies that at least one of Micah's unlawful images represents Yahweh or is involved with the worship of Yahweh—which sounds suspiciously like the first Deuteronomic Historian's view of Jeroboam's golden bulls.

The reforming priest-historian probably added "two" idolatrous images to the story to liken the unlawful worship in the early Israelite sanctuary at Dan to the later introduction of one of Jeroboam's "two" golden bulls. (We also should notice that the two idols in the story are described with language very like that which the priest-historian used for the "graven" and "molten" calf [small bull] made by Aaron in Ex 32:4.)

After Micah had entrusted his cult paraphernalia to the care of his highly prized Levitical priest of Mosaic descent, he had occasion to offer hospitality to five Danites whose tribe had been dispossessed of their territory in the south:

> And in those days the tribe of the Danites was seeking for itself an inheritance to dwell in. . . . So the Danites sent five able men . . . to spy out the land and to explore it. . . . And they came to the hill country of Ephraim, to the house of Micah, and lodged there. (Judg 18:1–2)

While lodging with Micah, the five Danites met Micah's priest and asked him to consult God to see if their mission would prosper. The Levite did so and gave them vague assurance that their journey would be successful (Judg 18:3–6). The Danites then spied out the city of Laish (later called Dan) to the north and found it very desirable. They returned to the other Danites in the south and gave their favorable report (Judg 18:7–10). All the Danites then traveled to the north to seize the city of Laish (Judg 18:11–12). While on their way, the five spies again passed by the house of Micah:

Judg 18:14, 17a

> Then the five men who had gone to spy out the country of Laish said to their brethren, "Do you know that in these houses there are an ephod, teraphim, a graven image, and a molten image?" . . . And the five men . . . entered and took the graven image, the ephod, the teraphim, and the molten image.

Judg 18:18b–20

> And . . . the priest said to them, "What are you doing?" And they said to him, "Keep quiet . . .and come with us, and be to us a father and a priest. Is it better for you to be priest to the house of one man, or to be priest to a tribe and family in Israel?" And the priest's heart was glad; he took the ephod, and the teraphim, and the graven image, and went in the midst of the people.

When Micah discovered the theft and the loss of his Levitical priest, he rallied his neighbors and overtook the Danites (Judg 18:22):

Judg 23–26

And they shouted to the Danites who turned around and said to Micah, "What ails you that you come with such a company?" And he said, "You take my gods which I made, and the priest, and go away, and what have I left? How then do you ask me, 'What ails you?'"

And the Danites said to him, "Do not let your voice be heard among us, lest angry fellows fall upon you, and you lose your life with the lives of your household." Then the Danites went their way, and when Micah saw that they were too strong for him, he turned and went back to his home.

Judg 18:27b, 28b, 29a, 30

The Danites came to Laish, to a people quiet and unsuspecting, and smote them with the edge of the sword, and burned the city with fire. . . . And they rebuilt the city . . . and they named the city Dan. . . . And the Danites set up the graven image for themselves; and Jonathan the son of Gershom, the son of Moses, and his sons were priests to the tribe of the Danites until the day of the captivity of the land.

The fierce opposition of the Jerusalem priests to Jeroboam's golden bulls vividly illustrates that what constituted acceptable worship of Yahweh by the twelve tribes of Israel was a matter of bitter dispute among Israelites during the monarchy. The folk religion of districts away from Jerusalem was usually at odds with the more restrictive henotheistic standards of the Jerusalem priests. Even various groups of Levitical priests held differing views.

The Levitical priests in the northern kingdom clearly did not perceive Jeroboam's golden bulls as a threat to exclusive worship of Yahweh. The evidence also suggests that many of the priests in both Israel and Judah (apart from Jerusalem) accepted the tradition of placing a stone pillar and an asherah in Yahweh's sanctuaries (2 Kgs 23:15; Jer 2:27). However, given Israel's complex origins, this should not surprise us. We will see in the next chapter that until the Exile to Babylon in 587 B.C., the Levitical priests who guarded Yahweh's ark in Jerusalem continued their tireless struggle against traditional practices which they perceived as violating or endangering Yahweh's exclusive right to worship.

Ancient Israel's history was such that the views of the Jerusalem priests finally prevailed. When these priests wrote and edited Israel's history (c. 600-580 B.C.), they regularly expressed their scorn for traditional religious practices which they had rejected. It is easy to see why they rejected some of these practices, such as child sacrifice and ritual prostitution. But other practices were ambiguous in varying degrees. As a rule, the Jerusalem priests were intolerant of any practice which they knew had once been associated with the worship of Baal, Astarte, or Asherah. Because they were folk historians, however, they never give the reasons why other Levitical priests allowed the ambiguous practices. The final editors of ancient Israel's written history had the last word.

Questions for Review and Discussion

1. What is the difference between exegesis and eisegesis?

2. Why is it important to distinguish between exegesis and eisegesis when reading evolving biblical statements about God?

3. Should the story of the capture of God's ark by the Philistines be read monotheistically or henotheistically? Justify your answer. Which part of the story is history and which part is theology?

4. Should the story in 2 Kings 3:27 about the king of Moab's sacrifice of his eldest son be read henotheistically or monotheistically? Justify your answer.

5. What behavior of King Solomon's was considered especially alarming to the priests of Yahweh in Jerusalem?

6. What unusual thing did the priests of Yahweh decide to do to try changing King Solomon's behavior?

7. What evidence suggests that only the man was tested and failed in an earlier form of the Genesis creation and fall story?

8. Why did King Jeroboam make two golden bulls and place one of them at Dan and the other at Bethel?

9. What is the connection between Jeroboam's golden bull at Bethel and the story in Ex 32:1–14 about Aaron making a golden calf [small bull] for the Israelites? What evidence in the Exodus story supports your answer?

10. What changes did a priest of Yahweh probably make in the story in Judg 17–18 about the founding of the city and sanctuary of Dan? Why did the priest-historian make these changes?

Chapter Four

Israel's Henotheistic Faith during the Last Half of the Monarchy

1.

We saw in the last chapter that Judah's priest-historians who wrote the Books of Kings regarded King Jeroboam's golden bulls as the beginning of the northern kingdom's great defection from Yahweh. It was because of that defection, they surmised, that the northern kingdom had been destroyed by Assyria in 721 B.C. As the later priest-historians remembered it, the apostasy begun by King Jeroboam reached its peak during the infamous reign of Ahab, son of Omri (c. 869-850 B.C.):

> In the thirty-eighth year of Asa king of Judah, Ahab the son of Omri began to reign over Israel. . . . And Ahab the son of Omri did evil in the sight of Yahweh more than all that were before him. And as if it had been a light thing for him to walk in the sins of Jeroboam the son of Nebat, he took for wife Jezebel the daughter of Eth-baal king of the

> Sidonians, and went and served Baal and worshiped him. He erected an altar for Baal in the house of Baal which he built in Samaria. . . . Ahab did more to provoke Yahweh the God of Israel to anger than all the kings of Israel who were before him. (1 Kgs 16:29–33)

Ahab's marriage to the Phoenician princess Jezebel was probably an expedient political alliance. Such an alliance brought commercial advantages but also was desirable because Israel was threatened at that time by the expanding Aramaean kingdom of Damascus. Jezebel, however, was a devoted worshiper of Baal, and she used her influence as queen to mightily encourage Baal's cult (which already existed among the remaining Canaanites and some Israelite farmers) in the kingdom of Israel.

Probably to please Jezebel and her royal father Eth-baal, Ahab built a temple for Baal in Samaria, his capital city. Ahab himself, however, was very likely not a worshiper of Baal. The names he gave his two sons, Ahaziah (= Yahweh has taken by hand) and Joram (= Yahweh is exalted), contain shortened forms of the name of Israel's covenant God. This evidence indicates that Ahab probably worshiped Yahweh not Baal. Ahab's generous toleration of Baal worship, therefore, was probably an expression of his foreign policy (somewhat like that of King Solomon).

The threat from Damascus notwithstanding, the priests and prophets of Yahweh looked with alarm at Ahab's official tolerance of Baal worship and Jezebel's active fostering thereof. We are told in 1 Kings 18:19 that four hundred and fifty prophets of Baal were fed at Jezebel's table (meaning they were subsidized by the royal treasury). We also learn that she actively persecuted groups of prophets who served Yahweh (1 Kgs 18:3–4, 13; 19:1–2, 14). Her persecution, however, was probably in response to the active hostility of these prophets to the Baal cult.

In the judgment of the priest-historians who wrote shortly after King Josiah's death (c. 600 B.C.) and during the Exile (c. 580 B.C.), Ahab had abandoned fidelity to Yahweh and was, implicitly if not explicitly, a worshiper of Baal. The zealous prophet Elijah also perceived that Ahab's tolerance and Jezebel's support of Baal worship had become a perilous threat to Israel's covenant with Yahweh. Accordingly, Elijah became the fiery champion of Yahweh's cause in the northern kingdom; he publicly rebuked King Ahab and challenged Jezebel's Baal-promoting activity.

The First Book of Kings recounts that Elijah, while acting in his capacity as Yahweh's prophetic champion, interpreted a severe drought that was parching the land during Ahab's reign as punishment sent by Israel's offended covenant God.

> Now Elijah the Tishbite . . . said to Ahab, "As Yahweh the God of Israel lives, before whom I stand, there shall be neither dew nor rain these years except by my word." (1 Kgs 17:1)

Near the end of the drought, we are told, Yahweh directed Elijah to challenge King Ahab and the prophets of Baal to a contest on Mount Carmel to determine whether Yahweh or Baal should be worshiped as the divine bestower of rain in Israel:

> **1 Kgs 18:1–2**
> After many days the word of Yahweh came to Elijah, in the third year, saying, "Go show yourself to Ahab; and I will send rain upon the earth." So Elijah went to show himself to Ahab. Now the famine was severe.

> **1 Kgs 18:17–19**
> When Ahab saw Elijah, Ahab said to him, "Is it you, you troubler of Israel?" And he answered, "I have not troubled Israel; but you have, and your father's house, because you have forsaken the commandments of Yahweh and followed the Baals. Now, therefore, send and gather all Israel to me at Mount Carmel, and the four hundred and fifty prophets of Baal . . . who eat at Jezebel's table."

A critical reading of this story, however, indicates that it was composed in folk fashion by Elijah's prophetic disciples and later expanded by the priest-historians to teach religious lessons which they considered urgent. The dramatic story was crafted to illustrate that Elijah was called by Yahweh to defeat Jezebel's promotion of Baal worship in Israel. The memory of a fierce struggle between

Elijah and the prophets of Baal, which underlies the legend, is reliable history. So also is the memory that Elijah publicly castigated Ahab and Jezebel and blamed them for the drought that was crippling the land. But the famous duel on Mount Carmel, with its mythical pyrotechnics, is a form of hyperbolized folk theology meant to promote and defend exclusive worship of Yahweh in Israel:

> **1 Kgs 18:20–21**
>
> So Ahab sent to all the people of Israel, and gathered the prophets together at Mount Carmel. And Elijah came near to all the people and said, "How long will you go limping with two opinions? If Yahweh is God, follow him, but if Baal, then follow him." And the people did not answer a word.

> **1 Kgs 18:23–24**
>
> Then Elijah said to the people . . . "Let two bulls be given to us; and let them choose one bull for themselves, and cut it in pieces and lay it on the wood, but put no fire to it; and I will prepare the other bull and lay it on the wood, and put no fire to it. And you call on the name of your god, and I will call upon the name of Yahweh. And the God who answers by fire, he is God." And all the people answered, "It is well spoken."

The story then relates that Elijah ridiculed the prophets of Baal who called unsuccessfully on Baal to send fire (lightning, the harbinger of rain) from heaven to consume the offering:

> And at noon Elijah mocked them saying, "Cry aloud, for he is a god; either he is musing, or he has gone aside, or he is on a journey, or perhaps he is asleep and must be awakened." And they cried aloud, and cut themselves after their custom with swords and lances, until the blood gushed out upon them. And as midday passed, they raved on until the time of the offering of the oblation [3 p.m.], but there was no voice, no one answered, no one heeded. (1 Kgs 18:27–29)

We are next told that Elijah laid his altar with wood and placed a slaughtered bull thereon. He also drenched the altar, the wood, and the bull with container after container of water:

> And at the time of the offering of the oblation, Elijah the prophet came near and said, "O Yahweh, God of Abraham, Isaac, and Israel, let it be known this day that you are God in Israel, and that I am your servant, and that I have done all these things at your word. Answer me, O Yahweh, answer me.". . . Then the fire of Yahweh fell and consumed the burnt offering, and the wood, and the stones, and the dust, and licked up the water that was in the trench. And when all the people saw it, they fell on their faces; and they said, "Yahweh, he is God; Yahweh, he is God." (1 Kgs 18:36–39)

The lightning that fell from heaven in the story symbolizes the storm activity by which Yahweh sent the rain that ended the drought as Elijah had promised. The legend of the contest on Mount Carmel between Yahweh and Baal was designed to emphasize that it was Yahweh not Baal who finally sent drought-ending lightning (and rain) from heaven:

> And in a little while the heavens grew black with clouds and wind, and there was a great rain. (1 Kgs 18:45a)

2.

After the deaths of Elijah and Ahab, the royal house of Ahab was brought to ruin as Elijah had predicted:

> Ahab said to Elijah, "Have you found me, O my enemy?" He answered, "I have found you because you have sold yourself to do what is evil in the sight of Yahweh. Behold I will bring evil upon you; I will utterly sweep you away, and will cut off from Ahab every male, bond or free, in Israel." (1 Kgs 21:20–22)

Ahab's dynasty was destroyed by a revolt instigated by Elijah's prophetic successor, Elisha. (The bloody excess of this revolt was approved of by Elisha but was later condemned by the prophet Hosea; 1:4.) Elisha encouraged Jehu, a zealous worshiper of Yahweh and a commander of Israel's army, to rebel (c 843 B.C.) against King Joram (also called Jehoram), the son of Ahab and Jezebel:

> **2 Kgs 9:1–3**
> Then Elisha the prophet called one of the sons of the prophets and said to him . . . "Take this flask of oil in your hand, and go up to Ramoth–gilead. And when you arrive, look there for Jehu the son of Jehoshaphat . . . and lead him to an inner chamber. Then take the flask of oil and pour it on his head, and say, 'Thus says Yahweh, I anoint you king over Israel.' Then open the door and flee, do not tarry."

> **2 Kgs 9:4–5**
> So the young man, the prophet, went to Ramoth–gilead. And when he came, behold, the commanders of the army were in council; and he said, "I have an errand to you, O commander." And Jehu said, "To which of us all?" And he said, "To you, O commander."

> **2 Kgs 9:6–7**
> So he arose and went into the house: and the young man poured the oil on his head, saying to him, "Thus says Yahweh the God of Israel, I anoint you king over the people of Yahweh, over Israel. And you shall strike down the house of Ahab your master, that I may avenge on Jezebel the blood of my servants the prophets, and the blood of all the servants of Yahweh."

> **2 Kgs 9:11–13**
> When Jehu came out . . . they said to him, "Is all well? Why did this mad fellow come to you?" . . . And he said, "Thus and so he spoke to me saying, 'Thus says Yahweh, I anoint you king over Israel.'" Then in haste every man of them took his garment, and put it under him on the bare steps, and they blew the trumpet and proclaimed, "Jehu is king."

Jehu accepted Yahweh's commission and moved swiftly against the house of Ahab; he slew Joram with an arrow (2 Kgs 9:24), and later ordered Jezebel's servants to throw her to her death from a high palace window (2 Kgs 9:30–33). He then saw to the execution of all of Ahab's remaining sons and grandsons (2 Kgs 10:1–7). Jehu thereby fulfilled Elisha's commission and secured his own claim to the throne.

Next, Jehu's zeal as a Yahwist prompted him to take action against the worshipers of Baal who had grown numerous in Samaria under the patronage of Jezebel. To accomplish his purpose, Jehu employed a ruse:

> Then Jehu assembled all the people, and said to them, "Ahab served Baal a little; but Jehu will serve him much. Now therefore call to me all the prophets of Baal, all his worshipers and all his priests; let none be missing, for I have a great sacrifice to offer to Baal.". . .But Jehu did it with cunning in order to destroy the worshipers of Baal. (2 Kgs 10:18–19)

After the summoned Baal worshipers had assembled and the sacrificial ritual had been carried out, Jehu ordered their execution:

> So as soon as he had finished offering the burnt offering, Jehu said to the guard and to the officers, "Go in and slay them; let not a man escape." So when they put them to the sword, the guard and the officers cast them out and went into the inner room of the house of Baal . . . and demolished the house of Baal and made it a latrine to this day. (2 Kgs 10:25, 27b)

The later priest-historians praised Jehu for punishing the house of Ahab (2 Kgs 9:36–37; 10:10, 17) and for taking vigorous action to eliminate Baal worship in Israel. Nevertheless, they faulted Jehu for not removing Jeroboam's golden bulls from the royal sanctuaries at Bethel and Dan.

> Thus Jehu wiped out Baal from Israel. But Jehu did not turn aside from the sins of Jeroboam the son of Nebat, which he made Israel to sin, the golden bulls which were in Bethel and in Dan. (2 Kgs 10:28)

Jehu, however, did not remove the golden bulls because they probably were not regarded as idolatrous by the Levitical priests in the northern kingdom. Recall that even Elijah seems not to have objected to the bull-pedestals for Yahweh at Bethel and Dan. It was the reforming priests in Jerusalem who later brought that judgment against Jeroboam's golden bulls. The priest-historians who shared that view condemned every king of Israel after Jeroboam for not removing his golden bulls.

3.

Before the northern kingdom fell to Assyria in 721 B.C., the prophet Hosea, who was from the northern kingdom, also decided that Jeroboam's golden bulls were an idolatrous abomination which had led Israel astray. We cannot say if Hosea was influenced by developing criticism in Israel or convinced by priestly or prophetic critics in Judah. It is possible that he arrived at his negative judgment independently through observing popular response to Yahweh's bull-pedestal at Bethel:

> And now they sin more and more, and make for themselves molten images, idols skillfully made of their silver, all of them the work of craftsmen. . . .They kiss young bulls! (Hos 13:2)

In the passage from Hosea that follows, the mention of "Samaria" in the first sentence stands in synonymous parallelism with the mention of "Israel" in the second sentence, just as Jerusalem and Judah were often paired by the prophets. The scornful mention of Samaria's bull is probably a reference to Israel's continued acceptance of the bull-pedestal for Yahweh placed by Jeroboam in Bethel's royal sanctuary:

> I have spurned your bull, O Samaria. My anger burns against them. How long will it be till they are pure in Israel?
>
> A workman made it; it is not God. The bull of Samaria shall be broken in pieces. (Hos 8:5)

There is a pejorative allusion to the bull at Bethel in another of Hosea's oracles. In this other oracle, there is a reference to an idolatrous bull at *Beth-aven,* "house of wickedness." Most exegetes agree that Hosea used this name to allude denigratingly to the controversial golden bull at Bethel, implying that Bethel (= house of God) was actually not a house of God but a house of wickedness. Samaria again stands as a poetic synonym for the northern kingdom, Israel:

> The inhabitants of Samaria tremble for the bull at Beth-aven. Its people shall mourn for it, and its idolatrous priests shall wail over it, over its glory which has departed from it. Yea, the thing itself shall be carried to Assyria, as tribute to the great king. Ephraim shall be put to shame, and Israel shall be ashamed of his idol. (Hos 10:5–6)

The Assyrians had probably destroyed the sanctuary at Dan in 732 B.C. Perhaps, then, Hosea made no reference to the bull at Dan because it no longer existed when he heaped scorn on the bull of Samaria at "Beth-aven." Hosea possibly continued to prophesy until the northern kingdom fell to Assyria in 721 B.C. If he lived to see that event, he doubtlessly concurred with the interpretation of Israel's destruction later assigned by a reforming priest-historian from Judah 120 years later:

> And this was so because the people of Israel had sinned against Yahweh their God. . . . And they forsook the commandments of Yahweh their God, and made for themselves molten images of two bulls; and they made an asherah, and worshiped all the host of heaven, and served Baal. . . . Therefore, Yahweh was very angry with Israel, and removed them out of his sight; none was left but the tribe of Judah only. (2 Kgs 17:7a, 16, 18)

4.

When the northern kingdom fell to Assyria in 721 B.C., Ahaz the son of Jotham, was reigning in Judah. Ahaz was remembered by the priest-historians of Judah as one of the wickedest of David's successors. We observed in an earlier chapter that Ahaz burned his son as a sacrifice (2 Kgs 16:3). It is usual to assume that Ahaz sacrificed his son to Baal (or Molech). Many scholars, however, think it probable that he sacrificed his son to Yahweh. (See *The Early History of God* by Mark S. Smith and John H. Hayes's commentary on Lev 20:1–5 in *Harper's Bible Commentary.*)

These scholars believe that the Israelite tribes who settled in Canaan before the arrival of Joshua and the Rachel tribes learned to practice child sacrifice from the Canaanites. When those tribes eventually agreed to worship Yahweh exclusively, some of them transferred to their worship of Yahweh practices which had traditionally been part of their worship of El and the fertility gods of Canaan. Offering one's firstborn child as first fruit of the womb along with the first fruits of fields and domesticated animals was probably such a transferred practice. This practice was intended to win the favor of the gods of fertility and induce them to bless one's family, fields, and flocks.

If we assume that such a transfer of child sacrifice to Yahweh's cult did occur in earliest Israel, we can account for the stern priestly admonitions in the law of Moses which forbid offering children to Yahweh along with firstborn animals:

> There shall not be found among you anyone who burns
> his son or daughter as an offering. (Deut 18:10)

It is traditional to explain that this injunction forbids the offering of one's children to fertility gods not Yahweh. That view, however, is probably eisegesis rather than exegesis. For a full review of the pertinent evidence justifies the opposite view—shocking though this may be to traditional assumptions.

The legal requirement in Deuteronomy 18:10 (quoted above) was very likely introduced by the Levitical priests to counteract the practice of child sacrifice which Israel had learned from the Canaanites. We quite possibly hear an echo of that pre-Joshua tradition in the very early Israelite cult prescriptions which follow:

Ex 13:1–2

> Consecrate to me all the firstborn; whatever is the first
> to open the womb among the people of Israel, both of
> man and of beast, is mine.

Ex 22:29b–30a

> The firstborn of your sons you shall give to me. You shall do likewise with your oxen and your sheep.

The tragic story of Jephthah and his daughter reminds us that in the period of the Judges it was still assumed by some in Israel that one could promise the sacrifice of a human life to Yahweh and, if one did so, Yahweh required that person to be sacrificed:

Judg 11:30–32

> And Jephthah made a vow to Yahweh and said, "If you will give the Ammonites into my hand, then whoever comes forth from the doors of my house to meet me when I return victorious from the Ammonites shall be Yahweh's, and I shall offer him up for a burnt offering." So Jephthah crossed over to the Ammonites to fight against them, and Yahweh gave them into his hand.

Judg 11:34–35, 39

> Then Jephthah came to his home at Mizpah; and behold, his daughter came out to meet him with timbrels and dances; she was his only child; besides her he had neither son nor daughter. And when he saw her he tore his garments and said, "Woe is me, my daughter, you have brought me very low, and you have become the cause of great grief to me; for I have opened my mouth to Yahweh, and I cannot take back my vow." . . . And . . . her father . . . did with her according to his vow which he had made.

Even near the end of the eighth century B.C., Micah the prophet knew that there were Israelites in the kingdom of Judah who believed that Yahweh would be pleased by the sacrifice of their first-born children:

> With what shall I come before Yahweh and bow myself before God on high? Shall I come before him with burnt offerings, with calves a year old? Will Yahweh be pleased with thousands of rams, with ten thousands of rivers of oil? Shall I give my firstborn for my transgressions, the fruit of my body for the sin of my soul? (Mic 6:6–7)

Probably from the beginning of the twelve-tribe league the Levitical priests rejected the custom of child sacrifice because they had not settled in the land of Canaan earlier with the other Leah tribes. Instead, they had very likely retreated from the central highlands (Gen 34:1–30; 35:5) and joined the still seminomadic Rachel tribes, probably in the region near Beersheba. They had not, therefore, learned to accept the custom of child sacrifice because of long exposure to Canaanite culture.

The Levites and the Rachel tribes (Joseph and Benjamin) who had been taught Yahweh's law by Moses at Sinai (You shall not kill [except in self-defense]) probably regarded the custom of child sacrifice as abhorrent and alien to the worship of Yahweh. It was very likely the Levites who guarded Yahweh's ark from the beginning (and eventually became Yahweh's only legitimate priests) and who continued to insist that such a practice was contrary to Yahweh's revealed will.

It was the inspired determination of the Levitical priests to eliminate child sacrifice in Israel that motivated them to create and teach the chilling story of Yahweh's request for the sacrifice of Isaac. This "justification" story is best understood as ancient Levitical theology, not historical memory of an actual event. God certainly concurred with the Levitical rejection of child sacrifice and encouraged the priests to struggle against it. We may assume that God did so by communicating the reinforcing experience of divine Presence and Love at decisive moments.

This well-known story relates that God "tested" Abraham by directing him to take his son Isaac to a designated mountain (high place) and there sacrifice him as a burnt offering to God:

Gen 33:1–3

> God tested Abraham and said to him . . . "Take your son, your only son Isaac, whom you love, and go to the land of Moriah, and offer him there as a burnt offering upon one of the mountains which I shall tell you." So Abraham rose early in the morning . . . and took . . . his son Isaac.

Gen 22:6–8

> And Abraham took the wood of the burnt offering and laid it on Isaac his son; and he took in his hand the fire

> and the knife. . . . And Isaac said to Abraham . . . "Behold the fire and the wood, but where is the lamb for the burnt offering?" Abraham said, "God will provide himself a lamb for the burnt offering, my son."
>
> **Gen 22:9–10**
>
> When they came to the place of which God had told him, Abraham built an altar there, and laid the wood in order, and bound Isaac his son, and laid him on the altar, upon the wood. Then Abraham put forth his hand, and took the knife to slay his son.
>
> **Gen 22:11–12**
>
> But the angel of Yahweh called to him from heaven, and said, "Abraham . . . do not lay your hand on the child or do anything to him; for now I know that you fear God, seeing that you have not withheld your son, your only son, from me."

Abraham then took a ram which Yahweh had marvelously provided nearby and offered it as an animal "substitute" for Isaac:

> And Abraham lifted up his eyes and looked, and behold, behind him was a ram, caught in a thicket by his horns; and Abraham went and took the ram, and offered it as a burnt offering instead of his son. (Gen 22:13)

When Abraham did as Yahweh ordained, his action constituted a divinely provided example for all of his descendants. They, too, the Levitical priests remonstrated, should offer an animal substitute to Yahweh in place of their firstborn children. To the same end, they added the following clarification to Israel's ancient tradition (probably learned from the Canaanites) of offering the first fruits of the womb to Yahweh:

> You shall set apart to Yahweh all that first opens the womb. All the firstlings of your cattle that are males shall be Yahweh's. Every firstling of an ass you shall redeem with a lamb. . . . Every human firstborn among your sons you shall redeem. (Ex 13:12–13; also, Ex 34:20; Num 18:15)

It took centuries, however, for the view of the Levitical priests to fully prevail. King Ahaz and King Manasseh still practiced child sacrifice in the last half of the monarchy. It is probably significant that when the reforming priest-historian who wrote after Josiah's death reported the abhorrent acts committed by these two kings (2 Kgs 16:3; 21:6), he did not state that they sacrificed their sons to Baal or some deity other than Yahweh. The shocking implication of his silence is that Ahaz and Manasseh probably had offered their sons to Yahweh in accordance with a pre-Levitical tradition still persisting in Judah.

Ezekiel the prophet recalled that child sacrifice had once been considered a lawful form of worship in Israel. But this memory troubled him, and he tried to explain it (unconvincingly by present standards) as an aberration which Yahweh had brought about temporarily to shock the Israelites into recognizing their sinfulness and Yahweh's contrasting holiness:

> Moreover, I gave them statutes which were not good and ordinances by which they could not have life; and I defiled them through their very gifts in making them offer by fire all their firstborn, that I might horrify them; I did it that they might know that I am Yahweh. (Ezek 20:25–26)

The prophet Jeremiah also reacted to the practice of child sacrifice with shame and horror. His view of the problem, however, was different from Ezekiel's. Yahweh, Jeremiah contended, never commanded or condoned such a hideous practice. Yet the very vehemence of Jeremiah's repudiation of the notion indicates that there were Israelites in the land who believed that such a practice could be pleasing to Yahweh:

> They have built the high place of Topheth, which is in the valley of the son of Hinnom, to burn their sons and daughters in the fire; which I did not command, nor did it come into my mind. (Jer 7:31)

We find another denunciation attributed to Jeremiah specifying that the high place at Topheth (just outside of Jerusalem) where children were burned was dedicated to Baal. We may reasonably suspect, however, that the priests who edited Jeremiah's prophecies during and after the Exile were anxious to obliterate the memory that child sacrifice had formerly been offered to Yahweh by some Israelites.

Accordingly, some scholars have concluded that Jeremiah's priest-editors may have added the brief statement (indicated in brackets in the passage below) that the high place in question was dedicated to Baal. If the references to Baal are removed, the passage reads essentially the same as Jeremiah 7:31 cited above. Furthermore, it would have made no sense for Jeremiah to assure his audience that Yahweh "did not command or decree" ritual practices carried out in honor of Baal. Such an observation would have been obvious and unnecessary. It requires, therefore, a Baal-free context in which such a reminder was deemed necessary:

> Because they have filled this place with the blood of innocents [and have built the high places of Baal to burn their sons in the fire to Baal] which I did not command or decree, nor did it come to my mind; therefore, behold the days are coming, says Yahweh, when this place shall no more be called . . . the valley of the son of Hinnom, but the valley of slaughter.(Jer 19:4b–6; see also 32:35)

So abhorrent was the post-Exilic memory of the valley of the son of Hinnom (a short distance from Jerusalem's southern wall) that the Israelites turned the valley into the city dump where all of Jerusalem's refuse and human waste were thrown daily. Later yet, the scribes used Jerusalem's foul-smelling, maggot-infested, and perpetually burning city dump (called "Gehenna" from the Aramaic gehinnam = valley of Hinnom) as a vivid metaphor for the lower part of Sheol where the wicked will be permanently tormented by unquenchable fire and gnawing worms.

5.

Although the northern kingdom (Israel) was destroyed by the Assyrians in 721 B.C., the southern kingdom (Judah) remained intact because King Ahaz had not rebelled against Assyria. It is one of history's ironies that Ahaz's son, Hezekiah, who succeeded him in 715 B.C. was praised as one of the two worthiest successors of David (the other was Josiah; see 2 Kgs 23:25):

> He trusted in Yahweh the God of Israel; so that there was none like him among all the kings of Judah after him, nor among those who were before him. For he held fast to Yahweh; he did not depart from following him, but kept the commandments which Yahweh commanded Moses. (2 Kgs 18:5–6)

Hezekiah received such exceptional praise from the priest-historians of Judah because soon after he began to reign he initiated an unprecedented religious reform: He restricted all worship in Judah to the central sanctuary in Jerusalem. The account of Hezekiah's reform in 2 Chronicles is much longer (chapters 29–31) than the account in 2 Kings (18:1–6).

It is evident that the later account in 2 Chronicles has been expanded with theological language and ritual concerns characteristic of the priest-historian who wrote it, known as the Chronicler (c. 350 B.C.). Nevertheless, the substance of his account of Hezekiah's reform is probably reliable and agrees essentially with the shorter account in 2 Kings. (The author of 2 Kings devoted more space to King Josiah's reform than to Hezekiah's because he wanted to present Josiah as the ideal model for all future kings.)

By limiting worship to Jerusalem, Hezekiah intended to ensure that unlawful worship would not occur in the land. Hezekiah's reform had the full backing of the Jerusalem priests whose authority to control worship (and income from tithes) increased considerably. The priests in outlying districts, on the other hand, bitterly opposed the reform, which deprived them of their customary livelihood. The reform was also extremely unpopular among lay people who lived away from Jerusalem.

Such an ambitious reform was judged to be necessary by pious King Hezekiah because of the recent destruction of the northern kingdom. The northern kingdom's fall had been prophesied by Amos and Hosea. Both these prophets had foreseen Israel's destruction and interpreted the coming calamity as punishment from Israel's jealous covenant God. Yahweh's commandments had been so seriously violated, they announced, that divine wrath would surely descend on unrepentant Israel. Moreover, the prophets Isaiah and Micah had recently warned the people of Judah that the same punishment awaited them if they failed to serve Yahweh worthily. Because the words of Amos and Hosea had been strikingly fulfilled,

Hezekiah and his priest-advisers were anxious to prevent Judah from suffering a similar fate.

Hezekiah and his priest-advisers knew that the planned reform would be exceedingly unpopular because it was contrary to long established Israelite custom. For centuries, every city and town had enjoyed its own local sanctuary maintained by a family of priests. Hence, the king and his advisers understood that if the proposed reform was to succeed it would have to carry the authority of Mosaic law with it.

Providentially, some of the priest-refugees from the northern kingdom who had fled to Judah had probably brought with them copies of a book consisting of exhortations to obey various aspects of Yahweh's covenant law. The material in this book had probably been collected by the Levitical priests in the northern kingdom for regular use in urging their communities to be faithful to Yahweh.

Temptations to defect from the exclusive worship of Yahweh were often experienced in the northern kingdom where many surviving Canaanites and some Israelites still worshiped Baal and his consort. In order to enhance the book's instructional authority, therefore, all of its admonitions were placed on the lips of Moses. This collection of laws and admonitions was the earliest form of the book we now call Deuteronomy. It is reasonable to assume that a copy of it was obtained by the Jerusalem priests from their priestly cousins who had fled as refugees from the northern kingdom to escape the invading Assyrian army.

Relatedly, the Book of Proverbs indicates that Hezekiah had been concerned to gather and preserve Israelite traditions:

> These also are proverbs of Solomon which the men of Hezekiah king of Judah copied. (Prov 25:1)

Hezekiah's priest-historians would have been involved in preserving any material brought from the northern kingdom that had religious significance. It was probably at Hezekiah's behest that the "Elohist document" (c. 800 B.C.), which contained the sacred traditions of the northern kingdom, was partially preserved by priest-editors in the Books of Genesis, Exodus, and Numbers. Copies of the Elohist document would have been brought to Judah by the Levitical priests who fled there from the Assyrians. Those portions of the Elohist document deemed compatible were combined by the Jerusalem priests with the "Yahwist document" (c. 950 B.C.), which preserved the sacred traditions of Judah.

Among the Mosaic exhortations in the recently arrived book from the north was a stern and reiterated command that Israelites were not to go to the "high places" where the Canaanites (and unfaithful Israelites) still worshiped the old fertility gods of the land. Instead, faithful Israelites were admonished to offer their sacrifices at a shrine which Yahweh had chosen (through a faithful priest or prophet) as an acceptable "place" of worship:

> You shall go to the place which Yahweh shall choose,
> and offer your burnt offerings, the flesh and the blood,
> on the altar of Yahweh your God. (Deut 12:26b–27)

A critical reading of Deuteronomy reveals that the original aim of such a directive was to insure that Israelites would worship at Yahweh's local shrines or high places rather than at forbidden high places dedicated to other gods. However, the Jerusalem priests who advised King Hezekiah saw a window of opportunity in the directive's nonspecific language.

They realized that if its wording were slightly expanded, it could become a command from Moses restricting worship to one central sanctuary: Jerusalem where Yahweh's ark was kept. (Jerusalem is never mentioned in Deuteronomy because the substance of the book took shape in the northern kingdom after the split of Solomon's kingdom into Israel and Judah.) Such a modification, the Jerusalem priests believed, would be fully approved by Moses if he were alive because it would ensure the exclusive worship of Yahweh required by the first and most important Mosaic commandment.

Accordingly, along with other noncentralizing directives like the one cited above (Deut 12:26–27; 15:20; 26:2; 31:11), we find in Deuteronomy amplified versions of essentially the same directive. These expanded versions (Deut 12:4–6, 13–14; 17:8–10; 18:6–7) were probably created by a priest-editor at the time of Hezekiah's reform (c. 700 B.C.). The expanded directive cited below was tactically located by that editor as the first of a series which speaks of the acceptable "place" where Yahweh may be lawfully worshiped. Its added centralizing language was intended to color all similar subsequent statements in the remainder of Deuteronomy—even those that essentially retain the original language of the noncentralizing directive cited above.

The words most likely added by Hezekiah's priest-editor to the second passage below are enclosed in brackets. If these words are omitted, the passage agrees essentially with the noncentralizing directive quoted above:

Deut 12:2–3a

> You shall surely destroy all the places where the nations whom you shall dispossess served their gods, upon the high mountains and upon the hills and under every green tree; you shall tear down their altars, and dash in pieces their pillars, and burn their asherim with fire.

Deut 12:5–6a

> But you shall seek the place which Yahweh your God shall choose [out of all your tribes to put his name and make his habitation there]; there you shall go, and there you shall bring your burnt offerings and sacrifices.

We have no way of knowing if the Jerusalem priests actually informed Hezekiah of the subtle editorial changes that they probably introduced into proto-Deuteronomy. The henotheistic determination of the Jerusalem priests who guarded Yahweh's ark should never be underestimated. They labored incessantly (with God's nonverbal encouragement) to establish Yahweh's exclusive worship in Judah. It is altogether possible that they urged Hezekiah to restrict worship to Jerusalem in obedience to the centralizing injunctions in their revised copy of proto-Deuteronomy after they had privately edited the book. In any event, there is little doubt that Hezekiah's reform was based on the authority of the "Mosaic" injunctions in a revised copy of proto-Deuteronomy.

Hezekiah enacted his reform by sending a delegation of priests and soldiers to every city and town in the kingdom of Judah. The priests first read and explained the "Mosaic" law of one sanctuary contained in their revised copy of proto-Deuteronomy. They then announced that all sanctuaries outside of Jerusalem must be destroyed. In the future, they declared, all lawful sacrifices must be offered at the Jerusalem temple.

We find in the First Book of Kings a telltale reference to Hezekiah's centralizing reform. The reference occurs in a remembered taunt made by an Assyrian official to the soldiers of Hezekiah who were defending the walls of besieged Jerusalem. This official assumed that Yahweh would be angry with Hezekiah for having recently abolished all of Yahweh's shrines in Judah except the Jerusalem temple:

> And the Rabshakeh said to them, "Say to Hezekiah, 'Thus says the great king, the king of Assyria: On what do you rest this confidence of yours? . . . But if you say to me, "We rely on Yahweh our God,"' is it not he whose high places and altars Hezekiah has removed, saying to Judah and to Jerusalem, "You shall worship before this altar in Jerusalem?" (2 Kgs 18:19, 22)

Hezekiah's reform promised the disenfranchised priests from outlying districts that they could come to Jerusalem and take their turn there in offering sacrifices to Yahweh and receiving tithes (Deut 18:6–8). This promise was probably honored during Hezekiah's reign. But during King Josiah's later renewal of the reform, the practice was suspended by the Jerusalem priests who disliked sharing their duties and tithes with the Levites from other districts (2 Kgs 23:8–9).

As long as King Hezekiah reigned, his unpopular reform was enforced by military might. But Hezekiah finally died in 698 B.C. and was succeeded by his son Manasseh. We should remember that Hezekiah's religious nationalism had brought political humiliation and economic disaster to Judah. When his attempt at independence from Assyria failed, he retained his throne only by agreeing to pay a crippling penalty of gold and silver (2 Kgs 18:13–16). The Assyrians also removed much of the territory of Judah from his jurisdiction and assigned it to their loyal allies in the region.

Manasseh knew that his father's religious reform was deeply resented in the remaining districts of Judah outside Jerusalem. He also realized that his subjects would serve him more readily and pay their burdensome taxes more willingly if they were less unhappy. In addition, Manasseh was possibly under pressure from the Assyrians to erect altars in the outer court of the Jerusalem temple so that the Assyrian ambassador and his entourage could worship Assyrian astral divinities.

Accordingly, Manasseh revoked his father's religious reform and allowed the priests and people in the outlying districts to restore their local high places or sanctuaries. He also allowed them to return to practices the Jerusalem priests harshly disapproved of but which had formerly been viewed as compatible with Yahwism, such as the presence of a stone pillar or a wooden asherah at a Yahweh shrine.

Moreover, if the account of Manasseh's reign in 2 Kings is substantially reliable, he might have allowed the remaining Canaanites in Judah to rebuild their Baal shrines (2 Kgs 21:3). It is probable that the priest-historians have vilified Manasseh's memory by attributing to him every unacceptable practice that occurred in the land after he ended his father's reform. But it seems unlikely that they would have accused him of sacrificing his son if he had not actually done so. Even folk historians are bound by some constraints.

The Jerusalem priests had no choice but to accept Manasseh's revocation of Hezekiah's reform. They conceded defeat for the moment and stored their revised copy of proto-Deuteronomy in Yahweh's house. The priest-historian who wrote later, after the reign of King Josiah, described Manasseh as the most wicked of Judah's kings. It is clear that this priest viewed Manasseh's repeal of Hezekiah's reform as the worst kind of apostasy. And Manasseh's heinous apostasy brought a host of additional abominations in its wake:

> Manasseh . . . did what was evil in the sight of Yahweh, . . . For he rebuilt the high places which Hezekiah his father had destroyed; and he erected altars for Baal and made an asherah, as Ahab king of Israel had done, and worshiped all the host of heaven, and served them. . . . And he built altars for the host of heaven in the two courts of the house of Yahweh. And he burned his son as an offering, and practiced soothsaying and augury, and dealt with mediums. (2 Kgs 21:1–6a)

After the kingdom of Judah was destroyed by the Babylonians in 587 B.C. the priest-historian who wrote during the Exile (the second Deuteronomic Historian) asserted that it was because of Manasseh's shocking sins that Yahweh had punished Judah with invasion and exile:

> And Yahweh said by his servants the prophets, "Because Manasseh king of Judah has committed these abominations . . . and has made Judah also to sin with his idols; therefore, thus says Yahweh, the God of Israel, Behold, I am bringing upon Jerusalem and Judah such evil that the ears of every one who hears of it will tingle. . . . And I will wipe Jerusalem as one wipes a dish, wiping it and turning it upside down. (2 Kgs 21:10–13)

Manasseh was a problem for the Jerusalem priests in more ways than one. Not only did he nullify Hezekiah's reform, he also reigned for fifty-five years (2 Kgs 21:1). Such a lengthy reign perplexed Judah's priest-historians. Because they considered Manasseh to be utterly evil; they believed he should have died quickly instead of enjoying the longest reign in Judah's history. Worst of all, Manasseh reigned much longer than either Hezekiah (twenty-nine years) or Josiah (thirty-one years), the two reforming heroes of the priest-historians.

A later priest-historian who wrote 2 Chronicles (c. 350 B.C.) created a story intended to resolve this embarrassing enigma. His legendary story related that God punished Manasseh and brought him to repentance. It was because Manasseh sincerely prayed to God for forgiveness, therefore, that he had been spared and allowed such a long reign:

> Yahweh spoke to Manasseh and to his people, but they gave no heed. Therefore Yahweh brought upon them the commanders of the army of the king of Assyria, who took Manasseh with hooks and bound him with fetters of bronze and brought him to Babylon. And when he was in distress he entreated the favor of Yahweh his God and humbled himself greatly before the God of his fathers. He prayed to him, and God received his entreaty and heard his supplication and brought him again to Jerusalem and to his kingdom. Then Manasseh knew that Yahweh was God. (2 Chr 33:10–13)

We may be justifiably skeptical about the historicity of this story in 2 Chronicles; the priest-historians who earlier wrote and edited 2 Kings knew nothing of Manasseh's conversion. Nor did they mention the humiliating journey to Babylon where his repentance purportedly took place. Experience suggests that they would have eagerly reported Manasseh's humiliation by the king of Assyria had they known of it. Sufficient temporal distance from Manasseh's reign had to accrue before the Chronicler could create and introduce his mitigating story.

6.

When Manasseh died in 642 B.C. he was succeeded by his son Amon. Amon's reign, however, was brief. He was assassinated in 640 B.C. and his empty throne was then given to his son Josiah. We read in 2 Kings 22 that in the eighteenth year of King Josiah's reign, a significant discovery was made in the Jerusalem temple. While supervising repairs of the temple, we are told, the chief priest Hilkiah found "a book."

This book was the revised copy of proto-Deuteronomy that the priests had stored in the temple after Hezekiah's reform was annulled. From the time of its discovery by Hilkiah the high priest, the revised book of proto-Deuteronomy was revered as "sacred Scripture" by Judah's priest-historians. It was the first book among the Hebrew Scriptures to be described as implicitly "canonical," officially recognized as sacred Scripture. As such it was the foundational volume of the eventual collection of five sacred books (Genesis, Exodus, Leviticus, Numbers, and Deuteronomy) called the Torah (the Hebrew word for the law of Moses) or Pentateuch (the Greek word for the *five books* that comprised the law of Moses).

Whether Hilkiah actually found the book or whether he and his priestly confreres decided that the time was right for an attempt to revive Hezekiah's reform is a moot question. It seems unlikely, however, that the Jerusalem priests had forgotten Hezekiah's reform or the book that had provided its "Mosaic" legitimization:

> And Hilkiah the high priest said to Shaphan the secretary, "I have found the Scroll of the Law in Yahweh's house." . . . And Shaphan the secretary came to the king, and reported . . ."Hilkiah the priest has given me a book." And Shaphan read it before the king.
> (2 Kgs 22:8–10)

According to the account in 2 Kings, King Josiah was deeply troubled when the book was read to him because he realized that its repeated insistence on the law of one sanctuary (and other of its requirements) was not being observed:

> And when the king heard the words of the Scroll of the Law, he rent his garments . . . saying . . . "Great is the wrath of Yahweh that is kindled against us, for our fathers have not obeyed the words of this book."
> (2 Kgs 22:11, 13b)

King Josiah decided accordingly that a reform must be imposed on Judah so that the requirements of the book of the Law might be fulfilled. Josiah's reform is recounted in detail and with obvious approval in 2 Kings 23:1–23. The henotheizing priest-historians who wrote after Josiah's reign bestowed unstinting praise on Josiah. He was the only king of Israel or Judah (including David) in whom they found no fault whatsoever. Their account of Josiah's reign presents him as the standard by which all future Israelite kings should judge themselves:

> Josiah put away . . . all the abominations that were seen in the land of Judah and in Jerusalem, that he might establish the words of the law which were written in the book that Hilkiah the priest found in the house of Yahweh. Before him there was no king like him, who turned to Yahweh with all his heart and with all his soul and with all his might, according to the law of Moses. Nor did any like him arise after him. (2 Kgs 23:24–25)

The priest-historians also tell us with scarcely concealed glee that Josiah journeyed to Bethel and both destroyed and defiled the sanctuary that remained there. For after the fall of the northern kingdom, the Assyrians had restored the sanctuary of Yahweh at Bethel in an effort to lessen the appeal and influence of Yahweh's temple in Jerusalem:

> Then the king of Assyria gave command, "Send there one of the priests whom you carried away from there; and let him go and dwell there, and teach them the law

> of the god of the land." So one of the priests whom they had carried away from Samaria came and dwelt in Bethel, and taught them how they should fear Yahweh. (2 Kgs 17:27–28)

We are probably correct if we suspect that the Jerusalem priests urged King Josiah to demolish and desecrate the rival sanctuary at Bethel. Josiah could dare to do so because the Assyrians were being threatened by enemies in Mesopotamia and were in no position to retaliate against Judah. The priests especially hated the Bethel sanctuary because of its past association with Jeroboam's golden bulls.

There is, however, no mention of Josiah destroying a golden bull when he demolished the Bethel sanctuary, for the Assyrians had probably carried the bull away as plunder in 721 B.C. after they demolished the rebellious northern kingdom. When they later rebuilt the Bethel sanctuary, they did not restore its costly golden bull:

> Moreover, the altar at Bethel, the high place erected by Jeroboam the son of Nebat, who made Israel to sin, that altar with the high place he [Josiah] pulled down and he broke in pieces its stones, crushing them to dust; also he burned the asherah. And as Josiah turned, he saw the tombs there on the mount; and he sent and took the bones out of the tombs, and burned them upon the altar and defiled it. (2 Kgs 23:15–16a)

7.

In 609 B.C., Josiah was slain near Megiddo during an encounter with the army of Pharaoh Neco II. The Pharaoh was on his way to assist the Assyrians who were being overwhelmed by the Babylonians and Medes. After Josiah's death, the political fortunes of Judah worsened rapidly; the death rattle of David's dynasty had begun.

Jehoahaz, the son of Josiah, was anointed as his father's successor. After only three months, however, he was deposed and taken captive by the Pharaoh who now claimed imperial authority over Judah. The Pharaoh then appointed Josiah's son Eliakim as king and assigned him the throne name Jehoiakim (to remind him that he ruled by the will of the Pharaoh).

Jehoiakim soon abandoned his father's reform policy; he allowed recently forbidden forms of worship to return to Judah (2 Kgs 23:37; Jer 7:9, 18, 30–31; 11:9–13). The law of one sanctuary, therefore, was never permanently enforced in Judah until the chastened Judahites returned from exile determined to fully observe Yahweh's covenant law, which by then included the Book of Deuteronomy.

When Jehoiakim had reigned eight years, he suffered a fateful change of fortune. After the Battle of Carchemish in 605 B.C., King Nebuchadnezzar of Babylon drove Pharaoh Neco II from Judah and imposed his own imperial authority on the land:

> And the king of Egypt did not come again out of his land, for the king of Babylon had taken all that belonged to the king of Egypt from the brook of Egypt to the Euphrates. (2 Kgs 24:7)

But after three years of subjugation to Babylonia, Jehoiakim of Judah revolted. He probably died, however, before the Babylonians could retaliate, and was succeeded by his young son Jehoiachin (2 Kgs 24:1–2, 6). When the punitive Babylonian army finally arrived and laid siege to Jerusalem, Jehoiachin quickly surrendered (c. 598 B.C.). He was taken captive to Babylonia together with several thousand other hostages (2 Kgs 24:10–16). Nebuchadnezzar then appointed Josiah's third son Mattaniah as king of Judah and gave him the throne name Zedekiah.

Zedekiah was the last king of Judah. Unfortunately, he rejected the antirevolutionary warnings of the prophet Jeremiah:

> To Zedekiah, king of Judah I spoke in like manner: "Bring your necks under the yoke of the king of Babylon, and serve him and his people and live. Why will you and your people die by the sword, by famine, and by pestilence, as Yahweh has spoken concerning any nation which will not serve the king of Babylon?" (Jer 27:12–13)

In the eighth year of Zedekiah's reign he rebelled against Babylonia. Nebuchadnezzar's patience with the house of David was now spent. The Babylonians came with a mighty army and, after a siege of one and one-half years, they captured, plundered, and destroyed Jerusalem:

> Nebuchadnezzar king of Babylon came with all his army against Jerusalem, and laid siege to it; and they built siegeworks against it round about. So the city was besieged till the eleventh year of King Zedekiah. . . . Then a breach was made in the city; the king with all the men of war fled by night by the way of the gate between the two walls by the king's garden. . . .
>
> But the army of the Chaldeans pursued the king, and overtook him in the plains of Jericho. . . . Then they captured the king and brought him to the king of Babylon at Riblah, who passed sentence upon him. They slew the sons of Zedekiah before his eyes, and put out the eyes of Zedekiah, and bound him in fetters, and took him to Babylon.
>
> Nebuzaradan . . . a servant of the king of Babylon, came to Jerusalem. And he burned the house of Yahweh, and the king's house and all the houses of Jerusalem; every great house he burned down. And all the army of the Chaldeans . . . broke down the walls around Jerusalem. (2 Kgs 25:1–10)

Moreover, Nebuchadnezzar realized that revolutions usually begin in cities where citizens and their leaders have more time and can easily gather and conspire. Accordingly, he compelled most of the survivors in Jerusalem and the other cities and large towns of Judah to go into exile to Babylon. However, he left the farmers in the countryside to grow crops which he could tax:

> And the rest of the people who were left in the city . . . [Nebuchadnezzar] . . . carried into exile. But [he] left some of the poorest of the land to be vinedressers and plowmen. (2 Kgs 25:11–12)

It took the Babylonians and their unwilling captives about one year to complete the journey to Babylon. A few years after the deportees from Judah had reached Babylon, one of the priest-historians from Jerusalem (the second Deuteronomic Historian) recorded the memory of Judah's final devastation and explained it as follows:

> Surely this came upon Judah at the command of Yahweh, to remove them out of his sight for the many sins which Manasseh had committed, and also for the innocent blood which he had shed. (2 Kgs 24:3–4)

Questions for Review and Discussion

1. In the judgment of the priest-historians of Judah, who was the most wicked king to rule over the northern kingdom, Israel? Why was this king considered the most wicked?

2. Who was the famous prophet in the northern kingdom who vigorously opposed another evil king and his equally evil wife? Who were the evil king and his wife?

3. Do contemporary biblical scholars think that the contest on Mount Carmel between Elijah, the champion of Yahweh, and the priests of Baal is history or theology? Explain your answer.

4. Who was the prophet who continued Elijah's work of opposing the royal house of Ahab? Who did this prophet anoint as king and command to destroy the heirs of Ahab?

5. When the northern kingdom fell to Assyria in 721 B.C., who was reigning as king in Judah? What evil deed of this king did the priest-historians of Judah especially abhor?

6. Explain why many scholars think that some Israelites offered child sacrifice to Yahweh during the period of the Judges and also during the period of the Kings.

7. Who wrote the famous story which recounts that God commanded Abraham to offer his son Isaac as a sacrifice? Why was this story written? Is it history or theology?

8. Why did the priest-historians of Judah praise King Hezekiah so generously?

9. Where did the Jerusalem priests get the "Mosaic" justification needed for Hezekiah's novel and unpopular reform?

10. Who ended King Hezekiah's reform and why? What happened to the book used to justify that reform?

11. In 621 B.C., what unusual discovery was made in the temple during the reign of King Josiah? What was the outcome of that discovery?

12. Who was the only king of Judah who was never criticized by the priest-historians of Judah? Why was he never criticized?

13. Why was wicked King Manasseh's extremely long reign a problem for the priest-historians of Judah? What unusual step did a later priest-historian take to deal with that problem?

14. Who was the last king of Judah? How did his reign end? Who was the prophet whose advice he tragically rejected?

Chapter Five

Israel's Discovery of Monotheism during the Exile

1.

When the weary expatriates from Judah finally reached Babylon, they were doubtlessly awed by the city's architectural splendors. The Euphrates River flowed through the city, and graceful palm trees lifted their fronds above her massive turreted walls. Nevertheless, to most of the Judahites, Babylon seemed alien and hostile. Their hearts were still filled with longing for the familiar sights and sounds they had left behind:

> By the waters of Babylon we sat down, and we wept when we remembered Zion. On the willows there we hung up our harps. For there our captors required songs of us, And our tormentors expected joyful sounds saying, "Sing to us one of the songs of Zion."
>
> How shall we sing Yahweh's song in a foreign land? If I forget you, O Jerusalem, let my right hand wither.

> Let my tongue cleave to the roof of my mouth if I fail to remember you, if I do not set Jerusalem above my highest joy! (Ps 137)

Although the Bible frequently states that the exiles from Judah were taken to Babylon (2 Kgs 24:16; 25:7; 1 Chr 9:1; 2 Chr 36:20; Jer 20:4–6; 29:1, 4), they were probably not assigned living quarters within Babylon's walls. Such a large group of captives was more likely settled in one or more of the towns just outside the city, in what today we would call the suburbs. They were allowed freedom of movement but, depending on their personal skills, they were probably assigned quotas of work to be done under the supervision of Babylonian overseers. They were also free to enter nearby Babylon and explore its wonders.

Prior to and after their arrival in Babylon, the Jerusalem priests would have reminded the discouraged Judahites that shortly before Jerusalem fell, Jeremiah the prophet had spoken a comforting word from Yahweh to the doomed city's inhabitants:

> Thus says Yahweh, "When seventy years are completed for Babylon, I will visit you, and I will fulfill to you my promise and bring you back to this place. For I know the plans I have for you, says Yahweh, plans for wellbeing and not for evil, to give you hope and a future." (Jer 29:10–11; see also 25:11–12)

Ezekiel the prophet had also promised the exiles from Judah that Yahweh would "restore them to life" as a people even though their national future presently seemed "dead" and devoid of all hope:

Ezek 37:1–2

> The hand of Yahweh was upon me, and he led me out by the Spirit of Yahweh and set me down in the middle of the valley; it was full of dry bones. And he led me about among them; and behold, there were very many upon the valley; and lo, they were very dry.

Ezek 37:11–14

> Then he said to me, "Son of man, these bones are the whole house of Israel. Behold, they say, 'Our bones are

> dried up, and our hope is lost; we are completely cut off.' Therefore prophesy and say to them, Thus says Yahweh God: Behold, I will open your graves, and raise you from your graves, O my people; and I will bring you home into the land of Israel."

The priests, therefore, admonished their fellow exiles to keep alive their faith in Yahweh and to strive to fulfill Yahweh's commandments so that the promise made through Jeremiah and Ezekiel would be fulfilled. To that end, the priests encouraged the Judahites to gather for prayer and instruction in each other's dwellings on the Sabbath, their traditional day of rest. At these Sabbath gatherings, the priests read and explained key passages from the law of Moses and the writings of the prophets. The Sabbath gathering in Babylon was the remote beginning of the weekly Jewish synagogue service. Israel's fidelity to the Sabbath gathering has helped preserve her religious identity till this day.

During that period of renewed devotion to Yahweh's law, the priests gathered all of the sacred writings and traditions which explained the nature of their relationship with Yahweh. Included in this material was the Book of Deuteronomy, which had been the basis of Josiah's reform. The resulting collection of sacred writings became known as the Torah, or instruction, which God had given to Israel through Moses.

When all of this sacred instruction had been joined together, it filled five "scroll" books. In the third century B.C., the Greek-speaking Jews who lived outside of Palestine named these five books Genesis, Exodus, Leviticus, Numbers, and Deuteronomy. Those names are still commonly used to designate the five books of the Torah. The priest-historians continued to edit and expand the Torah until shortly after 500 B.C.; thereafter, the Torah became relatively fixed and unchangeable.

2.

Forty years earlier, around 540 B.C., electrifying news came to the exiled Judahites: King Cyrus of Persia had successfully invaded the Babylonian Empire. He had already defeated several Babylonian armies and was even then marching to take Babylon. One of the exiles who received this news was the prophet called "Second Isaiah"

(Is 40–55). This prophet is called "Second Isaiah" because he was the second of several later disciples of the original Isaiah who added their teachings to their master's book. The other two are called "Third Isaiah" (Is 56–66) and "Apocalyptic Isaiah" (Is 24–27).

In several of his prophecies, Second Isaiah spoke with enthusiasm of King Cyrus's anticipated arrival in Babylon. The prophet's inspired intuition told him that Cyrus would be the instrument through whom Yahweh would end the captivity of the Judahites; Jerusalem would then be restored and Yahweh's temple rebuilt:

Is 44:24a, 26, 28

> Thus says Yahweh, your Redeemer, who formed you from the womb . . . who confirms the word of his servant [2 Isaiah], and performs the counsel of his messengers [Jeremiah and Ezekiel]; who says to Jerusalem, "She shall be inhabited," and of the cities of Judah, "They shall be built, and I will raise up their ruins" . . . who says to Cyrus, "He is my shepherd, and he shall fulfill all my purpose;" saying of Jerusalem, "She shall be built," and of the temple, "Your foundations shall be laid."

Is 45:1, 4

> Thus says Yahweh to his anointed one, to Cyrus whose right hand I have grasped. . . . For the sake of my servant Jacob, and Israel my chosen, I call you by your name, I surname you though you do not know me."

During the same period when Second Isaiah assured the Judahites that Yahweh would use King Cyrus to set them free, his message also included a series of startling declarations concerning Yahweh's *oneness.* Something new and profoundly significant began with these declarations—Second Isaiah was the first of Israel's prophets to teach exclusive *monotheism:*

Is 44:6–8

> Thus says Yahweh, the King of Israel and his Redeemer, Yahweh of hosts: "I am the first and I am the last; besides me there is no God. Who is like me? Let him proclaim it, let him declare and set it forth before me. . . . Is there a God besides me? There is no Rock; I know not any."

Is 44:24b

I am Yahweh who made all things; who alone stretched out the heavens, who spread out the earth—Who was with me?

Is 45:5–7

I am Yahweh, and there is no other, besides me there is no God; I gird you [Cyrus], though you do not know me, that people many know from the rising of the sun and from the west, that there is none besides me; I am Yahweh, and there is no other. I form light and create darkness, I make weal and create woe, I am Yahweh who do all these things.

Is 45:22

Turn to me and be saved, all the ends of the earth! For I am God, and there is no other.

Is 46:5–9

To whom will you liken me and make me equal, and compare me, that we may be alike? Those who lavish gold from the purse and weigh out silver in the scales, hire a goldsmith and make it into a god; then they fall down and worship! They lift it upon their shoulders, they carry it, they set it in its place, and it stands there; it cannot move from its place. If one cries to it, it does not answer or save him from his trouble. . . . I am God, and there is no other; I am God, and there is none like me.

One might object that the prophet Jeremiah had already taught monotheism before the Exile:

Jer 10:6–9

There is none like you, O Yahweh, you are great, and your name is mighty in power. Who would not fear you, O King of the nations? . . . Among all the wise ones [gods] of the nations and in all their kingdoms there is none like you. They are both stupid and foolish; the instruction of idols is but wood. . . . They are the work of the craftsman and the hands of the goldsmith.

Jer 10:10–12

> But Yahweh is the true God; he is the living God and the everlasting King. . . . The gods who did not make the heavens and the earth shall perish from the earth and from under the heavens. It is [Yahweh] who made the earth by his power, who established the world by his wisdom, and by his understanding stretched out the heavens.

These verses from the Book of Jeremiah manifestly share much with the teaching of Second Isaiah and are probably monotheistic in intent. However, they stand in stark contrast with the other teaching in the Book of Jeremiah and were most likely inserted in the Book of Jeremiah by a monotheistic priest-historian who wished to lend additional prophetic support to the new monotheistic teaching of Second Isaiah. There are also monotheistic passages in the law of Moses (Deut 4:35, 39) and the pre-Exilic historical books (e.g. 2 Sam 7:22), but these likewise were added later by the priest-historians who had embraced Second Isaiah's monotheism.

3.

A number of predisposing factors in the historical consciousness of Second Isaiah (and his community) contributed to his discovery (and their acceptance) of monotheism. Some of these factors were traditional and some were new. To begin with, (1) Israel had already decided henotheistically that she should worship only one God, Yahweh. Furthermore, (2) her henotheistic tradition insisted that Yahweh could not be represented by an image:

> You shall not make for yourself a graven image, or any likeness of anything that is in heaven above, or that is in the earth beneath, or that is in the water under the earth. (Ex 20:4)

The priest-reformers who wrote after Josiah's reform (the first and second Deuteronomic Historians) added to Israel's ban on images of Yahweh the view that (3) Yahweh does not actually dwell in any temple on earth. Rather, (4) Yahweh dwells in the highest heavens. It is only Yahweh's "name" that dwells in a particular "Yahweh" shrine on earth:

Deut 12:11

> To the place which Yahweh your God shall choose, to make his name dwell there, thither you shall bring . . . your burnt offerings and your sacrifices.

Deut 14:23

> And before Yahweh your God, in the place which he shall choose, to make his name dwell there, you shall eat the tithe of your grain, of your wine, and of . . . the firstling of your herd and flock.

1 Kgs 8:27–29

> But will God indeed dwell on the earth? Behold, heaven and the highest heaven cannot contain you; how much less this house which I have built. Yet have regard to the prayer of your servant . . . O Yahweh my God . . . that your eyes may be open night and day toward this house, the place of which you have said, "My name shall be there."

In addition, the henotheistic Israelites had revised their ancient creation story derived from Mesopotamia. This story had originally related that the "gods" were responsible for the work of creation. But after the Mosaic covenant, the henotheizing Levitical priests removed the story's plural pronouns. They left the plural noun "Elohim" (gods) in the story, but now interpreted it as a singular noun of henotheistic fullness (i.e., since the power of all the other gods is possessed by Yahweh in its fullness, Yahweh can be spoken of in the plural). In the revised story, the work of creation was attributed to Yahweh alone. (5) Yahweh, therefore, was believed to be the "sole" creator of humankind and all the other living creatures in the world.

When the Judahites were being taken away to Babylonia in 587 B.C., they probably assumed with localizing henotheistic logic that they would no longer experience Yahweh's mysterious Presence when they prayed to Yahweh in that faraway land. We should recall that it took one year for them to finally reach Babylon. By the time they arrived they must have felt that they were at the other side of the world—an immense distance from their homeland. Each region of the world, they believed, was governed by gods who controlled that part of the earth. Yahweh, by this reasoning, would remain in the land of Judah, for the gods of Babylonia would not allow a foreign god to enter their territory. If Yahweh attempted to do so, Yahweh would meet with fierce opposition.

We know that before Second Isaiah the Judahites still thought of Yahweh's Presence as being ordinarily limited by geography. The prophet Ezekiel, for example, described Yahweh's Presence (glory) leaving the land of Judah on a throne-chariot and traveling briefly to the land of Babylonia to communicate a revelation to him (Ezek 1–3:11). (Yahweh visited Ezekiel near the tiny hamlet of Tel-abib thirty miles south of Babylon, not in mighty Babylon herself where the great gods resided.) Afterward, Ezekiel recounts, the cherubim who bore Yahweh's throne-chariot swiftly carried Yahweh back to the land of Judah (Ezek 3:12–13).

Not surprisingly, the idiosyncratic Ezekiel disagreed with the Deuteronomic Historian cited above who insisted that Yahweh dwelt in the heavens and not in the Jerusalem temple (1 Kgs 8:27–29). Ezekiel preferred the older view that Yahweh did indeed dwell in the temple's Holy of Holies. Guided by his conviction, Ezekiel told of a revelatory vision in which he saw Yahweh's Presence (glory) depart from the temple before the Babylonians arrived to destroy it along with Jerusalem (Ezek 10:3–4, 18–19; 11:22–24).

Because of their historically limited preconceptions, therefore, when those among the exiles from Judah, who were deeply religious, centered themselves and prayed near Babylon, the result was no doubt unexpected: They experienced Yahweh's mysterious Presence just as they had in their homeland. The more curious among them very likely puzzled over this matter: Why are the gods of Babylon not opposing Yahweh's Presence just outside the city where their temples are located. Perplexingly, there were no signs of divine conflict in the sky above or near Babylon when Yahweh's Presence was experienced.

Eventually Second Isaiah (or possibly someone before him) would have wondered if the gods of Babylon did not oppose Yahweh's Presence because these gods did not truly exist. Moreover, Second Isaiah would have recalled that everywhere the Israelites had ever sojourned during the lengthy course of their history since the

Patriarchs, Yahweh had always been experienced as present in their midst. Could it be that Yahweh's Presence was experienced by Israel everywhere she went in history because Yahweh is already present everywhere? If so, that would explain why Yahweh's Presence was experienced by Second Isaiah and other Judahites when they prayed in faraway Babylon.

One final element in Second Isaiah's dramatically altered historical experience also helped him to grasp God's mysterious oneness and universal sovereignty over the nations. That element was his experience of "imperial kingship." Babylon was the capital city of the vast Babylonian Empire. She was the center from which the imperial king held sway over the nations compelled to serve him.

Imperial armies marched through the great processional avenue of Babylon and departed to impose the will of her king whenever and wherever the need arose. Also, tribute streamed into the imperial city from the far-flung corners of the empire. One man governed this vast process and controlled the destinies of all the nations known to Second Isaiah. Such an all-encompassing exercise of majesty helped his mind's eye to "see" how one God could rule omnipotently over all the earth. When we read the writings of Second Isaiah carefully, it is evident that he envisioned Yahweh as an imperial King who ruled over all nations as Lord of history.

4.

Shortly after Second Isaiah heralded the arrival of King Cyrus in Babylon, something extraordinary happened when Cyrus actually neared the city in 539 B.C. The citizens of Babylon, anxious to avoid useless carnage and the destruction of their magnificent city, threw open its gates and invited Cyrus to become their new imperial king. Cyrus, of course, was happy to accept their invitation.

In the following year (538 B.C.), Cyrus told the exiles from Judah (now increasingly referred to by foreigners as the "Jews"—because they came from Ju-dah) that they could return to their homeland if they wished. But they would not be allowed to rebuild the walls of rebellious Jerusalem. After careful consideration, however, most of the Jews declined this offer and chose to remain in Babylon. They did so for the following reasons.

The exiled Jews knew that the Babylonians had burned Jerusalem and broken down her walls. Accordingly, if they returned there but were not allowed to rebuild her walls and restore her gates, they would have no physical or economic security. The prospect of living in a ruined city without protective walls was not inviting. On the other hand, under Persian rule the Jews were now being paid well for their labor and the massive walls of Babylon promised security for their families.

In addition, we should not forget that most of the Jews who had to make this decision had been born and raised in Babylon. They were three or four generations removed from the experience of the original deportees. They did not remember or long for Jerusalem as had the original arrivals from Judah. Also, not to be overlooked is the fabled beauty of Babylon herself. Struggling for years to rebuild a burned-down city that provided no safety scarcely compared with the secure life they now enjoyed in Babylon.

Understandably, therefore, most of the Jews opted to remain in Babylon for the present. Only a small group of hardy pioneer types dedicated to rebuilding Yahweh's temple were willing to return to Jerusalem. The other Jews promised to support such courageous dedication with regular financial support.

The returning Jews organized a caravan and departed for Jerusalem in 537 B.C. They arrived in ruined Jerusalem the following year. The task of rebuilding Yahweh's house was their goal of highest priority. Their task, however, was unexpectedly delayed for sixteen years because it was vigorously opposed by the Samaritans who lived in the province north of Judah.

The people of Samaria were of mixed blood; they were the descendants of the Israelite farmers who had intermarried with foreigners brought to their land by the Assyrians after the northern kingdom fell. These Samaritans offered to help the Jewish returnees rebuild Yahweh's house. When their offer was rebuffed, they were deeply offended and temporarily prevented the project's completion:

> Now when the [Samaritans] heard that the returned exiles were building a temple to Yahweh, the God of Israel, they approached Zerubabbel [the leader of the Jews] and the heads of fathers' houses and said to them, "Let us build with you; for we worship your God as you do, and we have been sacrificing to him ever since the days of Esarhaddon king of Assyria who brought us here.

> But Zerubabbel, Jeshua [the high priest], and the rest of the heads of fathers' houses in Israel said to them, "You have nothing to do with us in building a house to our God; but we alone will build to Yahweh.
>
> Then the people of the land [the Samaritans) discouraged the people of Judah, and made them afraid to build. (Ezra 4:1–4)

Not until 520 B.C. when the prophets Haggai and Zechariah exhorted the Jews to return to their original task did they do so. (By that time the anger of the Samaritans had subsided.) They finally finished the temple in 515 B.C.

In the meantime, the Jews who remained in Babylonia prospered under Persian rule. Most of them kept their recently acquired monotheistic faith alive by attending the weekly Sabbath gatherings. Nevertheless, the glittering polytheism of Babylon had its seductive attractions and, inevitably there were defections from their ranks. After all, some concluded, the Babylonians had certainly prospered while serving the gods of Babylon, and so shall we.

Babylon was the most beautiful city in the Ancient Near East. Its imposing walls contained the celebrated hanging gardens, many splendid palaces, and an array of magnificent temples. The material prosperity of Babylon was undeniably impressive. There was a very real danger, therefore, that increasing numbers of Jews might be tempted to abandon their newly found monotheism and its stern ethical demands in favor of the material prosperity ostensibly bestowed by the gods of Babylon.

The power of Babylon to dazzle the Jews and invite their defection from monotheism would have intensified every springtime when the Babylonian new year festival was celebrated with twelve days of spectacular religious pageantry. During this celebration the polytheistic Babylonian myth recounting the creation of the world by the victorious god Marduk was solemnly recited and dramatically reenacted.

This solemn recital of the Babylonian creation myth was an essential part of the ritual deemed necessary to guarantee the renewal of creation and its annual cycle for the coming year. The Jews living in Babylon could hardly have failed to learn about the twelve-day festival and its creation myth. And curiosity in the young being what it is, some of the Jews probably joined the festivities as spectators, and others as worshipers.

This situation presented the priestly guardians of Israel's newly found monotheism with a serious challenge. Around 500 B.C., (perhaps a little earlier) one of these priests resolved to write a new creation account designed to defend and strengthen his community's monotheistic faith. (This priest is called the "Priestly Author" by biblical scholars. They give him that title because, while acting as the final editor of the Torah, he added to it the "priestly" rule book, Leviticus.)

The Priestly Author decided to write a new creation story as a preface to the old Yahwistic creation account (the one revised during the reign of Solomon). The Priestly Author's purpose in writing his new account was twofold: (1) He wished to encourage Sabbath observance as a means of safeguarding and strengthening Jewish monotheism; (2) he also wanted to present the Jewish community in and near Babylon with an impressive monotheistic creation story that would effectively counteract the Babylonian account by depriving it of credibility.

5.

To encourage Sabbath observance, the Priestly Author decided to present God's creative activity within a seven-day framework. He described God as engaged in the specific works of creation for six consecutive days and then declared solemnly that on the seventh day God rested from all of God's labors. God thereby provided a divine precedent for the observance of the seventh day (the Sabbath) as a hallowed time of rest set apart for worship of the one true God (Gen 2:2–3). The Priestly Author scrupulously avoids using God's personal name, Yahweh, throughout his creation account. He does so for fear of treating it with disrespect and violating the third commandment: You shall not take the name of Yahweh your God in vain.

The second goal of the Priestly Author, the repudiation and replacement of the Babylonian creation account, was a bit more complicated. We will better understand why he proceeded with his task as he did if we are familiar with the general outline of the Babylonian creation story, the Enuma Elish. In that account, the victorious god Marduk created the world from the colossal corpse of Tiamat, the great goddess identified with the primordial sea; it was she and her husband, Apsu (identified with the primordial river flowing phallically into the sea), who were the ultimate progenitors of all the gods.

When Tiamat threatened to destroy many of her divine offspring, they prevailed upon Marduk to meet her in battle. After he inflicted a mortal wound on the great goddess, he divided her huge corpse into halves. With one half he created the vault of heaven (the firmament), and with the other, the earth. Marduk then appointed stations in heaven for the gods and permanent places for the starry constellations that represented them. He also established the months, seasons, and years by creating fixed pathways for the sun, moon, and stars.

Finally, after consulting the god Ea, renowned for wisdom, Marduk created humans from the blood of Kingu, a god who had been allied with Tiamat. Kingu had also been defeated after Tiamat, and was later executed by being drained of his blood. Marduk created humans from Kingu's blood so that the gods might be freed from the burden of providing their own sustenance. Humans, therefore, were assigned the task of growing food for the gods and providing daily meals for them on the altar-tables of temple-houses built for them on earth.

It is highly unusual that the Babylonian creation story relates that Marduk created the moon. (The story probably implies but does not state that Marduk also created the sun.) Everywhere else in Mesopotamia the moon and the sun were understood to be gods in their own right. How should we understand their loss of divine status in the Babylonian account?

There are grounds for suspecting that the Enuma Elish describes the creation of the moon by Marduk for a defensive reason: Before Babylonia surrendered to Persian rule, the last Babylonian king, Nabonidus, had been an eccentric antiquarian who was deeply devoted to the moon god (called Sin in Akkadian and Nanna in Sumerian.) Nabonidus restored the ancient temples of the moon god Sin in the cities of Ur and Haran. He also attempted to make the moon god the new head of the Babylonian pantheon. Not surprisingly, however, Nabonidus's promotion of the moon god drew sharp protests in Babylon where Marduk was traditionally worshiped as king of the gods.

The powerful priests of Marduk were especially alarmed by Nabonidus's attempts to elevate the moon god to premier status in

Babylon. It seems likely, therefore, that after Babylon passed under Persian rule, the priests of Marduk seized the opportunity to rewrite the traditional Babylonian creation story in a manner calculated to eliminate the moon god as a contender for Marduk's preeminence: They adroitly demoted the moon from a god who had recently menaced Marduk's supremacy to a mere creation of Marduk. In a certain way, the revisers of the Enuma Elish can be said to have acted in a demythologizing manner. Their motive, however, was not monotheizing but polytheistic politics.

6.

The Priestly Author's monotheistic account of creation frequently reacts in deliberate and subtle ways to things stated in the Babylonian account, always intending to negate that account's polytheism. He begins by telling us that before God began to create, the earth was shrouded in darkness and covered by a primordial sea. This primordial sea recalls the role of Tiamat in the Babylonian story. As we would expect, Tiamat is not mentioned by the Priestly Author, but his word for the "deep sea," *tehom* from which the earth will emerge reminds us of her indirectly:

> In the beginning God created the heavens and the earth. The earth was without form and void, and darkness was upon the face of the deep; and the Spirit of God was moving over the face of the waters. (Gen 1:1–2)

We are told that the "Spirit of God" (not the creative power of Marduk) was moving in readiness over the deep waters (*tehom*) awaiting God's creative command. The Hebrew word for "Spirit" (*ruach*) basically means "wind" or "breath," but can also mean "Spirit," depending on its context. And while it is true that the worldview of the Priestly Author was such that he could use one word to signify all three of these invisible realities, it is also true that we cannot. We may justifiably infer that when the Priestly Author uses the word *ruach* in his story in conjunction with God's creative activity, he intends it to be understood as the invisible creative power (Spirit) of God about to be directed by divine commands, which will recur during the following six days.

On the first day God calls forth light from the encompassing darkness and names the light "Day" and the darkness "Night." Ancient Israel reckoned that a day ended with sunset, and that in the ensuing night the next day was already present, ready to emerge in full view at sunrise. For this reason, the Jewish tradition begins its Sabbath (Saturday) observance on Friday evening after sunset, and considers the Sabbath to be completed when the sun sets on Saturday evening. Accordingly, a solemn formula is used by the Priestly Author to call attention to the end of each of the six days of creation leading up to the divinely inaugurated seventh day of rest ("And there was evening and there was morning, one day."):

> And God said "Let there be light;" and there was light. And God saw that the light was good; and God separated the light from the darkness. God called the light Day and the darkness he called Night. And there was evening and there was morning, one day. (Gen 1:3–5)

On the second day God creates the solid vault of heaven called the "firmament." Its purpose is to separate and hold back the waters above heaven (which periodically fall through opened floodgates in the form of rain) from the waters still covering the earth below. (The Babylonian account also mentions the vault of heaven but says that Marduk created it from one of the halves of Tiamat's corpse.):

> And God said, "Let there be a firmament in the midst of the waters, and let it separate the waters from the waters." And God made the firmament and separated the waters which were under the firmament from the waters which were above the firmament. And it was so. And God called the firmament heaven. And there was evening and morning a second day. (Gen 1:6–8)

On the third day God causes the dry land to emerge from the deep water below the firmament:

> And God said, "Let the waters under the heavens be gathered together into one place, and let the dry land appear." And it was so. God called the dry land Earth and the waters that were gathered together he called Seas. And God saw that it was good. (Gen 1:9–10)

God then creates the various kinds of vegetation on earth that produce seed-bearing fruit. It is clear that the Priestly Author and his community are still close enough to the discovery of agriculture to be fascinated by the mysterious nature of seeds. A sense of wonder resonates in his repeated reference to God's creation of "fruit trees bearing fruit in which is their seed, each according to its kind":

> And God said, "Let the earth put forth vegetation, plants yielding seed, and fruit trees bearing fruit in which is their seed, each according to its kind, upon the earth." And it was so. The earth brought forth vegetation, plants yielding seed according to their own kinds, and trees bearing fruit in which is their seed, each according to its kind. And God saw that it was good. And there was evening and there was morning, a third day. (Gen 1:11–13)

The Babylonian creation story makes no mention of the creation of plants and trees by Marduk; their presence is merely implied when humans are assigned the task of providing food for the gods. By explicitly ascribing the creation of all green growing things to the one true God, the Priestly Author is reminding the ancient Jews that the one true God is the only source of the vegetation on which all higher forms of life on earth depend; vegetation is not provided annually by fertility gods.

On the fourth day God creates the great lights that travel across the firmament, separating day from night and determining the months, seasons, and years:

> And God said, "Let there be lights in the firmament of the heavens to separate the day from the night; and let them be for signs and for seasons and for days and for years, and let them be lights in the firmament of the heavens to give light upon the earth." And it was so. (Gen 1:14–15)

The Priestly Author deliberately avoids using the Hebrew words for "sun" and "moon" to further specify "the two great lights" because these words also served as personal names for astral deities who were worshiped throughout Mesopotamia and Syria-Palestine. He wishes to avoid any suggestion that astral phenomena are divine, for the worship of these phenomena had already plagued Israel before the Exile:

> At that time, says Yahweh, the bones of the kings of Judah . . . and the bones of those who dwell in Jerusalem . . . shall be spread before the sun and the moon and all the host of heaven which they have loved and served, which they have gone after, and which they have sought and worshiped. (Jer 8:2; cf. Zeph 1:5)

Fear that Israel might return to the worship of the sun, moon, and stars (see 2 Kgs 21:3–5) was also expressed by the Deuteronomic Historian who wrote during the Exile:

> And beware lest you lift up your eyes to heaven, and when you see the sun and the moon and the stars, all the host of heaven, you be drawn away and worship them and serve them, things which Yahweh your God has allotted to all the peoples under the whole heaven. (Deut 4:19)

We should also observe that even though light was created and separated from darkness on the first day, the creation of the "two great lights," which also separate light from darkness, was deferred by the Priestly Author until the fourth day. He probably arranged his account in this fashion to avoid connecting the sun, moon, and wandering stars (planets) with the first day. (The planets were thought to be gods who wandered through the heavens; *planetes* = Greek for wanderer.) He was thereby rejecting the polytheistic belief that these created beings are gods who existed before the world began:

> And God made the two great lights, the greater light to rule the day, and the lesser light to rule the night; he made the stars also. And God set them in the firmament of the heavens to give light upon the earth, to rule over the day and over the night, and to separate the light from the darkness. And God saw that it was good. And

> there was evening and there was morning, a fourth day. (Gen 1:16–19)

It is noteworthy that even though the Priestly Author is trying to avoid polytheistic language by speaking of the "two great lights," his fund of monotheistic language is still so new and limited that he describes the great lights as ruling over day and night, echoing polytheistic belief that astral divinities rule over the historical destiny of the nations:

> Come down and sit in the dust, O virgin daughter of Babylon. . . . You are wearied with your many counsels; let them stand forth and save you, those who divide the heavens, who gaze at the stars, who at the new moon predict what shall befall you. (Is 47:1, 13)

On the fifth day God creates the "swarms of living creatures" that fly through the sky above and swim in the seas below:

> And God said, "Let the waters bring forth swarms of living creatures, and let birds fly above the earth across the firmament of the heavens." So God created the great sea monsters and every living creature that moves, with which the waters teem, according to their kinds, and every winged bird according to its kind. And God saw that it was good. (Gen 1:20–21)

God then blesses the swarms of living creatures by commanding them to "be fruitful and multiply," which again reminds the ancient Jews that the one true God is the sole source of life and blessing, not the so-called gods of fertility mistakenly worshiped by other nations:

> And God blessed them saying, "Be fruitful and multiply and fill the waters in the seas, and let birds multiply on the earth." And there was evening and there was morning, a fifth day. (Gen 1:22–23)

On the sixth day God first creates the various kinds of animals that run and creep upon the earth:

> And God said, "Let the earth bring forth living creatures according to their kinds: cattle and creeping things and beasts of the earth according to their kinds." And it was so. And God made the beasts of the earth according to their kinds and the cattle according to their kinds, and everything that creeps upon the ground according to its kind. And God saw that it was good.
> (Gen 1:24–25)

After creating the animals, God's creative activity reaches its pinnacle, and God finally creates human beings. At this point in the Priestly Author's account, however, something surprising occurs. Whereas in the Yahwist's account (c. 950 B.C.) God mocks the disobedient humans because they have foolishly presumed to become "like" God ("Behold, the man has become like one of us;" Gen 3:22), the Priestly Author introduces a dramatic reversal of this earlier divine scorn by having God now declare (borrowing the same discrepant plural pronouns found in Gen 3:22): "Let us make humans in our image, after our likeness" (1:26). What prompted this reported change in God's attitude?

The one true God, the Priestly Author wished to remind the Jews, had called them through the law of Moses to a life of holiness in their Creator's service ("You must be holy, for I Yahweh your God am holy," Lev 19:2; see also 20:26; 21:6, 8). Moreover, just before King Cyrus released them from captivity in 538 B.C., God had called them through Second Isaiah to be God's servant-people (Is 41:8–10; 44:21) and to witness (Is 43:10, 12; 44:8) to God's oneness (Is 44:6–8) and holiness (Is 43:15; 47:4) among the nations. They were to fulfill their lofty vocation as God's witnesses by the uprightness and holiness of their lives.

The Priestly Author decided, therefore, that he must counteract the ancient view that it is absurd for frail humans made of clay to aspire to be "like" God. Instead of stressing the frail insufficiency of humans, the Priestly Author chose to emphasize our privileged possession of the creative power of reason and freedom of choice. It is our possession of a finite measure of God's creative power that makes us the "image" of our Creator. For this power enables us to cooperate with God's creative purpose and to share responsibly in God's "dominion" over the kingdom of creation. Notice that since the demise of the monarchy, it is no longer primarily the king but

God's covenant people at large who are called to share in God's righteous oversight of creation.

Accordingly, in the Priestly Author's majestic story of creation, God announces the divine intention to make humans in God's own "image" and "likeness" (Gen 1:26) so they may share in God's "dominion" over creation (Gen 1:28). To call attention to his inspired reversal of the earlier view expressed in Genesis 3:22, the Priestly Author deliberately borrows that verse's atypical plural pronouns in order to invest them with sublime new intent:

> Then God said, "Let us make humans in our image, and after our likeness and let them have dominion over the fish of the sea, and over the birds of the air, and over the cattle, and over all the earth, and over every creeping thing that creeps upon the earth." (Gen 1:26)

Placing plural pronouns in the mouth of God in an otherwise rigorously monotheistic account was countenanced by the Priestly Author only because of the urgency of his theological task and his conviction that such plural language would be understood as the "plural of majesty," the usage whereby the king who rules over all speaks officially in the first person plural.

The plural of majesty is probably the only interpretation of the plural pronouns in Genesis 1:26 that the Priestly Author would have allowed because the advent of monotheism meant the eclipse of henotheism and the attendant henotheistic use of the "plural of fullness" (i.e., using the first person plural when Yahweh speaks to imply that Yahweh possesses fully the power of all the other gods). Furthermore, angels are never mentioned in the biblical material attributed to the strictly monotheistic Priestly Author. Consequently, his plural language should not be understood as God addressing an angelic court as in 1 Kings 22:19.

Nevertheless, we can tell that the Priestly Author was still somewhat uneasy about using the plural language necessary to teach his urgent new theological lesson in Genesis 1:26. For in Genesis 1:27, lest anyone misunderstand, he immediately repeats essentially the same idea with synonymous parallelism, but now he carefully replaces the plural with singular pronouns for God:

Gen 1:26

> Then God said, "Let us make humans in our image, and after our likeness; and let them have dominion over the fish of the sea, and over the birds of the air, and over the cattle, and over all the earth, and over every creeping thing that creeps upon the earth."

Gen 1:27

> So God created humans in his own image, in the image of God he created them, male and female he created them.

After creating the humans in God's image, God blesses them and bestows awesome status and responsibility on them. They have become privileged participants in God's holy and righteous dominion over the kingdom of creation:

> And God blessed them, and God said to them, "Be fruitful and multiply, and fill the earth and subdue it; and have dominion over the fish of the sea and over the birds of the air and over every living thing that moves upon the earth." (Gen 1:28)

Finally, in Genesis 1:29 God gives the humans permission to eat plants and fruits for nourishment; animals are also allowed green plants for food in Genesis 1:30. The Priestly Author believed that before the arrival and spread of sin there was no violence or bloodshed on earth; it was his view that humans and animals were vegetarians and herbivores before the Fall:

Gen 1:29

> And God said, "Behold, I have given you every plant yielding seed which is upon the face of all the earth, and every tree with seed in its fruit; you shall have them for food."

Gen 1:30

> "And to every beast of the earth, and to every bird of the air, and to everything that creeps on the earth, everything

> that has the breath of life, I have given every green plant for food."

In the Priestly Author's religious interpretation of history, humans were not given permission to kill animals and eat their flesh until after the great Flood when God made a covenant with Noah:

> And God blessed Noah and his sons and said to them . . . "Every moving thing that lives shall be food for you; and as I gave you the green plants, I now give you everything." (Gen 9:3)

In the Yahwist's account of God's rebuke of the man (Gen 3:17–19) there is also a brief directive restricting the diet of humans to plants:

> Cursed is the ground because of you. . . . Thorns and thistles it shall bring forth to you; And you shall eat the plants of the field. (Gen 3:17b–18)

But because nothing resembling this directive occurs anywhere else in the Yahwist's writings and it disrupts the logical flow of the thoughts that precede and follow it, we may reasonably suspect that the Priestly Author inserted it when he acted as the Torah's final editor. Moreover, other material added to the Torah by the Priestly Author betrays his general concern for the observance of dietary laws (Gen 1:30; 9:3 above). Accordingly, it was probably he who added the dietary directive to Genesis 3:18 in the Yahwist's creation story when he prefaced that story with his own creation account. He wished to imply by this editorial strategy that dietary laws had been part of God's will for humans from the very beginning.

During the course of each of the first five days, except the second day, God finds that what God has made is "good" (Gen 1:4, 10, 12, 18, 21, 25). But on the sixth day, when the work of creation is completed, God surveys the results of the past six days and finds all that has been wrought to be "very good." The Priestly Author is thereby affirming the fundamental goodness of the gift of creation, and probably also rejecting the polytheistic violence that permeates the world's creation in the Babylonian account (fierce and deadly combat among the gods, Tiamat's sundered corpse, the violent appropriation of Kingu's blood):

> And God saw everything that he had made, and behold it was very good. And there was evening and morning, the sixth day. (Gen 1:31)

When the climactic seventh day arrives, we are told with great solemnity and didactic redundance, God "rested from all his work which he had done," and God "hallowed" or sanctified the seventh day, setting it apart as a time for humans also to rest from their labors and to worship their Creator:

> Thus the heavens and the earth were finished, and all the host of them. And on the seventh day God finished his work which he had done, and he rested on the seventh day from all his work which he had done. So God blessed the seventh day and hallowed it, because on it God rested from all his work which he had done in creation. (Gen 2:1–3)

Having achieved his goal of majestically describing (1) the monotheistic origin of the world and (2) the divine institution of the Sabbath, the Priestly Author tersely notifies us that his account is finished:

> These are the generations of the heavens and the earth when they were created. (Gen 2:4a)

It has possibly occurred to the reflective reader that it was odd for the Priestly Author to have allowed his account to spill over into the beginning of chapter 2, where it ends awkwardly at v. 4a. We must understand, however, that originally there were no chapter or verse divisions in the Bible. The chapter divisions found in Christian Bibles are thought to have been added by Stephen Langton, the archbishop of Canterbury, in the thirteenth century of the Christian era. (He was one of the signers of the Magna Carta in A.D. 1215.) The verse numbers now in use were not universally adopted until the sixteenth century.

This information explains the unseemly chapter divisions we occasionally find in the Bible. Stephen Langton had the best of intentions, but he sometimes lacked a sufficiently informed understanding of the text. Nevertheless, we are all indebted to his practical wisdom (and that of those who continued his work). Imagine trying to find a desired text in the Bible without the aid of chapter and verse numbers.

7.

Some Bible readers experience disappointment and confusion when they become acquainted with the contemporary reading of the Genesis creation stories. They sometimes conclude that because these stories were written to address specific problems in the distant past, the stories are no longer relevant for our faith needs today. Such a response is understandable but mistaken.

There are many good reasons why the creation stories will continue to express vital sacred meaning for all later ages. It would be inappropriate to review all of those reasons in this book. We will, however, consider a few that seem especially germane. (Those interested in learning more about the abiding religious meaning of the Genesis creation stories will find it explained in detail in *Exploring the Genesis Creation and Fall Stories* in this series.)

To begin with, the creation stories provide an illuminating record of the dedicated and creative efforts by which our spiritual forebears struggled to remain faithful to their more evolved understandings of God. For example, it is instructive to observe the Priestly Author groping for the new language needed to teach and defend the monotheism he and his community had only recently embraced. His was an extremely important task at a critical moment in the history of religion.

Pastorally speaking, the Priestly Author's monotheizing labors were astonishingly successful. Encouraged by his inspired masterpiece, the Jewish community in Babylon preserved their monotheistic faith, and the Jewish people became the first nation in history to grasp and practice exclusive monotheism. All later monotheists, including Jesus, are the spiritual beneficiaries of the Priestly Author's creative devotion to the one true God. We have already noted in an earlier chapter that, among other things, God had to wait patiently until the Jews understood monotheism before it was appropriate for

God to give us God's definitive answer to our ultimate questions through the Risen and Spirit-mediating Jesus.

Likewise, one is filled with admiration for the ingenuity and commitment manifested by the Yahwist when he earlier revised Israel's traditional creation story. His mission of defending Israel's superior henotheistic faith from the regressive tug of polytheism and the scandalous behavior of King Solomon was also preparation for the Christ Event. To the degree that we fail to recognize his pivotal contribution to God's Self-disclosure in history, our own understanding of God's creative Providence is impoverished.

Our appreciation should also reach back a step further to include the contribution of the Mesopotamian mythmaker who was doubtlessly encouraged by God to teach the earliest form of the traditional creation story revised by the Yahwist. We should recognize that the Mesopotamian mythmaker also was "inspired" by his polytheistic faith experience of Ultimate or Sacred causal power to provide his contemporaries with an account of creation and its tragic disruption by sin.

His story was an even earlier step in the process by which we humans have been prompted by our experience of God's reality to reflect on our relationship with our Sacred ground. It is fascinating to recognize that in the first three chapters of Genesis we find evidence of the polytheistic, henotheistic, and monotheistic stages through which human thinking about the mystery of God has evolved. It is almost impossible to exaggerate the cultural significance of these three chapters when they are understood against their historical background and when their impact on subsequent history is recalled.

Questions for Review and Discussion

1. When did the exiled Judahites depart for Babylon, and roughly how long did it take for them to arrive there?

2. Which two prophets from Judah had given a promise of hope to the exiled Judahites? What general form did each of their promises take?

3. What weekly practice did the priests from Judah initiate in Babylon to help the exiles from Judah keep alive their

faith in Yahweh? What lasting impact did this practice have on later Jewish history and later human history?

4. Who was the first literary prophet in ancient Israel's history to teach exclusive monotheism? Where would we find instances of his monotheistic teaching?

5. What predisposing religious elements were already present in the historical consciousness of the Israelite prophet who first taught exclusive monotheism? Explain the significance of those providential elements.

6. What "new" contributing elements entered the historical consciousness of the Israelite prophet who first taught exclusive monotheism. Explain the significance of those providential elements.

7. Who was the "Priestly Author" and why was he given that title?

8. Why did the Priestly Author consider ancient Babylon a source of special temptation for the ancient Jews who dwelt there after the Exile?

9. For what two important reasons did the Priestly Author write a new creation story as a preface to the old one?

10. Why did the Priestly Author say that God created the "two great lights" instead of being more clear by saying that God created the "sun and the moon?"

11. Why did the Priestly Author describe the creative activity of God within a seven-day framework?

12. If the Priestly Author was striving to write a strictly monotheistic creation story, why did he use plural pronouns in Genesis 1:26 where God declares the divine intention to make humans "in our image, after our likeness?"

Chapter Six

The Evolution of Philosophical Monotheism

1.

This chapter will digress briefly from the biblical history in the preceding five chapters. The reader is assured, however, that our digression is not totally unrelated to the Bible. Ancient Israel's ideas about God have had a pronounced influence on various of the philosophers we will be considering. (If the reader has no interest in philosophy, he or she can skip this chapter and move on to the next.)

By way of illustration, the reader might suspect that once philosophy took up the task of reflecting on God independently of ancient myths, the Genesis creation stories were left far behind. We will see, however, that this was not the case. The Genesis creation accounts influenced philosophical thinking about God from c. A.D. 20, when they were introduced to philosophical circles in Alexandria by the Jewish philosopher Philo, until c. A.D. 1670, when they were perceptively deliteralized by Benedict Spinoza, another Jewish philosopher. Even after Spinoza, the influence of the creation accounts lingered in the minds of some creationist philosophers (i.e., those who believe the world has been created).

In this chapter we will review some of the ideas that a select group of Western philosophers have adduced about God. These particular philosophers have been chosen because, directly or indirectly, each made a major contribution to the currently ascendant interpretation of God—Whitehead's dipolar theism. The reader should understand, however, that only a brief summary of each philosopher's views will be presented, and significant ideas about God held by many other philosophers will be omitted. Much more could be said than our modest purpose will allow. Proceeding in this manner includes an advantage and a disadvantage.

The obvious disadvantage is that the reader's exposure to a particular philosopher's views will leave many things unsaid. The advantage, however, is that the reader without a philosophical background will not be overwhelmed by a surfeit of daunting information well beyond his or her interest. Furthermore, we can realistically limit our attention to a small group of ideas specific to our purpose. The historical development of these ideas can then be followed to greater advantage.

The author hopes that such an overview will help the reader attain two goals: First, the reader should be able to grasp in a very general way how philosophical reasoning about God, which began with the ancient Greeks, evolved to its present stage. Second, the reader should be able to recognize the influence that biblical monotheism and creationism have sometimes exercised within our Western philosophical tradition.

(If the reader wishes to know more about the ideas of a particular philosopher, he or she is encouraged to consult Frederick Copelston's *A History of Philosophy.* Also, the author would like to acknowledge his indebtedness to Anthony Catenazzo. who improved this chapter by making several corrections and a number of helpful suggestions. Its remaining deficiencies are due solely to the limitations of the author.)

Before we begin with the principal subject of this chapter it will be beneficial if we pause to reflect on some of the circumstances that were conducive to the discovery of philosophical (i.e., abstract and dialectical) reasoning. (Dialectic is argumentive or critical dialog which facilitates the discovery of clarifying distinctions.)

Wallace Matson (*A New History of Philosophy*, vol 1) reminds us that philosophy was initiated by the ancient Greeks who had colonized Ionia (the western coast of Asia Minor or present-day Turkey). There were several factors which encouraged the more intellectually daring among them to break away from the mythological mode of thinking. That mode of thinking was explained in the first chapter; it still prevailed literally everywhere when the Ionian Greeks discovered dialectical reasoning:

1. The Ionian Greeks were adventurous colonists who had left their Greek homeland in search of a new and better life. Accordingly, they did not feel as bound by the customary ways of acting and thinking that still prevailed in the old country. It was easier, therefore, for these Ionian Greeks to become independent thinkers with ideas of their own.

2. Many of the Greeks in the cities of Ionia were engaged in commerce instead of agriculture. Since agriculture does not invite bold innovation, ancient farmers tended to be conservative. Enterprising Ionian merchants, however, were rewarded when they took risks, tried new ideas, and sought foreign markets for the goods they manufactured.

3. Their commercial ventures required the Ionians to learn about and respect the customs and viewpoints of many other nations. Their willingness to tolerate and even accept novel ideas was correspondingly enhanced. Even in Ionia they frequently had contact with visitors from distant lands.

4. Greek religion, for the most part, was not administered by a class of hereditary priests who possessed sacred authority and a professional motive for preserving ancient myths and rituals. The priestly supervision of Greek temples and religious traditions was usually in the hands of volunteers who supported themselves by other means. They did not, therefore, have an unconscious need to guard beliefs and customs on which their own social standing and security depended.

The philosophical reasoning introduced by the Ionian Greeks was a major departure from mythological thinking, but it was not a total departure. Mythological thinking had correctly grasped that human attempts to understand invisible forces or causes must employ the laws of "causality" and "resemblance." But such thinking still assumed naively that all invisible causes were supernatural in character. Philosophical reasoning learned to challenge that traditional assumption and to make a distinction between "natural" and "supernatural" invisible causes.

Philosophers will never finish inferring from their increasing knowledge of creation the clarifying attributions and distinctions that should be made about its Creator. We will be examining below some of the more significant steps that have been taken during the long history of this ongoing search.

2.

We observed at the end of chapter one that when Second Isaiah taught exclusive monotheism in Babylon (540 B.C.), almost simultaneously the Greek philosopher Xenophanes was teaching monotheism in southern Italy (536 B.C.). This dual discovery portended that eventually ancient Israel's view of God would become linked for more than a thousand years with Western philosophical attempts to understand God's nature.

Xenophanes was born at Colophon in Ionia, but he was probably driven from his homeland by the Persians. After a period of wandering, he seems to have finally settled in southern Italy. When we examine Xenophanes' ideas about God, we are required to be brief and tentative. For his views must be sifted carefully from the few fragments of his surviving poetry: Xenophanes taught that God is one, transcends bodily form, and is already present everywhere. God need not, therefore, move from place to place. Everything beyond these few ideas is somewhat obscure.

It seems that Xenophanes thought of the sky as the experienceable reality that best enabled one to grasp the nature of God: Both are invisible, encompass the world, and are distinct from the world. It is even possible that he identified God with the sky. Xenophanes has been called a pantheist, but he probably was not. (A pantheist believes everything in the universe is identical with God.)

Like almost all ancient Greek philosophers (Plato was the sole exception), Xenophanes did not think that God had created the world. Instead, he believed that God moves all beings in the world by the power of divine thought. Xenophanes probably thought that the world itself was eternal.

Xenophanes is also remembered for his rejection of the Homeric myths and his criticism of their *anthropomorphic* language. (Anthropomorphism is the likening of nonhuman beings to humans.) He noted scornfully that the immoral behavior which the myths attributed to the gods was unworthy of humans, not to speak of "gods." He also remarked that if animals could reason and create works of art, they would (projectively) depict the gods as supernatural animals. Philosophical demythologizing, therefore, probably began with Xenophanes.

We should note that ancient Greek philosophers who were monotheists sometimes spoke seriously of "gods." When they did, we should not assume that they were reverting to polytheism or being inconsistent. It was traditional among the Greeks to speak of any mysterious force in the world as a "god." For a time, therefore, the early philosophers used the word "gods" to signify invisible natural forces or causes. Accordingly, when Thales of Miletus said "all things are full of gods," he probably meant all things in the world are full of mysterious natural forces. This early Greek philosophical convention explains the following words of Xenophanes: "There is one God, the greatest of gods and humans, who neither in shape nor in thought resembles mortals." Xenophanes probably intended his words to mean that God is the greatest of all the beings, visible or invisible, who exercise causality in the world.

Second Isaiah succeeded in convincing most of the unlettered exiles from Judah that Israel's God is exclusively one. He succeeded, in large part, because he used concrete picture language which the Judahites could grasp with their mind's eye. The novel and abstract language of Xenophanes, however, was not easily understood by his preliterate Greek contemporaries. Only his fellow philosophers, we may surmise, truly comprehended his monotheistic teaching.

3.

Among the ancient Greek philosophers who agreed with Xenophanes's monotheism, it was Plato (429-348 B.C.) who exercised the greatest influence on the history of abstract thinking about God. Plato's exceptional influence was due primarily to his personal genius. But he was also admired by Jewish and Christian philosophers who came later because he taught that God had "created" the physical world (but not out of nothing). All other ancient Greek philosophers thought of the world as eternal and uncreated. Accordingly, because Plato essentially agreed with the creation stories in Genesis, Jewish and Christians philosophers revered his teaching as highly authoritative.

In Plato's view, God formed the various beings in the physical world from preexistent matter. This preexistent matter was patterned by God after eternal and unchanging "Ideas" or "Forms" contained in a supreme Idea called the "Good." These immutable Ideas or Forms exist, Plato believed, in a transcendent realm. But they exist independently of God and are the timeless and perfect Exemplars from which God copied the imperfect forms possessed by all temporal beings.

By describing God as the world's Creator, Plato was clearly acting as an innovator. Yet he did not depart completely from the ancient Greek view that the world is uncreated. For the matter from which God "formed" the world was preexistent and probably thought of by Plato as eternal (like the eternal Ideas which gave it form). Nevertheless, when Plato asserted that God had created the physical world, he broke rank with his ancient Greek peers.

Eventually Plato's disciples realized that the eternal Exemplars he postulated are best understood as God's own Ideas. Guided by the laws of causality and resemblance, they recognized that it makes good sense to assume with Plato that the design or essence of a temporal being is patterned after eternal Ideas. But these Ideas, they decided, constitute the creative knowledge of God. For Plato's Ideas are ultimately difficult to account for—difficult to reconcile with monotheism—if construed as eternal Beings on which God's creativity depends.

4.

Aristotle (384-322 B.C.) is probably the best known of the philosophers who attended Plato's Academy in Athens. His fame eventually rivaled that of his illustrious teacher. Aristotle, however, was a decidedly independent thinker who disagreed with much he had learned from Plato. It should come as no surprise, then, that he did not share Plato's view that God created the physical world.

In Aristotle's thought, God did not create the world; the world simply "is" eternally and requires no Creator. Instead, God is the Unmoved Mover who eternally causes all beings in the world to be set in motion. God, however, does not engage in any activity which produces movement in the world. Rather, all beings are attracted by the beauty of God's absolute perfection. It is their natural striving to imitate God's fully actualized Being (by actualizing their own potential) that sets all things in motion.

As envisioned by Aristotle, God is eternally and necessarily immutable; because God is absolute perfection, God cannot engage in any kind of activity other than Self-contemplation. For any other kind of activity would require "change," and change, according to Aristotle, always involves "imperfection." Change requires some potentiality to be actualized. But God is already absolutely perfect and can have no potentiality for further development. God, therefore, is Pure and Eternal Act devoid of any potential for change or improvement.

Because "spiritual consciousness" is superior to less conscious or nonconscious forms of being, God's perfection requires that God must be absolute and unchanging spiritual consciousness. Aristotle concluded, therefore, that God is Absolute Thought eternally thinking Itself. God's Self-thinking, he believed, is static not dynamic; it admits of no change and requires no increase. God already knows absolutely everything that can be known; there is simply nothing else for God to learn.

It follows for Aristotle that the only object worthy of God's contemplation is God. Consequently, God knows and cares nothing about the world, for the world is inferior and unworthy of God's consideration. (It would do no good, therefore, to pray to Aristotle's God.)

One might conclude that Aristotle's God, instead of attracting everything in the universe, is remote, Self-absorbed, and unattractive. For Aristotle, however, God is the ultimate paradigm of Self-sufficient Perfection. It is probably no coincidence that Aristotle's God resembles a divine philosopher who serenely and eternally contemplates divine Truth and Beauty.

We will notice as we proceed that a number of philosophers who came after Aristotle agreed that God is, in a certain aspect, immutable and Self-thinking. But most of them decided that God's Self-contemplation must somehow include an awareness of the world.

Eventually the "dipolar" theists (those who posit "two" contrasting poles or dimensions in God's nature, one immutable and the other mutable) further modified Aristotle's ideas. They asserted that God's Self-knowledge is not static but dynamic and always increasing. Dipolar theists do not object to the view that God can enjoy a (nonessential) knowledge of the world, which continually undergoes change or increase.

Furthermore, dipolar theists maintain that the universe, even though not identical with God, is nevertheless contained within God and is part of God. They believe that God created the world out of God's very own Being, not out of nothing—*ex Deo, non ex nihilo.* In their judgment, therefore, God is intimately related to the world and delights in learning more about it at every moment. We will return to dipolar theism below and consider it at greater length.

5.

The next philosopher to come within our purview is Philo of Alexandria (30 B.C.-A.D. 50). Philo was a hellenized Jew who had been born into a wealthy and prominent family. To be hellenized means to have adopted the Greek language and other aspects (but not necessarily all aspects) of Greek culture. He received a good education in rhetoric and philosophy, and was well informed about his own Judaism.

In a number of his books, Philo tried to demonstrate the essential agreement between the truths revealed in the law of Moses and those advanced by various philosophers, especially Plato. To accomplish this task, Philo used the allegorical method of explaining ancient religious texts by assigning edifying meaning to the concrete elements in the ancient biblical stories. This method had been introduced by the Stoic philosophers as a way of finding positive meaning in the increasingly outmoded Homeric myths.

When Philo undertook to philosophize about God, he already possessed several firm and non-negotiable religious convictions. As a devout Jew, he believed above all else in God's oneness (Deut 6:4–5; Is 44–46). He also believed that God had revealed to Moses that the world had been created by God (Gen 1–3). And because Plato also held that God had created the world, Philo found Plato's philosophy especially attractive.

Philo had enormous respect for Plato, but his respect for Moses and the authority of sacred Scripture was even greater. Tension was inevitable, therefore, between Philo's theology and Plato's philosophy: For example, Philo's Jewish monotheism maintained that God alone is eternal. Plato, on the other hand, taught that God had created the world from preexistent matter commonly thought of as eternal, and that this matter was given forms derived from eternal Ideas.

To resolve this incompatibility, Philo made two tactical accommodations; one was profoundly insightful but the other merely expedient. First, he moved Plato's eternal Ideas into the mind of God—if the eternal Ideas are God's own Ideas, he realized, they pose no problem. (An impressive array of later philosophers have endorsed Philo's decision; they agree that Plato's Ideas have their true home in God's mind.)

Second, Philo decided that God had created the world in two distinct stages: To begin with, God created matter; God then created the world out of that preexisting matter. By positing these two stages of creation, Philo preserved his belief that only God is eternal. And yet he also was able to advance a view of creation fairly close to that of Plato: Matter is not eternal, but Plato is correct when he asserts its preexistence.

We are never told by Philo what he thought God had made matter out of. But since he read the Old Greek version of the Jewish Scriptures (also called the Septuagint), he very likely believed that God had created matter "out of nothing":

> Look at the heaven and the earth and see everything that is in them, and recognize that God made them out of things that did not exist [*ex ouk ontōn*].
> (2 Macc 7:28)

If Philo did indeed believe in *creatio ex nihilo,* he probably avoided saying so in order not to call attention to a further discrepancy between his own views and those of Plato.

A far greater problem confronted Philo when he undertook to describe God as the world's Creator. For Philo agreed with Aristotle that God absolutely transcends the world and is absolutely immutable. This assumption made it difficult for Philo to explain, therefore, how God could have contact with or create the world without engaging in "activity," which would contradict God's absolute transcendence and immutability.

Philo solved this problem by an ingenious strategy: Plato had taught that the eternal Ideas are contained within the supreme Idea of the Good. Correspondingly, Philo declared, all of God's Ideas reside within a supreme Idea or Thought called the "Logos" (logos = Greek for thought, word, or reason). According to Philo, the divine Logos emanated mysteriously from the fullness of God's mind without any activity on God's part. (Philo himself did not use the term "emanation," which later played such an important role in Neoplatonic philosophy. The term, however, correctly expresses his meaning.)

The Logos then became the agent who undertook the work of creation for God. It was the Logos who created matter and then created the world out of that preexistent matter. All of the beings which the Logos created for God were patterned after the copies of God's eternal Ideas present in the Logos. It is also through the Logos that God exercises the providential care for creation spoken of in sacred Scripture. Even though God transcends the world with sovereign immutability, God knows about the world with eternal omniscience and cares for creation through the eternally foreintended mediation of the Logos.

Philo's choice of the "Logos" as the mediating agent of God's creative purpose was probably determined by the Old Greek version of the Jewish Scriptures and by Stoic philosophy. In the Greek version of the Scriptures, Philo found that *logos* was the term used for the Word through which God created the world:

Ps 33:6

> By the word [logos] of the Lord the heavens were made,
> and all their host by the breath of his mouth.

Ps 33:8–9

> Let all the earth fear the Lord. . . . For he spoke, and it
> came to be; he commanded, and it stood forth.

Psalm 33:6–9, we should note, is faith-inspired reflection on the Genesis creation account wherein God calls creation into being by a "word" of command:

Gen 1:3

And God said, "Let there be Light;" and there was light.

Gen 1:6

And God said, "Let there be a firmament in the midst of the waters, and let it separate the waters from the waters."

Gen 1:9

And God said, "Let the waters under the heavens be gathered together into one place, and let the dry land appear."

Moreover, the Wisdom literature in the Old Greek Scriptures personified God's creative Word (Logos) and described "him" as proceeding from God's throne to act as God's agent:

Wis 9:1–2

O God of my fathers and Lord of Mercy, who have made all things by your Word [*logos*], and by your Wisdom [*sofia*] have formed humans to have dominion over the creatures you have made.

Wis 18:14–15

While gentle silence enveloped all things, your all-powerful Word [*logos*] leaped down from heaven, from the royal throne.

In addition, Philo also knew that Stoic philosophy described the divine agent who orders and governs the world with universal "Reason" as the "Logos." Because Philo was eager to demonstrate the agreement between the Jewish Scriptures (in Greek translation) and Greek philosophy, he thought it fitting to designate God's supreme Idea as God's Logos instead of the Good (Plato's term for the supreme Idea).

Finally, Philo vigorously asserted that God's transcendence is such that God is essentially unknowable to inquiring human minds. Humans can recognize dimly that God exists, but their unaided reason can never know anything further about the mystery of God's Being. All we can know clearly about God is what God is not. God is not like the imperfect and inferior world of finite beings. Philo thought he found scriptural authority for his "negative theology" in the law of Moses (Philo is considered the originator of "negative theology."):

Ex 33:17a, 20

> And the Lord [Kurios] said to Moses . . . "You cannot see my face; for a human may not see me and live."

Ex 33:17a, 23

> And the Lord [Kurios] said to Moses . . . "You shall see my back, but my face you shall not see."

Accordingly, humans could never have learned anything about God if God had not graciously conferred the gift of revelation on Moses and the prophets. Apart from revelation, Philo believed, there is no way that humans could ever have learned anything about God's essential Being. He concluded, therefore, that because Plato knew about God's creation of the world, Plato must have learned about it from the creation account revealed to Moses in the Book of Genesis.

It was Philo's deeply held conviction that humans should learn from sacred Scripture and philosophy to live virtuous lives in God's service. Our major task in life is to become as much like God as possible through the practice of virtue and the guidance of wisdom. If we learn to live in such a manner, we can experience a divinely conferred ecstasy in which we enjoy mysterious contact with God's Being. This ineffable experience confirms our belief in God's transcendent otherness and provides a preview of the immortal life that awaits the soul when it is finally freed from the body.

Philo is a minor but significant philosopher in the process we are examining, for he is regarded by historians as the father of "classical" theism. Classical theism interprets God's nature as monopolar rather than dipolar. The substance of Philo's monopolar view of God was the dominant philosophical paradigm for explaining God's nature, from its acceptance by Augustine of Hippo (c. A.D. 400) till its rejection by Benedict Spinoza (c. A.D. 1670). It is still the model preferred by many traditional thinkers.

A classical or monopolar theist believes that there can be only "one" time-transcending pole or dimension in God's nature. And to this pole or dimension may be assigned only those attributes considered "strong" and "perfect" (Absoluteness, Infinity, Eternity, Transcendence, Immutability). The polar opposites of these strong attributes are thought to be "weak" and "inferior" (relatedness, finitude, temporality, immanence, mutability). Classical theism insists that these "inferior" attributes must be excluded from our understanding of God.

Dipolar theists (e.g., the twentieth-century philosophers Alfred North Whitehead, Charles Hartshorne, and Paul Tillich) obviously do not agree with the conclusions of monopolar theism. They believe that there are good reasons for positing "two" poles or contrasting dimensions in God's nature instead of only one. They insist that both ultimate categories involving polar opposition must be attributed to God: eternality and temporality, transcendence and immanence. If we fail to do so, they conclude, we will not be able to understand God's nature adequately or grasp how God can relate intimately to us and all else in the world.

Further, dipolar theism rejects the notion that one of two polar opposites must always be regarded as inferior and excluded necessarily from God. There are circumstances, it maintains, in which either pole can be seen as strong and enhancing. No ultimate category expressing polar opposition, therefore, is intrinsically inferior or weak if correctly understood.

6.

The next philosopher of note whom we will consider is Plotinus (A.D. 205-270), the founder of *Neoplatonism.* As the term itself suggests, Neoplatonism was a movement which carried the thought of Plato in new directions. Plotinus was probably born in Egypt; we know that he studied philosophy in Alexandria under Ammonius Saccas. He eventually traveled to Rome and established his own school. Although Plotinus was not a Christian, he exercised considerable influence on many Christian philosophers. We will see below that various of his views were linked to classical theism by Augustine of Hippo (c. A.D. 400).

Plotinus decided that the supreme Idea of the Good in Plato's philosophy could be described more fittingly as "the One." He was very likely led to this conclusion by Plato's own reflections in the *Parmenides* on the ultimately inclusive nature of the One.

Neopythagorian speculation on the primary and divine significance of the One (from which all other numbers and beings derive) was probably also a motivating factor. (The Neopythagorians were philosophers who modified and developed ideas of the philosopher-mathematician Pythagoras. They were influential from the first century B.C. until the end of the second century A.D.)

"The One" is Plotinus's preferred way of designating the mysterious reality of God. He conceives of the One as the ultimate metaphysical principle that absolutely transcends the world. For Plotinus, the reality of the One is so exalted that it is beyond all being, all multiplicity, and all distinctions. Therefore, it is impossible for human reason to describe the One. Nevertheless, we must think about the One, albeit inadequately, for the One is the ultimate source of the power by which we and all other beings exist.

To safeguard the exalted transcendence of the One from any suggestion of contact with the inferior realm of matter, Plotinus envisioned a series of emanations which began with the One and became increasingly inferior as they neared the realm of bodily beings. We are assured by Plotinus that this series of emanations in no way diminishes the indescribable fullness of the One. Nor does it compromise the One's sublime immutability.

The reader should understand that there is nothing "temporal" about the emanations that Plotinus envisioned. Instead, he understood them to be atemporal and eternal. That is, from all eternity these emanations have proceeded from highest to lowest in a simultaneously completed manner. The "priority" in Plotinus's descriptions, therefore, is "logical" or "mental" rather than temporal. Even though the world of material beings is the "last" in a series of emanations, Plotinus still regarded the world as eternal, that is, without temporal beginning.

The divine fullness of the immutable One is such, we are told, that it flows forth in the form of an eternal emanation called the divine Intelligence or Mind (*Nous*). The Intelligence knows only Itself and the ineffable One from whose fullness It eternally proceeds. It also knows that It contains the eternal Ideas of all classes of beings as well as all individual beings. (Plato thought the Ideas were Exemplars of all classes of beings but not of all individuals.)

From the divine Intelligence then emanates the divine Soul (*Psyche*) or Life Power. This Soul, however, must be distinguished into a higher part and a lower part called the World Soul. It is only the World Soul that comes into contact with the world. The higher Soul continues to contemplate the divine Intelligence without distraction.

In turn, human souls and the souls of all other living beings then emanate from the World Soul. The various living beings in the world are able to participate in their eternal Ideas because dim copies of these Ideas are mediated to their souls when they emanate from the World Soul. Finally, matter emanates from the souls of living beings (and embodies the soul from which it emanates). And matter, Plotinus tells us, is the source of all the evil in the world.

Evil, however, is not something that actually exists in its own right. Rather, evil is the absence or privation of some possible and appropriate goodness just as darkness is the absence of light. (Augustine and Aquinas both inherited this view of evil from Plotinus.) The moral darkness that issues from matter, therefore, can blind human souls and prevent them from contemplating the higher realm of divine Intelligence, and finally the One.

Plotinus taught that the individual human soul can learn to free itself from the blinding influence of matter by a life of virtue, the study of philosophy, and contemplation of the One. When the human soul has successfully prepared itself, it can periodically experience mystical union with the One. This ineffable union is a foretaste of the uninterrupted union with the One awaiting a wise and illuminated soul beyond death.

In agreement with Socrates, Plato, and Philo, Plotinus taught that when philosophy is truly the "love of wisdom," it is far more than mere intellectual pursuit of theoretical knowledge. It must always include an ethical component which aids us in orienting our lives toward God and the attainment of ultimate meaning and joy: True wisdom assures that only the honestly examined and virtuous life is truly worth living.

7.

Augustine of Hippo (A.D. 354-430) was born at Tagaste in North Africa and later became the Christian bishop of Hippo, also in North Africa. He tells us in his well known *Confessions* that it was his reading of Neoplatonic philosophy that freed his mind from skepticism and convinced him of the reality of the spiritual realm. After Augustine became a Christian, he gradually abandoned some

Neoplatonic ideas he had formerly accepted. However, many of the ideas in his philosophical framework remained Neoplatonic.

The teaching of Augustine was a peculiar blend of Christian faith experience and philosophical reflection meant to clarify that experience. He was primarily interested in theology rather than philosophy. But even though Augustine produced no formal philosophical system, he nevertheless taught a number of ideas which contributed significantly to Western philosophical reflection on God.

In essential agreement with Neoplatonism, Augustine affirmed that God is transcendent, eternal, infinite, and immutable. He also found it necessary, however, to stress God's omnipotence and omniscience when discussing God's creation of the world from nothing and God's foreknowledge of free human choices. Augustine was probably led to the view that God created the world out of nothing by his reading of 2 Maccabees 7:28 (already quoted above when discussing Philo). He would have had access to that book in Latin translations (the Old Latin version and Jerome's Latin Vulgate which appeared in A.D. 405) as well as in the Old Greek version of the Scriptures.

When Augustine was asked by the skeptics how God could create from nothing, he replied that God is omnipotent and free to create in whatever mysterious way divine Wisdom deems best. And when pressed further about what God was doing "before" creation, he answered that the question involved a misconception. For the term "before" is inseparable from the temporality of our finite world. Time, therefore, did not exist "before" God created the world.

In addition, Augustine was asked how God could engage in the "act" of creation without contradicting God's transcendent immutability. He replied (with dipolar intuition) that God is both transcendent and intimately present within creatures; God remains immutable yet is acting in our hearts. In some mysterious way, therefore, God was able to engage in creative activity while remaining transcendent and immutable. That these opposites can be reconciled in God may seem impossible to humans, Augustine observed, but such difficulty is due to the limitations of our finite minds.

Augustine was the first philosopher to assert that God always "foreknows" what we humans will do with our freedom of choice. But God's foreknowledge, he insisted, does not interfere with our freedom. To solve this problem, he advised, we must understand that God's eternal omniscience envisions the past, present, and future simultaneously. What God eternally foresees, then, is precisely what we will decide to do with our freedom when some future situation requires us to make a free choice. (We will learn below why dipolar theists find Augustine's reasoning about this matter unconvincing and unnecessary.)

One of Augustine's most important "theological" innovations was his likening of God's inner life of knowledge (the divine Word) and love (the divine Spirit) to the inner life of a human being. Augustine, like Philo and the Neoplatonists, agreed that Plato's eternal Ideas should be located in God's mind. He was further led by the Gospel of John to conclude that the divine "Word" is the necessary repository of God's eternal Ideas:

> When time began, the Word was already there, and the Word was face to face with God; and the Word was God's own Word. He was with God when time began; all things were made through him, and nothing that has been made was made without him. (Jn 1:1–3)

Augustine had also learned from Scripture to personify God's Self-communication as love, the Holy Spirit:

> If you love me, you will keep my commandments. And I will pray to the Father, and he will give you another Counselor to be with you forever, even the Spirit of truth whom the world cannot receive, because it neither sees him nor knows him; you know him, for he dwells with you, and will be in you. (Jn 14:15–17, see also 26)

Guided further by Genesis 1:26 ("Let us make humans in our image and after our likeness") and working with the law of resemblance, Augustine believed that he could "see" the image of God's inner life reflected in our spiritual souls. For we humans also possess the power of spiritual "life." And we "know" that we possess this spiritual life. Moreover, we "love" the spiritual life which we know we possess. Therefore, it is our inner life of knowledge and love that enables us to "image" the Eternal Life, Knowledge, and Love of the Triune God. (In the thirteenth century A.D., Aquinas inherited this trinitarian view of God's nature from Augustine and developed it further in his *Summa Theologica.*)

It is quite possible that using this psychological analogy was suggested to Augustine by the two divine emanations that proceed consecutively (but nontemporally) from the Plotinian One: Just as the divine Intelligence emanates eternally from the One, and the divine Soul or Life-Power emanates from the divine Intelligence, so also, the divine Word is eternally "thought" by the divine Father, and the Life-giving Spirit is breathed forth or "spirated" as the eternal "love" of the Father for the divine beauty and goodness eternally known in the divine Word.

We should note, however, that Augustine himself rejected the Neoplatonic notion of passive emanations from God. He thought of the divine Word and Spirit as eternal activities in God's Mind. Eight and a half centuries later, Aquinas interpreted the two divine mental activities postulated by Augustine as two eternal processions "within" God that are sent on two temporal missions "outside" of God.

8.

Thomas Aquinas (A.D. 1225-1274) was the greatest of the medieval philosopher-theologians. Such an appraisal of Aquinas, however, was not immediate. During his lifetime, various of his views were considered dangerously novel and even heretical. Within a decade of his death several of his conclusions were condemned by the archbishops of Paris (1277) and Canterbury (1284). His ideas were especially suspect in the eyes of some because Aquinas ordinarily preferred the philosophy of Aristotle to that of the Neoplatonists. And Aristotle could, with good reason, seem menacing to church leaders of that age. A recent "interpretation" of Aristotle's work by the Arabic philosopher Averroes (A.D. 1126-1198) had advanced ideas in serious conflict with Christian beliefs.

Most of the works of Aristotle had been lost in the West after the barbarian invasions. Neoplatonic philosophy, especially as interpreted by Augustine, had fared much better. It was the Muslim conquerors of southern Spain who reintroduced Aristotle's writings to the West. Gradually his works were translated from Arabic and Greek into Latin and began to circulate among Christian scholars. By the thirteenth century most of Aristotle's writings were available in reliable translations.

Aquinas perceived that the empirically grounded philosophy of Aristotle could better serve the changing intellectual needs of thirteenth-century Europe than the "otherworldly" emphasis of Neoplatonism. He understood, however, that Aristotilianism would have to be modified before it could serve as the rational undergirding of a Christian interpretation of reality.

Aristotle had rejected Plato's view that God created the world. He also had rejected the transcendence of Plato's eternal Ideas or Forms by asserting that "forms" exist only in actually existing beings. Aquinas agreed with Aristotle that each existing being possesses its own form. But he also agreed with Augustine that Plato's eternal ideas are present in God's mind as Exemplars which guided God's eternal creative decrees. And, of course, Aquinas agreed with Genesis that God is the world's Creator. In deference to Aristotle, however, he taught that we could not know of the world's creation apart from revelation, for unaided reason would have to conclude that the world is eternal.

Also, even though Aquinas accepted Aristotle's view that God is Pure and Immutable Act, he qualified the related notion that God is Eternal Thought thinking only Itself. In agreement with the Bible, Aquinas concluded that God's Self-contemplation includes knowledge of the world. For in knowing the divine Self, God also knows the eternal divine decrees concerning the world's creation and providential oversight. Aquinas had learned from Augustine how to make this Christian accommodation to ancient Greek philosophical insistence on God's absolute immutability. Furthermore, Aquinas accepted Augustine's opinion that God absolutely foreknows the free choices of all humans in a manner that does not violate their freedom. For God sees all things from an eternal perspective which simultaneously includes past, present, and future.

On the other hand, Aquinas was not willing to accept Augustine's view that God is intimately related to the world. (Augustine taught that God is present within all creatures and yet transcends them.) As Aquinas saw it, God exercises providential care through eternal decrees but has no direct relation to the world. In agreement with Aristotle, Aquinas believed that God's sacrosanct immutability and transcendence would be contradicted if God were "related" to the world.

After the synthesis achieved by Aquinas between Aristotle and Christian theology, the influence of Augustinian Neoplatonism began to diminish. Aristotilianism as modified by Aquinas increasingly provided the philosophical framework for classical or monopolar theism.

9.

The philosophy of Baruch (Benedict) Spinoza (A.D. 1632-1677) marks a jarring transition in the history of Western thought about God. He dealt classical theism a blow from which it never completely recovered. The full impact of Spinoza's highly idiosyncratic view of God was not at first evident. But near the end of the eighteenth and during the first half of the nineteenth centuries modifications of his ideas began to appear in German Idealism (which will be discussed below).

To appreciate the role that Spinoza played in undermining the authority of "classical theism," it helps to be aware of the following:

1. Spinoza was a mystic who communed habitually with God's indwelling presence; he knew from personal experience, therefore, that God is immanent (intimately present within), not utterly transcendent and unrelated to the world;

2. He was not a Christian but an excommunicated Jew. He accordingly felt less hesitation in rejecting the established Christian (and Jewish) philosophical orthodoxy;

3. He lived in Protestant Holland where he was free from the Roman Catholic Church's claim to absolute authority in matters of religion. In Holland there was greater freedom than anywhere else in the Protestant Europe to dissent from traditional orthodoxy without fear of harsh, even lethal, reprisal;

4. Classical theism affirmed four ideas about God which had always been rejected as unreasonable by critics inside and outside of Christianity. With the passage of time these ideas were more vigorously opposed and, consequently, more rigorously imposed by ecclesiastical authority. All of these ideas were *in some sense* repudiated by Spinoza:

    a. God created the world out of nothing.

b. God is absolutely immutable and yet created the world without undergoing change.

c. God has absolute foreknowledge of the free future actions of humans, but God's foreknowledge does not deprive humans of freedom.

d. God absolutely transcends the world and is in no way related to it. The world exists infinitely apart from and outside of God.

Spinoza was especially repelled by the "deistic" notion that God is the First Cause and Mover of the universe who then retreats into transcendence and no longer has anything to do with the world. Such a world did not require the sustaining presence of God in order to continue to be. It continued by itself in accordance with divinely established laws of nature which operated mechanistically; it did not, therefore, require the continuous sustaining power of God. Spinoza the mystic was unconvinced.

In continuity with classical theism, Spinoza affirmed the existence and oneness of God. He also agreed that God is eternal, infinite, perfect, and immutable. But having granted that much, he conceded nothing more. In reality, Spinoza's view of God was radically different from the God of traditional theism.

Spinoza emphatically rejected the notion that God infinitely transcends the world. So determined was he to bring God down from the empyrean heaven to earth that he antithetically identified God with the world (or nature). In other words, Spinoza postulated pantheism. God, for Spinoza, is totally immanent rather than totally transcendent. He would never allow, therefore, that God is unrelated to the world, for God is the world. God and nature are two words for naming the same infinite reality (*Deus sive natura* = God or nature).

According to Spinoza, the entire universe is one infinite substance, the substance of God. And all the individual beings in the world are finite modes of God's infinite substance. Humans, therefore, are finite modes of God, and our minds are finite modifications of God's infinite mind. (We will see below that these ideas, while not accepted by the German Idealists, nevertheless had an impact on their thinking.) Spinoza believed that he had eliminated

God's transcendence while preserving God's immutability. However, he did not truly explain how God's finite modes can derive from God's infinite substance without violating God's immutability.

If we object that a pantheistic interpretation of God is rendered unlikely by all the evil and suffering in the world, Spinoza assures us that if we possessed the infinite knowledge of God we would know that what looks like evil from our finite vantage point is actually part of an infinite totality that is perfectly ordered and good. The experience of evil and tragedy, therefore, is an illusion resulting from the ignorance and distortion which impede our finite minds.

Classical theism believes that God freely created the world and could have chosen *not* to create it. For Spinoza, however, the world is as eternal and necessary as God, for God and the world are one; God, therefore, did not create the world. And when we humans assume that we are free, what we take to be our freedom is actually the set of circumstances that move us to act as we must in conformity with the overall requirements of God's infinite nature. Freedom of choice, therefore, is just as illusory as the experience of evil. Both of these mistaken notions, according to Spinoza, result from the limitations inherent in our finitude.

Spinoza also provided his age with a surprisingly insightful critique of the Bible. The Bible, he observed, was not dictated by God. Instead, its ancient authors wrote it to explain their historically conditioned understanding of God to their contemporaries. He noted that such a book is necessarily filled with many primitive ideas which a philosophically educated person can no longer accept.

And yet, the Bible still has positive religious value for society as a whole: Its primitive threats of punishment and promises of reward can still motivate the unlettered masses to abide by law and to practice virtue. Because many of Spinoza's ideas contradicted orthodoxy and were considered alarming in the seventeenth century, he prudently asked his friends to publish his more disturbing views after his death.

10.

The next philosophers who contributed significantly to the process we are examining are the German Idealists: Fichte, Schelling, and Hegel. These three men are called Idealists because they agreed that "reality" and "thought" (the "real" and the "ideal") are somehow identical. It seemed evident to them that the world is permeated with the ordering power of reason and purpose. On that basis, they inferred that a Supreme Mind exists whose Reason and Purpose are manifest in the universe. This Supreme Mind, of course, is God's Mind.

Moreover, these three men held in common the extraordinary insight that the world is the visible expression of God's eternal Self-thinking. They manifestly agreed with Aristotle, in their various ways, that God is Eternal Thought thinking Itself. But they concluded with bold innovation that God's Self-thinking is dynamic and world-inclusive, not static and world-exclusive. Furthermore, it is God's very Self-thinking that has eternally called the world into being (in nontemporal fashion, i.e., the world has always been here).

Aristotle also believed that the world is eternal, but he thought that the world had not been created by God and was unworthy of God's consideration. In a stunning reversal, the German Idealists maintained that the world is precisely what God is eternally thinking about. Indeed, it is God's eternal act of Self-reflection that eternally "creates" the world.

The German Idealists had learned several important lessons from Spinoza. They disagreed with his decision to identify God with the world. But they agreed with his rejection of God's total transcendence of the world. They also accepted his denial that God "freely decided" to create the world at some "arbitrary beginning" and need not have created the world at all. Instead, they concluded, God is eternally creating the finite world within God's infinite Mind as the essential means to God's Self-thinking. Although Fichte, Schelling, and Hegel concurred that the world is necessarily involved in God's eternal Self-contemplation, each understood God's Self-discovery-through-the-world in a somewhat different manner.

Johann Fichte (A.D. 1762-1814) was the father of German Idealism. With intellectual daring, he introduced the *dynamic* paradigm for understanding God that was accepted, with secondary modifications, by Schelling and Hegel. God, Fichte concluded, is an Absolute Mind eternally discovering more about Itself through a world of finite "others" who possess subjective consciousness. When finite subjects are conscious of God's perfection as the goal of their moral striving, God becomes more conscious of God's Self in a way that involves *dialectical* development. (In this context, dialectic is a conscious activity that reconciles one's own ideas and their apparent oposites into a new and always-increasing unity.).

Fichte, as we noted above, followed Spinoza in rejecting the biblical view of creation which assumes that the world did not exist before God decided to create it. Instead, the world of others is the eternal opposite through which God's Self-knowledge proceeds to a richer synthesis. The world of conscious subjects, therefore, is the necessary consequence of God's eternal Self-contemplation. (Because of the exclusive role assigned by Fichte to finite "subjects" in God's Self-thinking, Schelling called Fichte's philosophy "Subjective Idealism.")

It was Fichte, then, who introduced dialectical process into Western philosophy's understanding of God's Inner Life. Fichte envisioned God's eternal Self-exploration as proceeding dynamically through *thesis* (God's act of Self-reflection) and *antithesis* (the world of "others" in whom God sees God's Self reflected) to *synthesis* (the unceasing increase in God's Self-knowledge). Because the finite world of conscious "others" through whom God contemplates God's Self is contained "within" God's infinite Being, Fichte's paradigm for God is implicitly dipolar.

The dipolar model for God is also called *panentheism.* Pan-en-theism (all-is-*in*-God) is not to be confused with pantheism (all-*is*-God). Panentheism is the view that everything in the universe is contained within God and is part of God. But not everything that is part of God is identical with God. For God has given a relative measure of freedom and independence to created beings. And God, panentheism concludes, did not create the world "out of nothing." (From nothing one gets nothing.) Rather, God is eternally creating the world out of some aspect of God's very own Being.

By way of illustration, just as children are parts of their parents yet are distinct from their parents, so also, by analogy, creatures are parts of God but are "distinct" from God. A major step forward in grasping God's immanence *and* transcendence occurred when Fichte launched German Idealism. For the German Idealists provided a rational basis for Augustine's earlier intuition that opposites can and do co-exist in God. It was they who began to articulate the distinctions necessary for grasping panentheism.

A panentheist infers that all created beings (and God's temporal attributes) are present in God's temporal pole or dimension. God's eternal Ideas, however, (and God's eternal attributes) are present in God's time-transcending pole or dimension. Schelling is the first philosopher who taught "explicit" panentheism. Both Fichte and Hegel are "implicit" panentheists, for they do not clearly make all the dipolar distinctions essential for fully articulated panentheism.

Initially, Friedrich Schelling (A.D. 1775-1854) was a disciple of Fichte, but disagreement arose between the two, and Schelling's construal of Idealism moved in a different direction. He agreed with Fichte that God is an eternal act of dynamic Self-thinking, but he rejected Fichte's view that God attains conscious knowledge only through the thoughts of finite subjects.

Schelling believed that Nature also should be assigned a role in the process by which God eternally engages in Self-thinking. For Nature provides the conditions for its own self-reflection in human consciousness. Nature, therefore, is "slumbering Spirit" which awakens as Human Spirit. And through the reflective power of Human Spirit, God comes to Self-knowledge. Fichte had regarded Nature as nothing more than the context for human self-discovery and moral striving which contribute to God's Self-knowledge. Schelling, on the other hand, understood Nature as the visible manifestation of Divine Intelligence seeking Self-knowledge.

In Schelling's view, God's eternal act of Self-thinking involves *three* logically distinguishable (but nontemporal) moments. (1) In the first moment, the Absolute (or Divine Reason) "objectifies" Itself in the realm of Nature. (2) Then the Absolute manifests Itself in the "subjective" realm of Human Spirit which can recognize the Absolute's Self-objectification in Nature. (3) Finally, the Absolute knows Itself in and through Human Spirit's conscious recognition of the Absolute. Because Schelling sees "objective" Nature as an essential moment in God's Self-thinking, he called his philosophy "Objective" Idealism to distinguish it from Fichte's "Subjective" Idealism.

Georg Hegel (a.d. 1770-1831) preferred to understand God as "Absolute Spirit." By Absolute Spirit, however, Hegel did not mean the absolutely transcendent Spirit spoken of by traditional theism. Rather, he meant the totality of all reality contained within Absolute Mind. (The German word used by Hegel to speak of Spirit is Geist, which means both spirit and mind.) So central was the concept of Absolute Spirit to Hegel's thought that he named his system "Absolute" Idealism.

The infinite Life of Absolute Spirit or Mind was thought of by Hegel as an eternally unfolding process wherein the Absolute departs from Itself and objectifies Itself in the realm of Nature. The "material" realm of Nature is alien to Absolute Spirit but is the necessary precondition for the emergence of Human Spirit. And it is through the subjective consciousness of Human Spirit that the Absolute then returns to itself and knows Itself as Absolute Spirit. Human Spirit's *historical* striving to understand the Absolute is the means by which Absolute Spirit actualizes Its potential for Self-discovery. Accordingly, when humans raise their consciousness to thoughts of the Absolute, their thoughts are moments in the life of Absolute Spirit's Self-thinking.

11.

Alfred North Whitehead (A.D. 1861-1947) is the philosopher whose interpretation of God is best known and most widely discussed in the twentieth century. Whitehead agreed with the German Idealists that God is both immanent and transcendent (and therefore has a dipolar nature). He also agreed that God is eternally thinking about God's Self through the world. However, Whitehead articulated these shared convictions in a manner that surpassed the historical limitations of the German Idealists. As a twentieth-century philosopher, Whitehead possessed scientific knowledge about evolution and cosmology (the study of the universe's origin and history) that was unknown a century earlier.

Whitehead did not share the assumption of the German Idealists that God's Self-consciousness must always involve the consciousness of some "other" thinking subject. Consequently, he did not limit God's knowledge to human thinking about the Absolute. Instead, he concluded that God has always been thinking about absolutely *everything* in the universe.

Nothing in the universe is unworthy of God's concern because every actual entity other than God is ultimately created out of God for the sake of God's Self-exploration. To be sure, humans are the actual entities about whom God is most concerned. For we, as self-transcending beings, can recognize and freely cooperate with God's purpose by consciously contributing to an increase of creative novelty and satisfaction in the world.

Whitehead was a panentheist, and it was he who introduced the terms *primordial* and *consequent* into the Great Dialog about God. God's dipolar nature includes a primordial or time-transcending dimension and a consequent or temporal dimension. Understanding the relation between these two dimensions in God enables one to solve the vexing problems that have arisen from attempts to reconcile developing historical consciousness with traditional (monopolar) theism—the conflict between: (1) God's transcendence and immanence; (2) God's immutability and creative activity; (3) God's foreknowledge and our freedom of choice; (4) God's goodness and the presence of evil in the world.

God's *primordial dimension* contains God's abstract, purely spiritual knowledge of the infinity of creative possibilities eternally present in God's Mind. (Whitehead expressly says that these eternal possibilities are the equivalent of Plato's eternal Ideas. For that reason he also calls the dimension which contains them the "mental" pole of God's nature.) This dimension, then, is characterized by all of God's time-transcending attributes such as Absoluteness, Eternity, Immutability, and Metaphysical Infinity. Whitehead assures us that the infinity of creative possibilities in God's primordial dimension is the reason why the universe never runs out of potentiality for further duration and creative novelty.

Conversely, in God's *consequent dimension* God is continually engaged in creative interaction with the world. This dimension contains God's concrete knowledge of God's creative activity in the past and present, as well as God's *statistically probable* foreknowledge of the future (especially the free future actions of humans).

God's consequent dimension also contains all the "physical" entities God is even now creating and sustaining within God's nature. (For that reason God's consequent dimension is also called God's "physical" pole.) This dimension is characterized by God's finite (but supereminently so) and temporal attributes such as Immanence, Mutability, and Relatedness. These (and other) temporal attributes are the polar opposites of God's timeless primordial attributes.

These polar opposites co-exist necessarily in the creative unity of God's nature. Guided by the laws of causality and resemblance, Whitehead insists that God is not the only exception to the universal interdependence of polar opposites. Rather, God is the chief exemplification of polar interaction. In other words, polar opposition is present in the world because it is eternally present in God.

Whitehead acknowledges that God is omniscient in the qualified sense that God possesses total knowledge about all past and present actualities and all future probabilities. But because the future is not yet actual, God does not yet have actual knowledge of it. God does not, therefore, have absolutely certain foreknowledge of the free future actions of humans. However, God does possess a highly probable statistical foreknowledge of what we will very likely do with our freedom in the future. But this knowledge is relative, not absolute, for the free future has not yet been decided, and we sometimes surprise God.

In Whitehead's system, the category of "creativity" is assigned the supreme and overarching role in God's Life. He agrees with Schelling that God is necessarily creative and, consequently, has been creating eternally. Whitehead concludes therefore, that God is eternally exploring the divine creativity through a universe of creatures who are free in varying degrees to contribute to God's creative purpose.

We humans can either cooperate or interfere with God's creative purpose, but our interference (which produces the moral evil in the world) cannot ultimately thwart God's quest for increasing creative novelty and satisfaction in the world. On the contrary, God has so provided actual entities with creative possibilities that any interference with a positive outcome in a particular instance contributes indirectly to the emergence of other opportunities for creative novelty. (Evil, therefore, is temporary interference which God allows for the sake of our freedom of choice, which is essential to our participation in God's creative purpose.)

This conclusion further implies that creatures are continually contributing, directly or indirectly, to an *increase* in God's knowledge and joy (in God's consequent dimension). Any *specific* increase is not essential as such to God's nature, but is nevertheless real and causes genuine growth in God's satisfaction.

Creative novelty can emerge from the evolutionary process because God has provided all actual entities with the creative possibilities necessary for its attainment. When favorable circumstances develop, the creative possibilities ingredient in actual entities are actualized and contribute to an increase of novelty in the world *and* in God's knowledge of the world.

Whitehead maintains the provocative view that God is always creating the world, and *the world is always creating God.* He states his case in this fashion to jar us into realizing that all created entities (and especially we humans) truly cause or "create" a nonessential but real increase in God's Self-knowledge and happiness.

The reader probably agrees that, compared to the remote God of classical theism, Whitehead's view of God bears much greater resemblance to the dynamic biblical God who is everywhere present, active, and intimately caring in history:

Gen 12:1–2

> Yahweh said to Abram, "Go from your country and your kindred and your father's house to the land that I will show you. And I will make of you a great nation and I will bless you."

Gen 28:15

> Behold I am with you and will keep you wherever you go. . . . I will not leave you until I have done that of which I have spoken to you.

Acts 17:27–28

> God . . . is not far from any one of us, for "In him we live and move and have our being."

Lk 12:6

> Are not five sparrows sold for two pennies? And not one of them is forgotten before God. Why, even the hairs of your head are all numbered.

12.

The final philosopher we will consider briefly is Paul Tillich (A.D. 1886-1965), a philosopher-theologian in the tradition of Augustine and Aquinas. Tillich, like Whitehead, was a twentieth century philosopher *and* a dipolar theist, but he disagreed significantly with Whitehead about several matters having to do with God and the God-human relationship.

Because Whitehead was a process philosopher, he believed that the category of *becoming* should be given the highest *ontological* rank in our understanding of reality. (Ontology is the branch of philosophy that studies the order and structure of reality most broadly considered.) Tillich objected; he acknowledged the importance of universal becoming, but he insisted that Absolute and Eternal *Being* is necessarily prior to all relative and temporal becoming and should, therefore, be assigned the highest rank. (The priority in question is logical not temporal.) For if Absolute Being were not eternally able to prevent absolute nonbeing from swallowing all being, nothing at all would be. And there would then be nothing to undergo process or becoming. God, accordingly, is the Absolute Being who is eternally able (1) to overcome all nonbeing *and* (2) to creatively ground all becoming.

In addition, Whitehead seems to have held the skeptical philosophical opinion that God has not destined humans for "subjective" immortality (i.e., conscious participation after death in God's Eternal Life). He granted that there is no intrinsic reason why such hope is not possible, and that one might adduce satisfying reasons of one's own in favor of such a belief (presumably, religious reasons). Philosophically speaking, however, the most that one could hope to successfully defend is belief in "objective" immortality (i.e., one's personal existence will be everlastingly remembered by God after one ceases to exist).

Once more, Tillich dissented and advanced an impressive case to the contrary. He maintained that the self-transcending design possessed by humans implies that God has destined us for unending participation in God's Life. The fact that our self-transcending reason enables us to think about infinity, eternity, and immortality suggests that God has probably destined us to participate consciously and unendingly in God's own infinity, eternity, and immortality. In Tillich's judgment, *design implies destiny,* and our self-transcending design indicates that we have a death-transcending destiny. Intuitive awareness of our death-transcending destiny contributes to our experience of ultimate concern.

Human beings, in Tillich's view, are self-transcending beings because we are endowed with that astonishing power that philosophers call *spirit.* By "spirit" Tillich means the power of unlimited self-transcendence, i.e., the power that enables us to engage in creative discovery and attainment with mathematical infinity. We humans are destined by our spirit-inclusive design to transcend limits. If transcending some limit would be beneficial and would not violate our nature's creative intent, then we are destined to aspire to transcend that limit. We can always learn more than we know and attain more than we have attained. And we are obviously meant to do so.

This recognition underlies all the creative progress that we humans have made throughout our history. It is the reason we successfully undertook to transcend the physical and technological limits that had earlier prevented us from going to the moon and back. Tillich would say that we were destined to accomplish that astounding feat in virtue of our design.

And because spirit-bearing beings are limit-transcending by their very nature, we humans have inevitably aspired to transcend that final physical limit: death. Our design implies that to aspire to immortality is an essential part of our destiny. For that same design confers on us our amazing ability to think about participating in the infinity, eternity, and immortality of our Ultimate Source (who is also our Ultimate Aim). It seems likely that beings whose nature enables them to recognize transcendent reality and meaning, and who can yearn to participate unendingly in that sublime reality and meaning, are also able to attain that goal.

Moreover, Tillich observed, our human capacity for *unlimited* self-transcendence indicates that we already possess the power requisite for *everlasting* participation in God's Life of unending creative discovery. Accordingly, when humans in the ancient world assumed that immortal gods could exist in superhuman form, those humans were unconsciously projecting onto personified forces in nature the immortal destiny implicit in their own design.

Tillich agreed that none of his philosophical conclusions about subjective immortality can be verified experimentally. But he countered that they can be verified *experientially* by pointing to the indications in our experience that imply their probability. For Tillich, something is *probable* when it is not demonstrably certain but is likely to some degree because of indirectly corroborating evidence in our experience. Such probability cannot provide absolute certitude, but it can provide various degrees of relative or partial certitude, depending on the nature of the case. Belief in immortality, therefore, is not irrational and unfounded; rather, it is grounded in our inferential awareness of the implications of our astonishing design.

Questions for Review and Discussion

1. List some of the factors which contributed to the discovery of philosophical reasoning by the Ionian Greeks.

2. Who was the first ancient Greek philosopher to teach monotheism, and what critical observations did he make about the Homeric myths?

3. Who was the first ancient Greek philosopher to teach that God created the world? How did he say that God had performed this task?

4. What is Aristotle's God doing eternally, and why did Aristotle think that this must be so?

5. What significant thing did Philo decide to do with Plato's Eternal Ideas or Forms? Did later philosophers in general approve or disapprove of his decision?

6. How did Plotinus account for the existence of the material world without ascribing any change to the transcendent and immutable "One" who is the ultimate source of all beings?

7. Did Augustine completely agree with the Neoplatonists that God is absolutely transcendent and immutable? Explain your answer. In what way was Augustine's view of this matter anticipatory?

8. Who was the greatest of the medieval philosopher-theologians? What significant innovation did he introduce, and why did he think it was wise to do so?

9. What was highly unusual about Spinoza's view of God? What were some of the reasons that motivated him to present his unusual view?

10. Who were the German Idealists? How did they agree and disagree with Aristotle? How did they agree and disagree with Spinoza?

11. How does monopolar theism differ from dipolar theism?

12. How does pantheism differ from panentheism?

13. What did Whitehead mean when he spoke of the "primordial" and "consequent" dimensions in God's nature?

14. According to Whitehead, why is it that the world never runs out of potentiality for further duration and creative novelty?

15. What did Whitehead mean when he asserted that not only is God always creating the world, but the world is also always creating God?

16. How would Tillich "verify" his philosophical conviction that God has conferred a death-transcending destiny on humans?

Chapter Seven

Prophetic Universalism Versus Post-Exilic Legalism

1.

We established in chapter five that the Jews finished rebuilding the Jerusalem temple in 515 B.C. However, since Jerusalem still had no walls for security, the city did not come back to life. It was not until Nehemiah succeeded in restoring the walls in 445 B.C. (Neh 1–6) that the city slowly began to revive. Only then did increasing numbers of merchants and artisans seriously consider locating themselves and their families in Jerusalem. Even then, much strenuous labor remained before the ruined city could be considered truly habitable.

During the period of Jerusalem's restoration, before Ezra's religious reform began (c. 398 B.C.), the high priest (who now also acted as governor) did not always enforce the standards called for by the current interpretation of Mosaic law. This conclusion is easily inferred from indications in the books of Ezra, Nehemiah, and some of the post-Exilic prophets (Mal 1:13). The high priest probably decided that everyday life in Jerusalem involved such economic hardship and social tension that it would not be expedient to impose the additional burden of full Mosaic observance.

Many Jewish farmers from the outlying districts of Judah had been prevailed upon by Nehemiah in 445 B.C. to live in Jerusalem so it could be successfully defended. The high priest knew that most of these people had not been deported to Babylon. Consequently, they were unfamiliar with and sometimes resented some of the developments of Mosaic law created by the zealous priest-reformers in Babylon. If these Jews were held to strict standards that were novel and seemed arbitrary, they might abandon underpopulated Jerusalem. In time, the high priest's compromising attitude allowed practices to develop which seriously diminished the quality of religious observance in Jerusalem. (Some of these practices will be listed below.)

In the meantime, the monotheistic Jews who had remained in Babylon had prospered under Persian rule. For years these Jews had contributed generously to the rebuilding of God's temple and the restoration of Jerusalem. Moreover, they had continued to gather on the Sabbath to strengthen their monotheistic faith through prayer and instruction based on the law and the prophets. Accordingly, they were well informed about the requirements of proper Mosaic observance.

The Babylonian Jews understood that the law of Moses could not be imposed on a large foreign city like Babylon. But they assumed that if there was a city in the world where Mosaic law was fully observed, and a holy hush prevailed on the Sabbath, it would be Jerusalem. Furthermore, their cultural isolation encouraged them to envision distant Jerusalem in an ideal and sacred light.

Some of these devout Jews eventually visited Jerusalem on business or as devout pilgrims and were shocked by the lax observance of Mosaic law which they encountered there:

1. Some of the Jews labored openly on the Sabbath;
2. Farmers and merchants were allowed to enter Jerusalem to sell their produce or wares on the Sabbath (Neh 10:31; 13:15–19);
3. The tax levied for maintaining daily worship in the temple went largely uncollected (Neh 10:32–33);
4. Tithes were not brought to the Jerusalem temple for support of the priests and Levites (Neh 10:35–39; Mal 3:8–10);

5. Unpaid priests and Levites had left the city to support themselves by other means (Neh 13:10);
6. Worship in the temple was conducted with insufficient priests and Levites (Neh 13:10; the Levites assisted the Aaronic priests in the sanctuary and also acted as doorkeepers, tithe collectors, singers, and musicians);
7. Blemished animals (blind or crippled) were sometimes offered to God as sacrificial gifts (Mal 1:13–14);
8. Intermarriage with foreigners (usually polytheists who were ignorant of the law of Moses and God's oneness) had become common (Ezra 9:1–4; 10:1–17; Neh 13:23–27);
9. Jewish children born of mixed marriages frequently could not speak either Hebrew or Aramaic and, therefore, were beyond the pale of instruction about God's law (Neh 13:23–24). The Jews who were taken to Babylon had to learn Aramaic to survive there. When they returned to Judah, they continued to speak Aramaic, and Hebrew was gradually abandoned.

Reports of these and other religious aberrations brought back to Babylon by visitors were deeply disturbing to the devout Jewish community in Babylon and its zealous priest-historians.

We should realize that the priest-historians in Babylon had strenuously encouraged the Jewish community there to avoid all unnecessary contact with foreigners and to abhor mixed marriages. They encouraged ethnic exclusiveness in an effort to preserve Jewish identity and prevent the loss of recently discovered Jewish monotheism. The priest-historians understandably feared that if Jews married polytheistic foreigners they could be tempted to abandon their own religious tradition. To discourage marriage to foreigners, the priests pointed to the Mosaic prohibition of mixed marriages with polytheistic Canaanites in the Book of Deuteronomy:

> You shall not make marriages with them, giving your daughters to their sons or taking their daughters for your sons. For they would turn away your sons from following me, to serve other gods. (Deut 7:3–4)

They also cited the example of King Solomon's folly with his foreign wives, which had been recorded with bitter disapproval by one of the Deuteronomic Historians:

1 Kgs 11:1–2, 4

> Now King Solomon loved many foreign women . . . from the nations concerning which Yahweh had said to the people, "You shall not enter into marriage with them, neither shall they with you, for surely they will turn away your hearts after other gods;" Solomon clung to these in love. . . . When Solomon was old his wives turned away his heart after other gods; and his heart was not wholly true to Yahweh his God as was the heart of David his father.

Neh 13:25b–26

> You shall not give your daughters to their sons, or take their daughters for your sons or for yourselves. Did not Solomon king of Israel sin on account of such women? Among the many nations there was no king like him . . . yet foreign women made even him to sin.

The Jews in Babylon were alarmed, therefore, when they learned of the many mixed marriages in Jerusalem and Judah.

The tension between Jews in Babylon and Jerusalem was probably further aggravated by differences in the written Mosaic law used to govern the geographically separated communities. The written law of the Jews in Babylon had almost certainly been expanded in minor but significant ways after the first group of returnees had departed for Jerusalem in 537 B.C. (The law of Moses as we now know it—Genesis, Exodus, Leviticus, Numbers, and Deuteronomy—was not essentially completed by the Priestly Author until c. 500 B.C.) Accordingly, Jews from Babylon who later visited Jerusalem probably held a number of religious beliefs which were neither known nor observed in Jerusalem.

The Babylonian Jews apparently decided that they were entitled to expect full compliance with Mosaic law in Jerusalem in return for the years of moral and financial support they had provided (and were still providing) for the returnees. They insisted, therefore, on a religious reform in Jerusalem and Judah. To ensure that the reform would satisfy their standards, they sent their own reformer, Ezra the priest-historian, who was "learned in the commandments of Yahweh and his statutes for Israel" (Ezra 7:11):

> For Ezra had set his heart to study the law of Yahweh, and to fulfill it, and to teach his statutes and ordinances in Israel. (Ezra 7:10)

The author of the Books of Ezra and Nehemiah is called the Chronicler. (He also wrote 1 and 2 Chronicles.) He incorrectly wrote (either deliberately or mistakenly, probably deliberately, in order to glorify Ezra's memory) that Ezra came to Jerusalem before Nehemiah, and that he and Nehemiah labored together to restore and reform Jerusalem and Judah. In reality, Nehemiah arrived first in 445 B.C. during the reign of the Persian king Artaxerxes I. Only after Nehemiah had ceased to govern (and was possibly dead) did Ezra arrive in 398 B.C. during the reign of Artaxerxes II.

For whatever reasons, the Chronicler interwove and embellished traditions about Nehemiah and Ezra. Both men were correctly remembered as instrumental in establishing sacred law and order in restored Jerusalem, but there were significant differences in their respective missions. Nehemiah had authority from the Persian king to restore Jerusalem's walls and to serve as governor of Judah. Ezra, however, probably had Persian approval only to reform the Jerusalem cult in accordance with the essentially completed Torah (the law of Moses), and to impose the Torah's requirements on Jews who chose to participate in the official cult.

When Nehemiah rebuilt Jerusalem's walls and served as governor, he certainly established civil order in Jerusalem and Judah that reflected the requirements of Mosaic law. It was Ezra, however, who rigorously and thoroughly reformed post-Exilic Jerusalem and Judah on the basis of the *completed* Torah. It is for that reason that he was remembered by the later scribes as the founder of scribal or rabbinic Judaism. (As a group, the scribes were not called rabbis until after Jerusalem's destruction in A.D. 70. Prior to that event, they could be addressed honorifically with the title Rabbi, but were still spoken of professionally as scribes.)

After Ezra and a large group of like-minded supporters arrived in Jerusalem in 398 B.C., Ezra presented his letters of introduction to the Jewish high priest. He then arranged for a compulsory assembly in Jerusalem of all Jewish returnees and their leaders from throughout Judah (Ezra 10:7). When they had all assembled in Jerusalem, he solemnly read and explained to them selected passages from the completed Torah, which he had brought from Babylon for that purpose:

> And all the people gathered as one man into the square before the Water Gate; and they told Ezra the scribe to bring the Scroll of the Law of Moses which Yahweh had given to Israel. And Ezra the priest brought the law before the assembly. . . . And he read from it facing the square before the Water Gate from early morning until midday . . . and the ears of all the people were attentive to the Scroll of the Law.
>
> And Ezra the scribe stood on a wooden pulpit which they had made for the purpose. And Ezra opened the book in the sight of all the people, for he was above all the people; and when he opened it all the people stood. (Neh 8:1–5)

Ezra informed the returnees that this official copy of the Torah was to be the basis of Jewish religious life throughout the land, and to insure that it would be so, he had been authorized to carry out a religious reform in Jerusalem and Judah.

Among the Jews who had come from Babylon with Ezra was a large group of priest-scribes and Levites who were also well informed about the requirements of the completed Torah. These men had come to assist Ezra with his reform by providing supplementary instruction and correction to the priests, Levites, and people of Jerusalem and Judah who were not aware of all the requirements in the completed Torah (Neh 8:7–8).

The Chronicler relates that almost all of the Jews and their local leaders meekly accepted the terms of Ezra's Torah-based reform (Ezra 10:1–17; Neh 8:13; 10:28–39). Nevertheless, we may suspect that the cooperation of some was not readily forthcoming (Ezra 10:15). For Ezra demanded that all mixed marriages between Jewish men and foreign women must be dissolved; foreign wives and their children, Ezra insisted, had to be sent away (Ezra 10:3, 11, 44). The problem of intermarriage between Jewish women and foreign men (Neh 13:25) was not vigorously addressed because the reforming Jewish scribes had no jurisdiction over foreign men who were heads of households.

In reality, the implementation of this requirement would have been extremely difficult, and some men undoubtedly refused to comply. The pious Chronicler, however, wishes to suggest in the idealizing manner of folk historians that the returnees almost unanimously submitted obediently to the authority of the Torah as interpreted by Ezra and his cohorts (Ezra 10:9–13).

2.

That Ezra's harsh method of dealing with mixed marriages discriminated unfairly against women, children, and foreigners is painfully evident at our time in history. His policy made no distinction between foreign spouses who respected or even accepted the monotheistic faith of their Jewish spouses and those who did not. Nor did he seem to realize that the danger of being swallowed up by Canaanite culture, which had called forth the old law against mixed marriages in Deuteronomy 7:3–4, no longer existed.

However, given the assumptions then current about the authority of the Torah and its learned priest-interpreters, the majority of the Jews believed that Ezra's policy represented the will of God. Nevertheless, there are indications that the Jews who disagreed with Ezra's policy (Ezra 10:15) continued to grow in number and influence. They eventually became a formidable source of prophetic opposition within the Jewish community in Judah.

The historical consciousness of these dissenting Jews had evidently evolved to the stage where they could transcend tribal exclusivism and the unquestioning acceptance of priestly strictures. Yet their admirable moral progress was still historically limited. For the evidence suggests that it was Ezra's total rejection of all mixed marriages and his implicit condemnation of all foreigners that the dissenters rejected as unjust. They gave no definite indication of having grasped the injustice of patriarchal discrimination against women in general. (Malachi's slightly earlier protest [c. 420 B.C.] against abandoning the wife of one's youth is the first stirring of such a recognition; see Mal 2:13–16.)

The dissenting prophetic circles found confirmation for their protest in the Torah, which they believed Ezra had interpreted too narrowly. The sacred covenant which God had made with Abraham contained evidence that God loved and intended to bless righteous Gentiles along with Abraham's faithful children. (Everyone who is not a Jew is a Gentile.):

> Now Yahweh said to Abram, "Go from your country and your kindred and your father's house to the land that I will show you. And I will make of you a great nation, and I will bless you, and make your name great so that in you all the families of the earth shall be blessed." (Gen 12:1–3)

They also remembered the inspired words of Second Isaiah by which God had called Israel to be God's witness to the nations:

Is 42:5a, 6

> Thus says God . . . "I am Yahweh, I have called you in righteousness, I have taken you by the hand and kept you; I have given you as a covenant to the people, a light to the nations."

Is 49:1, 3, 5a, 6

> Listen to me, O coastlands, and hearken, you peoples from afar. Yahweh called me from the womb, from the body of my mother he named my name. . . . And now Yahweh says . . . "I will give you as a light to the nations, that my salvation may reach to the end of the earth."

Moreover, the dissenting prophets recalled that King David's grandmother, Ruth, had been a foreign woman, a Moabitess. According to tradition, Ruth had been not only an exemplary wife and daughter-in-law; she also had been instrumental in giving Israel her greatest king. Surely, then, God approved of this "foreign" woman and the mixed marriage from which David had descended. Therefore, shortly after Ezra's policy against foreign wives was enforced, a literate member of one of the groups who opposed Ezra's harsh policy (probably a Levite or priest; cf. Ezra 10:15) composed the Book of Ruth as a form of prophetic protest. The book pointedly contradicted Ezra's view of mixed marriages.

The indications are that the scribes who succeeded Ezra (one of whom, the Chronicler, wrote the Book of Ezra) continued to enforce the xenophobic legalism of Ezra's reform. And their unqualified hostility to foreigners continued to invite prophetic opposition. The prophetic circles that opposed the scribes probably did so regularly at the Sabbath gatherings in Jerusalem and throughout

Judah. The members of these circles would not have been slow to quote the Scriptures which they believed contradicted the narrow nationalism of the scribes. These dissenters probably included charismatic leaders who were regarded as prophets and whose teaching, oral and written, was revered as divinely inspired. One suspects that these prophets expressed their views at worship services in a spirited manner that challenged and embarrassed Ezra's successors.

3.

Around 300 B.C., the conflict between the intolerant exclusivism of the scribes and the universalism of their prophetic opponents reached such a pitch that the scribes apparently decided to take measures that would silence them. Indirect evidence suggests that they prevailed upon the high priest to assemble the Jewish religious leaders in the province of Judah to deal with the dissent that threatened the ongoing success of Ezra's reform.

Some scholars infer that the scribes prevailed upon this assembly to legislate that prophetism had ceased with the death of Ezra: Ezra, they contended, had brought the word of God to Israel in its final and perfect form—the completed Torah. There was no further need, therefore, for prophets to speak a word for God (especially if it challenged Ezra's interpretation of the Torah). Accordingly, no written or oral religious teaching which postdated Ezra should claim or be assigned prophetic authority. By this strategy, the scribes hoped to retroactively discredit all the prophetic dissent in Judah since the time of Ezra's reform.

(It is very likely that the memory of this assembly called by the high priest in collaboration with Ezra's successors underlies the ancient rabbinic tradition of the Great Assembly presided over by Ezra himself in Jerusalem. In legendary fashion, the "Great Assembly" was probably fused with the religious assembly convened by Ezra as reported in Nehemiah 8–10. Also, the decision of Ezra's successors to limit the prophetic canon (official list) probably accounts for the tradition that it was Ezra who determined the entire canon of Scripture for Judaism. As is usual with legends, these two Ezra traditions probably contain a significant grain of truth.)

In effect, the later scribes attempted to deny that God would ever again raise up a prophet to speak out in defense of truth or justice, or to interpret some new situation on behalf of God. The dissenting prophets, however, were evidently not silenced by this scribal tactic, for they believed that the voice of Moses was on their side:

> Yahweh your God will raise up for you a prophet like me from among you, from your brethren—him you shall heed. (Deut 18:15)

Accordingly, the prophets devised a counterstrategy of their own—pseudonymous authorship. They borrowed the name of some earlier prophet who antedated Ezra's death and ascribed their teaching to that prophet. A legally acceptable prophet in this scenario was one who had been named somewhere in the accepted Scriptures (even though he had written no book) or whose prophecies had been gathered into an accepted book which bore his name.

Pseudonymous authorship could take either of two forms: (1) *Attributive authorship* was used by the pseudonymous prophets when they "attributed" a book, which contained their own teaching, to some earlier prophet or renowned teacher who had lived before the death of Ezra. (2) *Insertive authorship* was employed when the pseudonymous prophets "inserted" their own written teaching in the book of some literary prophet who had predeceased Ezra. In either case, the writing of a prophet who came after Ezra could then legally be considered as prophetic, and could be read and explained at public worship services.

(Ironically, a number of later authors who postdated Ezra attributed their writings pseudonymously to Ezra himself in hope of winning acceptance for them as legitimate prophecy.)

The reader might wonder how newly written material, whether a new book or new material inserted into an older book, could have been presented as "older" material derived from an earlier prophet without detection. Accomplishing this task was not as difficult as we might think, for ancient scribes could avail themselves of *palimpsests.* Palimpsests were *vellum* (leather) sheets taken from an old and badly worn scroll-book. The writing on these retrieved sheets was scraped off so that they could be written on again, for vellum was very expensive.

When the prophets wished to introduce their pseudonymous writings to a worshiping community, they sorted through the supply of palimpsests usually available in a *scriptorium* and selected those of roughly the same age and patina desired. Authors had to insure that the palimpsests which contained their writing matched the age of the book into which they were to be inserted. Because the ancient scroll-books contained no page, chapter, or verse numbers, it was easy to sew the palimpsests into the older book without detection. The new leather thread so used could be stained to approximate the color of the threads already in the book.

It also helps to remember that this covert introduction of pseudonymous writings took place in an essentially preliterate society. Precritical standards of judgment about the age of written material characterized all members of such a society, even the few who could read and write. Ancient Israel had not yet acquired our scientific standards of paleography or learned to ask our critical questions, and library science as we know it did not yet exist.

4.

The historical background provided in the preceding sections enables us to understand the form and intent of the highly unusual Book of Jonah. If one compares this book to the other prophetic books in the Bible, it clearly stands by itself. A critical reading of the Book of Jonah assures us that its bizarre narrative is not history but theology.

To begin with, the account of Jonah being swallowed by a great fish and emerging intact after spending three days and nights in its belly is patently absurd if taken literally. Moreover, ancient Nineveh is described in the Book of Jonah as "an exceedingly great city, three days journey in breadth" (Jon 3:3). But archeologists have long known where the ruins of Nineveh lie, proving that Jonah could have walked from one side of the city to the other in an hour. The city described in the Book of Jonah is clearly a legendary memory of the Nineveh which no longer existed. The Babylonians destroyed the city in 612 B.C.

In addition, Jonah receives a prophet's call from God but refuses to obey until he is terrified by God into doing so; he is nowhere called a prophet in the book that bears his name, nor is he located in history by the usual reference to a reigning king. All these traits are highly irregular and are further indications that the book does not contain history.

In reality, the Book of Jonah was probably written pseudonymously by a member of the prophetic circle that rejected the narrow nationalism of Ezra and his priest-scribe successors. Because the anonymous author of Jonah wrote after the scribal declaration (c. 300 B.C.) that prophetism had ceased, he had to employ a pseudonym. He assumed the name of an actual prophet named Jonah who wrote nothing that has survived. The historical Jonah is briefly mentioned in 2 Kings as active in the northern Kingdom during the reign of Jeroboam II (786-746 B.C.); he lived, therefore, well before Ezra's death, which probably occurred around 380 B.C.:

> Jeroboam [II] the son of Joash, king of Israel, began to reign in Samaria, and he reigned forty-one years. . . . He restored the border of Israel from the border of Hamath as far as the Sea of the Arabah, according to the word of Yahweh, the God of Israel, which he spoke by his servant Jonah the son of Amittai, the prophet who was from Gath-hepher. (2 Kgs 14:23, 25)

Correctly understood, the Book of Jonah is a sacred parable created to expose the ugly narrowness of scribal exclusivism and to affirm God's approbation of prophetic universalism. The parabolic story dramatically illustrates that there are Gentiles with righteous hearts and, if given a chance, they, too, will acknowledge and serve Israel's God. Furthermore, those who deny this truth are violating the true intent of God's covenant with Abraham and Israel and are deserving of divine rebuke.

The Book of Jonah begins with Jonah's commission by God to deliver a prophetic message to the Gentile inhabitants of Nineveh, the original capital city of Assyria. Jonah is told to announce that God's punitive wrath will soon descend upon the city because of its many sins:

> Now the word of Yahweh came to Jonah the son of Amittai, saying, "Arise, go to Nineveh, the great city, and cry against it; for their wickedness has come up before me." (Jon 1:1-2)

Jonah, however, is unwilling to accept this commission and attempts to flee to a faraway country:

> But Jonah rose to flee to Tarshish from the presence of Yahweh. He went down to Joppa and found a ship going to Tarshish; so he paid the fare, and went on board, to go with them to Tarshish, away from the presence of Yahweh. (Jon 1:3)

We are not initially told why Jonah decided to flee, but we learn later in the story that it is because he suspected that the Ninevites would repent, plead for mercy, and God would forgive them:

> When God saw what they did, how they turned from their evil way, God repented of the evil which he had said he would do to them; and he did not do it.
>
> But it displeased Jonah exceedingly, and he was angry. And he prayed to Yahweh and said, "I pray you, Yahweh, is not this what I said when I was in my country? This is why I made haste to flee to Tarshish; for I knew that you are a gracious God and merciful, slow to anger, abounding in steadfast love, and always ready to forgive." (Jon 3:10–4:2)

God is determined, however, that Jonah shall fulfill the prophetic commission he has received:

> But Yahweh stirred up a great wind upon the sea, and there was a mighty tempest upon the sea, so that the ship threatened to break up. (Jon 1:4)

Jonah, we are told, was sleeping below in the ship's hold when the storm broke, so the captain came and roused him:

> What do you mean, you sleeper? Arise, call upon your god! Perhaps the god will give thought to us, that we do not perish. (Jon 1:6)

The alarmed sailors then cast lots to determine which of them had angered the god who sent the storm. The lot finally fell upon Jonah, who thereupon confessed that he was a runaway prophet fleeing a commission from Yahweh, the God of heaven. Jonah then suggested that the sailors throw him overboard so they might be saved from Yahweh's pursuing wrath:

> Take me and throw me into the sea; then the sea will quiet down for you; for I know that it is because of me that this great tempest has come upon you. (Jon 1:12)

The Gentile sailors (who comport themselves in righteous fashion throughout the crisis) initially refused to follow Jonah's advice. Instead, they rowed valiantly against the raging wind in a generous attempt to save Jonah's life. But when the storm grew even more alarming and threatened to destroy them all, they capitulated:

> "We beseech you, O Yahweh, let us not perish for this man's life, and lay not on us innocent blood; for you, O Yahweh, have done as it pleased you." So they took up Jonah and threw him into the sea; and the sea ceased from its raging. Then the men feared Yahweh exceedingly, and they offered a sacrifice to Yahweh and made vows. (Jon 1:14–16)

In the meantime, Yahweh provided a great fish to swallow Jonah and carry him back to land so that he might undertake his mission to Nineveh:

Jon 1:17

> And Yahweh sent a great fish to swallow up Jonah; and Jonah was in the belly of the fish three days and three nights.

Jon 2:1, 10

> Then Jonah prayed to Yahweh his God from the belly of the fish. . . . And Yahweh spoke to the fish, and it vomited out Jonah upon the dry land.

The chastened Jonah is now of a mind to heed Yahweh's call, and he willingly accepts the renewal of his commission:

> The word of Yahweh came to Jonah the second time saying, "Arise, go to Nineveh, the great city, and pro-

> claim to it the message that I tell you." So Jonah arose and went to Nineveh, according to the word of Yahweh. (Jon 3:1–3a)

When Jonah arrived at Nineveh, he began to walk through the great city and proclaim the message of impending doom which God had given him. When the Gentile inhabitants of the city heard the word of God, they all repented of their sins, put on sackcloth, and undertook a penitential fast in hope of receiving God's mercy:

> When God saw what they did, how they turned from their evil way, God repented of the evil which he had said he would do to them; and he did not do it. (Jon 3:10)

Jonah (we have already learned above) was profoundly embittered by the repentance of the Ninevites and his anticipation that God would surely forgive them:

> But it displeased Jonah exceedingly, and he was angry. And he prayed to Yahweh and said, "I pray you, Yahweh, is not this what I said when I was in my country? This is why I made haste to flee to Tarshish; for I knew that you are a gracious God and merciful, slow to anger, and abounding in steadfast love, and always ready to forgive.
>
> Therefore, O Yahweh, take my life from me now, I implore you, for it is better for me to die than to live." And Yahweh said, "Is it right that you should be angry?" (Jon 4:1–4)

By now it has probably occurred to the reader that Jonah is intended to represent the narrow intolerance of scribal exclusivism, and God's willingness to love and forgive righteous Gentiles as well as Jews represents the anonymous prophet's conviction that God's love and mercy are universally extended.

In a fit of churlish pique, Jonah exits Nineveh and sits on the vast treeless plain outside its walls to wait to see for certain what its fate might be:

> Then Jonah went out of the city and sat to the east of the city . . . till he should see what would become of the city. (Jon 4:5)

God's patient wisdom then provided sulking Jonah with a lesson calculated to help Jonah recognize the wrongness of his unwillingness to accept that God should show mercy to the foreign Ninevites:

> And Yahweh God appointed a castor bean plant, and made it come up over Jonah, that it might be a shade over his head, to save him from his discomfort. So Jonah was exceedingly glad because of the plant.
>
> But when dawn came up the next day, God sent a worm which attacked the plant so that it withered. When the sun rose, God sent a sultry east wind, and the sun beat upon the head of Jonah so that he was faint; and he asked that he might die and said, "It is better for me to die than live."
>
> But God said to Jonah, "Is it right for you to be angry over the plant?" And he said, "It is right for me to be angry, angry enough to die."
>
> And Yahweh said, "You pity the castor bean plant, for which you did not labor, nor did you make it grow, which came into being in a night, and perished in a night. And should not I pity Nineveh, that great city, in which there are more than a hundred and twenty thousand persons?" (Jon 4:6–11)

When we deliteralize the story of Jonah, we free it to be understood as it was intended by its inspired author—a parable that discerns and defends God's universal love. The Book of Jonah, then, is remote preparation for the related insight in the New Testament summarizing the sublime teaching of Jesus about God's love:

> Beloved, let us love one another; for love is of God, and whoever loves is born of God and knows God. He who

does not love does not know God; for God is love.
(1 Jn 4:7–8)

Questions for Review and Discussion

1. After the Exile to Babylon in 587 B.C., when were the walls of Jerusalem finally rebuilt? Who succeeded in carrying out this important task? Why was it crucial that he succeed? Would the history of Jesus in the Gospels be significantly different if Jerusalem had not been restored?

2. Why were the Jews from Babylon shocked when they visited Jerusalem three or four decades after the restoration of its walls? Describe some of the objectionable practices they found there?

3. Why were the Jews in Babylon in a position to demand a reform in Jerusalem and Judah? Who did they send as their reformer? In what year did he probably arrive?

4. What was the most problematic of this reformer's demands?

5. Did all of the Jews agree with all of this reformer's demands? Explain your answer.

6. Why did this reformer's successors probably ask the high priest and his advisors to authorize them to teach prophetism's retroactive cessation?

7. According to this probable retroactive legislation, when was prophetism assumed to have ceased? Why did this cutoff date seem appropriate to those who chose it?

8. What does the evidence suggest that the prophets did when the successors of Ezra tried to silence them by teaching that prophetism had ceased?

9. When and why was the Book of Jonah probably written? Does the book contain history or theology? What reasons can you advance to justify your answer?

10. What literary form should be assigned to the Book of Jonah? What famous teacher later used this same literary form with great success?

11. In the Jonah story, the words and deeds of Jonah are probably intended to represent what group? What evidence can be adduced in support of this conclusion?

12. In the Jonah story, the words and deeds of God are probably intended to represent what group? What evidence can be adduced in support of this conclusion?

Chapter Eight

Israel's Discovery of Eschatological Hope

1.

Late in the post-Exilic period of ancient Israel's history, a series of painful events unfolded which dramatically changed her understanding of the fate of humans after death. As a result of these developments, most of the Jews began to hope that God would restore at the end of history the immortality that they believed Adam and Eve had lost for all humans at the beginning of history. This new hope was expressed as belief in the "resurrection" of the righteous dead to Everlasting Life and Joy in the New Creation. By the New Creation they meant God's ultimate restoration of the Old Creation to its original freedom from evil, suffering, and death.

Belief in the eventual attainability of Everlasting Life after death did not exist in ancient Israel until the Book of Daniel was written in 165 B.C. Before the Book of Daniel, the Israelites believed that death involved two stages: The first stage was the death of the body, which one suffered briefly on earth. One's body then went back to dust, but one's conscious center (*nephesh*) survived the body's dissolution and went to Sheol, the subterranean abode of the dead.

Continued existence in Sheol was not thought of as "life" after death. Rather, in Sheol one suffered the second and unending part of death as punishment for Adam and Eve's failure to believe and obey God in the garden of Eden:

Gen 2:15–17

> And Yahweh God took the human and put him in the Garden of Eden to till it and keep it. And Yahweh God commanded the human saying, "You may freely eat of every tree of the garden, but of the tree of knowledge of good and evil, you shall not eat, for in the day that you shall eat of it you shall die."

Gen 3:3–6

> Now the serpent . . . said to the woman, "Did God say, 'You shall not eat of any tree of the garden?' And the woman said to the serpent, "We may eat of the fruit of the trees of the garden; but God said 'You shall not eat of the tree which is in the midst of the garden, nor shall you touch it lest you die.'" But the serpent said to the woman, "You will not die. For God knows that when you eat of it your eyes will be opened, and you will be like God, knowing good and evil."
>
> So when the woman saw that the tree was good for food, and that it was a delight to the eyes, and that the tree was to be desired to make one wise, she took of its fruit and ate. And she also gave some to her husband, and he ate.

Gen 3:22, 24

> Then Yahweh God said, "Look, the human has become like one of us, knowing good and evil. And now he may presume to put forth his hand and also take of the tree of life and eat, and so live forever." Therefore Yahweh God sent him forth from the Garden of Eden to till the ground from which he was taken. He drove out the human; and at the east of the Garden of Eden he placed

> . . . a flaming sword which turned every way to guard
> the way to the tree of life.

Resurrection hope originated in ancient Israel as a prophetic response to a major crisis in her faith life. This crisis was experienced by devout Palestinian Jews who endured a hideous religious persecution. To understand this crisis and its impact on the religious thinking of ancient Judaism, we must briefly review the events that caused it.

2.

When Alexander the Great invaded the Persian Empire in 334 B.C. he met with extraordinary success. By 332 B.C. the Jews in the Persian province of Judah had submitted to his authority. Nine years later, however, Alexander died in Babylon at the age of thirty-three. His Macedonian-Greek empire was then divided by four of his generals, called the *Diadochi* (the Successors). These four generals are symbolized by the four heads of the third beast (Alexander) described in Daniel 7:6. They are also symbolized by the four conspicuous horns that replaced the broken horn of the he-goat (Alexander) in Daniel 8:8. Only two of these generals need concern us here: Ptolemy and Seleucus.

From the division of Alexander's empire (c. 323 B.C.) until 198 B.C., the Jews in the province of Judah were subject to Ptolemy and his successors, who ruled from "Alexandria" in Egypt. In 198 B.C., however, Antiochus III of Syria (a descendant of Seleucus) compelled Ptolemy V of Egypt to surrender Palestine to Syria. The Jews in Palestine then came under the authority of the Seleucid dynasty which ruled from Antioch in Syria. In 175 B.C., the Syrian king Antiochus IV began to rule over the Jews in Palestine. Conflict soon erupted between this cruel hellenizing king and his monotheistic Jewish subjects. (To hellenize is to encourage or impose Hellenistic, i.e., Greek, culture.)

In 168 B.C., King Antiochus ruthlessly began to persecute the Jews in an attempt to make them abandon the law of Moses and to embrace Greek polytheism. This persecution led to the Maccabean uprising in 167 B.C. (There is a very readable account of the Syrian persecution and Jewish revolt in 1 Maccabees. In Roman Catholic and Eastern Orthodox Bibles, 1 Maccabees is found in the Old

Testament; in Protestant Bibles it is found among the Apocrypha. Because this book was written in Greek, it is not included in Hebrew Bibles). In addition to triggering the Maccabean uprising, the Syrian persecution caused the major "religious crisis" for devout Jews mentioned above.

Traditional Jewish religious belief had long assumed that those who faithfully served God would be rewarded unfailingly by a long and happy life in this world. Blessing from God was expected only during one's sojourn on earth. After death one had to go to Sheol, the subterranean abode of the dead. In the silent gloom of Sheol, one experienced unending deprivation of life and joy as punishment for Adam's sin.

During the Syrian persecution, however, it became painfully evident that this belief was being contradicted. Large numbers of Jews who were determined to remain faithful to the one true God were put to death. Apostates, on the other hand, were spared and even rewarded. Suddenly, devout Jews were confronted by massive amounts of evidence which undermined an important part of their traditional belief system.

An anonymous Jewish prophet was inspired to resolve the resulting faith crisis by creating *Apocalyptic theology*. (Apocalyptic theology presents itself as a revelation from God which announces the imminent end of the world and tells how and when the end-time will occur.) This anonymous prophet, however, was faced with an additional problem. Jewish tradition held that the canon, or official list, of prophetic writings had been "closed" at the time of Ezra's death (c. 380 B.C.). Consequently, the anonymous prophet had to write his teaching pseudonymously by using the name of a famous wise man, Daniel, who antedated the death of Ezra and was mentioned in the canonical Scriptures:

> You are indeed wiser than Daniel; no secret is hidden from you. (Ezek 28:3; see also 14:14, 20)

The suggestion in this passage that Daniel possessed "secret" wisdom was especially congenial to the author of the Book of Daniel because his apocalyptic message claimed to reveal "secrets" about God's mysterious purpose at the end of history. Only by means of this covert stratagem could the anonymous prophet hope that his teaching would be read in the synagogue to instruct and comfort the discouraged Jews.

Apocalyptic theology then made its debut in the Book of Daniel in 165 B.C. It was influenced by the eschatological teaching introduced several centuries earlier by the Persian prophet Zoroaster. *Eschatology* is the study of the events that will happen when God ends the world.

The Book of Daniel was written to provide hope and meaning to faithful Jews during the nightmarish Syrian persecution. It teaches, therefore, that the world will end someday soon (Dan 12:4, 13); and on that day the dead will be raised and judged along with the living (Dan 12:2). After the final judgment, the righteous will enjoy unending life (Dan 12:2) in the New Creation (Dan 2:44). The wicked, however, will receive unending punishment as recompense for their deeds (Dan 12:2):

> And many of those who sleep in the dust of the earth shall awake; some to everlasting life, some to shame and everlasting contempt. And those who are wise shall shine like the brightness of the firmament; and those who turn many to righteousness, like the stars for ever and ever. (Dan 12:2–3)

The new resurrection hope found in Daniel was fully embraced by the Pharisees but was never accepted by the Sadducees (see Mk 12:18; Acts 23:6–8). By the time of Jesus, this hope had become widespread among the Jews. It is presupposed in Jesus' teaching about the coming Judgment which will inaugurate the restoration of God's Kingly Reign over creation. Accordingly, when the Risen Jesus began appearing to his apostles and disciples after his death, the idea of the "resurrection" of the body was already known to them; they instinctively reached for it to interpret Jesus' appearances.

Obviously the apocalyptic idea of our bodies being "resurrected" or "raised up" from the sleep of death involves symbolic imagery. Apocalyptic symbolism should be taken seriously but not literally. Such symbolism intends to assure us that God will bring us safely through the threat of self-loss on the occasion of our death by enabling us to enter a new and higher state of conscious existence.

The apocalyptic use of "resurrection" symbolism was historically appropriate at the time when it was introduced. But future ages are not bound to a literal understanding of such historically conditioned language when they attempt to understand the New Life beyond death promised in the Book of Daniel and confirmed by the Risen and Spirit-mediating Jesus. Later generations of Christians may legitimately use explanatory ideas that differ from those employed by ancient Judaism and early Christianity. As long as these later ideas agree essentially with the apostolic experience of Jesus' "appearances" and their sublime revelatory import, they are permissible and sometimes necessary.

3.

The author of Daniel was prepared by various elements in his historical experience to create his apocalyptic answers to questions being asked by the persecuted Jews. To begin with, he and other devout Jews believed that God had promised Israel a number of covenant blessings in exchange for covenant fidelity and trust. If we read the Torah with care, we find five promises which are made recurrently to Israel. The language in which these promises are couched varies somewhat but, essentially, the same promises are reiterated:

1. God will continually dwell with you and watch over you;
2. God will deliver you from all your enemies;
3. God will save you from death;
4. God will give you length of days and fullness of blessing;
5. God will give you and your descendants everlasting possession of the land in which you dwell.

Before the Book of Daniel was written, the Jews assumed that God would infallibly bestow these covenant promises on all who served God with a right and good heart. But, as we already observed, it became clear during the Syrian persecution that these promised blessings were not being received as expected. The Jews who were most devoted to keeping faith with God were the ones most likely to be executed by the evil minions of King Antiochus.

The anonymous author of Daniel wondered how this could be. His perplexity was probably compounded when he quieted his soul and prayed to God, for he experienced God's Presence and Love in his personal center as usual. He realized, therefore, that the first and most important of the covenant promises in the Torah was experiencably being conferred. Why, then, were not the other four?

The author of Daniel probably brooded prayerfully over this problem. Finally, his abiding experience of God's Presence and Love encouraged him to grasp the essentially correct solution. God certainly intended to bless him and the other anguished Jews as the Torah repeatedly assured them. But if the blessings promised in the Torah (and implicit in his experience of God's Self-communication as Love) were not forthcoming in the present, that could only mean that God actually intended to confer those blessings in the future.

However, if the fullness of God's covenant promises could only be received in the future, then the fate of humans in Sheol had to be reconsidered. Sheol could no longer be understood as the place where all humans were punished everlastingly for Adam's sin. Only the wicked would be punished there forever. If there were to be future blessing and vindication for the righteous Jews being slain by the Syrians, those Jews would have to be freed someday from Sheol.

It seemed likely to the anonymous prophet, therefore, that all of history since Adam's fall had been a test. During this test God had been searching the hearts of all humans to determine which are righteous and which unrighteous. Finally, the prophet concluded (with nonverbal divine encouragement), God will end the present age of the world, raise all the dead from Sheol, and judge the living and the dead with Divine Justice. This Ultimate Justice will finally right all wrongs and correct all of history's injustices; all of history's victims will ultimately be vindicated.

The righteous will then be given an inheritance of Unending Life and Joy in the New Creation. In this way, the author of Daniel surmised, the absurd contradictions of the present would be resolved and the promises in the Torah would finally be received by the righteous.

The Jewish scribes who concurred with the end-time teaching in Daniel decided that Sheol must be divided into two distinct parts: The righteous are waiting in upper Sheol for their vindication at the end of history. The wicked, on the other hand, are consigned to lower Sheol and are devoid of any future hope.

To comfort the families and friends of Jews who were executed by the Syrians, the scribes referred to upper Sheol as "Abraham's

Bosom" or (anticipatory) "Paradise." Jesus is described in Luke's Gospel as using both expressions: In the parable about Lazarus the beggar and the selfish rich man, Lazarus is "carried by the angels to Abraham's Bosom" when he dies (Lk 16:22). When the rich man dies, however, he is sent to lower Sheol (Greek = *hadēs*) where he is tormented with everlasting fire.

Also, as Jesus is dying on the cross, one of the two thieves crucified with him asks Jesus to remember him when Jesus enters into his Kingdom. Jesus replies, "This day you will be with me in Paradise" (Lk 23:43). The early church believed that after Jesus died on Good Friday he was in upper Sheol or anticipatory Paradise awaiting his Resurrection on "the third day." (Because of that belief, the Apostles' Creed created by the ancient church states that Jesus "descended into hell" [upper Sheol] after his death.)

The scribes called lower Sheol, Gehenna, after the steep ravine which served as the city dump just south of Jerusalem. All of Jerusalem's refuse and human waste were thrown into Gehenna, and a foul-smelling fire was kept burning there perpetually in an effort to reduce the city's waste. Moreover, in the warmer months the garbage and human waste of Gehenna were filled with maggots. Therefore, the "uncleanness" of Gehenna, its perpetual fire, and its repulsive maggots provided the scribes with a vivid set of negative images for describing the torment of the wicked in lower Sheol (cp. Is 66:24; in the synoptic Gospels Jesus is remembered as ordinarily calling lower Sheol, Gehenna. Matthew [11:23] and Luke [10:15; 16:23] changed the Aramaic word Gehenna to the Greek word Hades on a few occasions so Greek-speaking Gentile converts in their churches could better understand it.)

The last four of the five covenant promises listed above, therefore, were interpreted eschatologically by the author of the Book of Daniel. By doing so, he believed, one discovered their true meaning: In the second promise, the enemies that God promises to save us from are the powers of darkness who try to destroy us by tempting us to infidelity and sin. In the third, the death God promises to save us from is everlasting death in lower Sheol. In the fourth, the length of days promised by God in the Torah is actually Everlasting Life in the New Creation. And in the fifth, the land which we shall inherit everlastingly is our portion in the New Creation. The New Creation will arrive when God's Reign is finally restored over the Kingdom of Creation at the end of history. The eschatological reading of these four promises was accepted by Jesus and is presupposed when he announces that God's Kingly Reign is drawing near:

Mk 1:14–15

> Now after John was arrested, Jesus came into Galilee preaching the Good News of God and saying . . . "The Kingdom of God is drawing near."

Lk 10:9

> The Kingdom of God has come near to you.

Lk 11:20

> But if it is by the finger of God that I cast out demons, then the Kingdom of God has come upon you.

4.

It seems appropriate to pause briefly and reflect on the problem of end-time expectation in the Book of Daniel and the teaching of Jesus. Jesus and his apostles, in agreement with the Book of Daniel, solemnly warned their contemporaries that the end of the world and the Final Judgment were imminent (Mk 1:14–15; 9:1: Mt 10:23; 1 Thess 4:15–17; 1 Cor 15:51–52). Everyone, they announced, should prepare his or her heart to enter God's approaching Kingdom through faith and repentance.

And yet, the world continues to exist. Does this undeniable fact mean that the eschatological teaching of Jesus and his disciples was mistaken? An adequate response must be one which answers both "no" and "yes." When correctly understood, the eschatological warnings in the message of Jesus and his apostles were mysteriously true at the time when they were proclaimed, and they remain profoundly true for all future generations. However, one can only grasp the truth of their warnings if one is willing to understand them in a nonliteral, or figurative, way. It is obvious that the entire world did not end in the lifetime of Jesus or his apostles. Nevertheless, the *individual world* of every person who heard their end-time warning did come to an end.

Jesus and his apostles were evidently inspired by God to accept the eschatological teaching in the Book of Daniel (and the preaching of John the Baptizer). God encouraged them to proclaim a message of eschatological hope and warning to the world even though God knew that their understanding of the timing involved would suffer secondarily from their historically limited assumptions. Jesus himself refused to predict the precise time of the end (Mk 13:32). Yet one gets the impression that he expected God's approaching Kingdom to arrive in the lifetime of his contemporaries (Mk 1:14–15; Lk 10:9; 11:20).

The apostles understood that the essential substance of Jesus' end-time teaching was confirmed when God "raised" Jesus from the dead and empowered him to begin mediating the foretaste of God's Holy Spirit (God's Self-communication as Love). When the Risen Jesus began appearing to his apostles, they concluded that the world was already beginning to end because the resurrection of the dead had already begun with Jesus' appearances. Accordingly, they thought the Risen Jesus would quickly return in glory to conclude history and gather the righteous into God's Eternal Kingdom. They mistakenly announced, therefore, that the whole world would "literally" end in their lifetime.

However, despite their mistaken assumptions about the time when the whole world will end, the end-time teaching of Jesus and his apostles was (and remains) an essential and profoundly true part of God's saving purpose in history. For God knew that when Jesus did not return in the lifetime of the apostles, the church would have to reconsider the apostolic declaration of the world's impending end. She would then be forced to realize (with the help of the figurative language in Ps 90:4) that eschatological language should be construed in a nonliteral, or symbolic, manner:

Ps 90:4

> For a thousand years in your sight are but as yesterday when it is past, or as a watch in the night.

2 Pet 3:3–5

> First of all you must understand this, that scoffers will come in the last days with scoffing, following their own passions and saying, "Where is the promise of his coming? For ever since the fathers fell asleep, all things have continued as they were from the beginning of creation."

2 Pet 3:8–10

> But do not ignore this one fact, beloved, that with the Lord one day is as a thousand years, and a thousand years as one day. The Lord is not slow about his promise as some count slowness, but is forbearing toward you, not wishing that any should perish, but that all should reach repentance.
>
> But the day of the Lord will come like a thief, and then the heavens will pass away with a loud noise, and the elements will be dissolved with fire, and the earth and the works upon it will be burned up.

Eschatological symbolism remains valid for every generation of ultimately concerned humans till the end of time. For even though it is true that the entire world did not end in the lifetime of Jesus or his apostles, we noted above that the *individual world* of every person in the apostolic age did come to an end. Likewise, the *individual world* of every member of the present age is rapidly moving toward its conclusion, irrespective of whether we will still be alive when the whole world ends.

God's word, then, contains a salutary warning that our allotted time in this world is short and that all too soon we will have to give an account of our stewardship. The time remaining, therefore, should be wisely used in accordance with God's creative purpose to become authentically human and to make our personal contribution to society and to the future. (We become authentically human by striving honestly to complete the maturation process, i.e., by being habitually committed to the practice of truth, justice, and love in the changing circumstances of our lives.)

Accordingly, the Kingdom of God and the Final Judgment which precedes it are always drawing near. Each successive generation must prepare to submit to God's Final Judgment in order to enter God's always-approaching Kingdom. For this reason the Christian tradition teaches that there is a *particular judgment* which precedes the *General Judgment*. And the General Judgment is a powerful eschatological symbol which reminds us that God's Justice and Love will have triumphed unfailingly at the end of human history:

> Then I saw thrones, and seated on them were those to whom judgment had been committed. Also I saw the souls of those who had been beheaded for their testimony to Jesus and for the word of God. . . . They came to life and reigned with Christ a thousand years. . . . This is the first resurrection. Blessed and holy is he who shares in the first resurrection! Over such the second death has no power. (Rev 20:4–6)

5.

We noted above that apocalyptic belief in the resurrection of the dead was a departure from traditional religious teaching in ancient Judaism. Until the Book of Daniel was written, the Jews did not believe in the possibility of unending Life and Joy beyond death. We also observed that the new hope introduced in the Book of Daniel was accepted by the Pharisees but rejected by the Sadducees. The Sadducees correctly objected that there was no basis for such novel teaching in sacred Scripture or Jewish tradition prior to the Book of Daniel.

The author of the Book of Daniel anticipated that the novel eschatological hope which he had introduced would be challenged by the conservative guardians of tradition. To justify his new teaching, therefore, he had recourse to an established method of interpreting Scripture called *midrash*. Midrash was a post-Exilic teaching device developed by the ancient Jewish scribes (biblical scholars). They created this theological teaching device so they could find contemporary meaning in the ancient and increasingly outmoded Jewish Scriptures.

Whenever some later development in belief or practice required legitimization, a text in sacred Scripture which seemed to foreshadow it was sought as its authorization. Midrashic teaching was increasingly employed after the priest-historians gave the Torah and the other sacred Scriptures their final and fixed form.

Midrashic teaching could be either oral or written, and could take the form of *halakah* (interpretations of law) or *haggadah* (nonlegal religious lessons). Although midrashic teaching existed before the rise of apocalyptic theology (for example, Zech 3:8 and 6:12 are alluding midrashically to Is 11:1), it received an added measure of importance and was assigned a deeper level of meaning when it was used to validate the new hope presented in the Book of Daniel.

In its fully developed form, the midrashic method of teaching claimed that everything God intends to do in history is mysteriously foreshadowed in the law of Moses and the other sacred writings. Therefore, interpretations of law and developments of religious belief which could be shown to have a midrashic adumbration in Scripture were regarded in Pharasaic circles (but not in Sadducean circles) as divinely revealed.

The midrashing scribes searched the Scriptures for texts that seemed to portend and corroborate their interpretations of legal and nonlegal religious matters. They then either quoted the text which they thought validated their teaching, or they alluded to it by weaving one or more of its key words into their presentation. Either way, the confirming text was always indicated in a manner recognizable by those familiar with the Scriptures and the midrashic method of theologizing.

The author of Daniel, for example, justified his novel teaching about the resurrection of the dead by appealing midrashically to the covenant promises made by God to Abraham in the Torah. God promised to give Abraham descendants more numerous than the dust of the earth (Gen 13:16), the sand on the seashore (Gen 22:17), and the stars in the sky (Gen 15:5; 22:17; 26:4). Daniel 12:3 allusively implies that Abraham's children are like the dust of the earth and the sand on the seashore in this life, but will be transformed like the stars in the sky when they are finally raised in glory:

> And many of those who sleep in the dust of the earth shall awake; some to everlasting life, some to shame and everlasting contempt. And those who are wise shall shine like the brightness of the firmament; and those who turn many to righteousness, like the stars for ever and ever. (Dan 12:2-3)

The author of Daniel sincerely believed that the promise of final resurrection from the dead was already mysteriously fore-intended in the covenant promises given by God to Abraham. The Book of Daniel legitimizes its other eschatological innovations by means of similar midrashic allusions: The mysterious "stone" in

Daniel 2:34–35,44–45 which becomes a mighty mountain and symbolizes God's end-time Kingdom, is based on Isaiah 28;16 and 2:2. The "dominion" restored to one like a "son of man" in Daniel 7:6,12–14 is based on Genesis 1:26 and Psalm 8:3–6. The "seventy weeks of years" in Daniel 9:24–27 is based on Jeremiah 29:10–11 (see Dan 9:2). The eschatological "time of trouble" in Daniel 12:1b is based on Isaiah 33:2. The doomsday "book" in Daniel 12:1c is based on Exodus 32:32–33; Psalm 69:28; Malachi 3:16–4:3. The "awaking" from "sleep" in Daniel 12:2 is based on Psalm 3:5. The "time of the end" in Daniel 12:4a is based on Zephaniah 1:18b.

During the period in the early church when the Gospels were being written, midrash had become the prevailing theological method among Palestinian Jews for teaching about God's purpose in history. We should bear in mind that the first Christians were Jews who had learned about midrash in the synagogue. These Jewish Christians also carried out the major part of their witnessing to the Jews while attending the synagogue (Acts 6:9; 13:13–43; 17:17; 18:4; 19:8). It was inevitable, therefore, that they would appeal to the authority of midrash in order to advance and defend their claims about the vigorously contested Messiahship of Jesus.

For the Jewish Christians who constituted the earliest church, it was the crucified and Risen Jesus who had conclusively fulfilled all of the "promises" of salvation (both manifest and hidden) found in the Scriptures. These Jewish Christians were utterly convinced that Jesus and his unexpected Messianic destiny were secretly foreshadowed in the law and the prophets. We should not be surprised to learn, then, that the Gospels in general, and the Passion and Resurrection narratives in particular, are filled with midrashic teaching about Jesus.

Sometimes this teaching takes the form of explicit quotations (Mt 1:22–23; 2:5–6; Jn 19:24, 37). But more frequently midrashic allusions are woven into stories or events being narrated to avoid interrupting them (Lk 1:26–27; 32–33; Mk 14:20; 15:24; Jn 1:29, 35; 20:13, 15).

Theologizing in the midrashic mode may strike us as strange. Nevertheless, to the earliest Christians it seemed to be the only way to successfully bring their faith claims about Jesus to the Jews, especially when witnessing in the synagogue. Unless we are well versed in the Scriptures and informed about midrash, we will frequently fail to grasp what the Gospels truly intend to teach about Jesus. We also will fall into historical and theological error by taking nonliteral statements literally. If we make the effort to understand the viewpoint of Jewish-Christian midrash, we will discover that it is filled with theological meaning and beauty, and is often the key that unlocks the authentic meaning of the Gospel narratives.

6.

The New Creation promised by the Book of Daniel was eagerly anticipated as the final and permanent establishment of God's Kingly Reign over creation. Adam's sin had disrupted God's Kingly Reign, but the coming of God's eternal Kingdom would soon restore it. God's victorious "end-time" Kingdom is mentioned for the first time in Daniel:

> The God of Heaven will set up a kingdom which shall never be destroyed, nor shall its sovereignty be left to another people. It shall break in pieces all these kingdoms and bring them to an end, and it shall stand forever. (Dan 2:44)

It is this everlasting kingdom which Jesus had in mind when he announced that the Kingdom (or Reign) of God is near (Mk 1:15). The actual expression, "Kingdom of God," does not occur in the Hebrew Scriptures. It is mentioned in the Old Greek canon of the Old Testament only in Wisdom 10:10. The *pseudepigraphal* book called the Psalms of Solomon (written c. 50 B.C.) also speaks of the "Kingdom of God" in 17:1.

(The Pseudepigrapha are ancient Jewish religious books that were not accepted into either the Hebrew or the Old Greek canons of the Old Testament. The formidable word "pseudepigrapha" means "pseudonymous writings." These writings are all pseudonymous for essentially the same reason given above for the Book of Daniel: They were attributed to some ancient authority who antedated Ezra's death in the hope that they would be accorded prophetic authority.)

The Book of Daniel discloses that God's end-time Kingdom will be presided over by a mysterious king who is presented as the New Adam. After creation has been cleansed from all the evils inflicted on it by the Old Adam, especially the persecuting Syrians, the New

Adam will reign forever over the New Creation as God's gerent. The New Adam is not explicitly assigned the role of end-time Judge in the Book of Daniel. He is, however, a king (Dan 7:14), and in ancient Israel the reigning king was always understood to be the chief judge who upheld God's law in the kingdom (2 Sam 8:15; 15:2).

In Daniel 7:13, the New Adam is alluded to midrashically as a "son" or descendant of the Old Adam. In order to grasp this allusion we must remember that the Hebrew word for human being (or "man" in the inclusive sense) is *adam*. By the time the Book of Genesis was translated into Greek (c. 250 B.C.), Jewish scribes had begun treating this common noun as the personal name of the first human, "Adam."

The passage we are about to read indicates that the New Adam is a mysterious human who is authorized by God to be the end-time representative of God's restored Reign over creation. God confers upon him, therefore, the "dominion" taken from the Old Adam after his fall:

> I saw in the night visions, and behold, coming with the clouds of heaven was one like a son of man; he came to the Ancient of Days and was presented before him.
>
> And to him was given dominion and glory and kingdom, that all peoples, nations, and languages should serve him; his dominion is an everlasting dominion, and his kingdom one that shall not be destroyed.
> (Dan 7:13-14)

Daniel's reference to "one like a son of man" (or son of Adam) who receives "dominion" from God over the "kingdom" of creation assumes that we are familiar with the traditional Israelite theme of Adam as the divinely appointed king of creation. This royal Adamic theme is stated explicitly in Genesis 1:26–28 where Adam is given "dominion" by God and told to "rule" over creation:

> So God created man [Heb = *adam*] in his own image, in the image of God he created him; male and female he created them. And God blessed them, and God said to them, "Be fruitful and multiply, and fill the earth and subdue it; and have dominion over the fish of the sea

> and over the birds of the air and over every living thing that moves over the face of the earth." (Gen 1:27-28)

Adam's primeval kingship is also spoken of in one of the psalms which adverts to the same passage in Genesis:

> When I look at the heavens, the work of your fingers, the moon and the stars which you have established; what is man [*adam*] that you are mindful of him, and the son of man that you care for him?
>
> You have made him little less than God, and you crown him with glory and honor.
>
> You have given him dominion over the works of your hands; you have put all things under his feet, all sheep and oxen, and also the beasts of the field, the birds of the air, and the fish of the sea. (Ps 8:3–8)

The Book of Daniel also added that ancient Israel, because of the promises God had made to her through the prophets, would be associated with the Son of Adam in a privileged way in ruling over the nations gathered into God's end-time Kingdom.

> And the kingdom and the dominion and the greatness of the kingdoms under the whole heaven shall be given to the people of the saints of the Most High; their kingdom shall be an everlasting kingdom and all dominions shall serve and obey them. (Dan 7:27)

It is sometimes suggested that the "one like a son of man" who comes "with the clouds of heaven" and receives "everlasting dominion" in Daniel 7:13–14 is an "angel" rather than the mysterious descendant of Adam elected by God to be the New Adam. This claim is advanced because the "interpreting angel" who periodically instructs Daniel is said to have the "appearance of a man" (Dan 8:15b; see also 9:21; 10:5, 18; 12:6, 7).

However, likening angels to humans was an established literary convention well before Daniel was written (see Ezek 9:1–11; Zec 1:8–2:3). Furthermore, the same book also calls the prophet Daniel a "son of man" (Dan 8:17) and a "man" (Dan 10:19) in recognition of his humanity.

The claim that the "one like a son of man" is an angel fails to recognize the deliberate midrashic allusions in Daniel 7 meant to contrast the original Adam with the New Adam appointed by God as king of the New Creation. As the original king of creation, Adam of old received "dominion" over the "beasts" (Gen 1:26–28). It is for that reason, therefore, that the Gentile kings and kingdoms which have subjugated Israel since the Exile are likened in Daniel 7:3–7, 11–12, 17–19 to "beasts." These Gentile "beasts" are destined to be ruled over by the New Adam who is God's "image" when God's Reign over creation is finally restored.

These four Gentile kingdoms are also said to have received temporarily the "dominion" (Dan 7:6, 12) taken from the Old Adam and, later, from David's sons at the time of the Exile. Daniel taught that this dominion would finally be taken from the "beasts" and restored to the Son of Adam (Dan 7:13–14) and to faithful Israel (Dan 7:27). Because there were no descendants of David on the horizon who possessed political or military power when Daniel was written, it probably seemed more realistic to its author to base Israel's hope for final salvation on a "Son of Adam" rather than a "Son of David."

In addition, it seems reasonable to conclude that because the "four great beasts" spoken of in Daniel 7:3–7 represent "four kings" (Dan 7:17) who rule over four successive Gentile kingdoms, then the "one like a son of man" also represents a human (a son of Adam) who is destined to rule as king over God's end-time Kingdom. The ancient Jews could not envision a divinely authorized kingdom, even an everlasting kingdom, without a king appointed by God as the representative of God's Reign on earth.

So true is this observation that even after the Exile, when the house of David lost its dominion over Israel (587 B.C.), it was assumed by Daniel that God gave that forfeited dominion to the four successive kings (Dan 7:17) who subjugated Israel. An earlier prophecy in Isaiah 45:1–4 had already announced that Israel's God had appointed King Cyrus of Persia to conquer Babylonia and rule over Israel:

> Thus says Yahweh to his anointed, to Cyrus, whose right hand I have grasped, to subdue nations before him

> and ungird the loins of kings, to open doors before him that gates may not be closed:
>
> "I will go before you and level the mountains, I will break in pieces the doors of bronze and cut asunder the bars of iron, I will give you the treasures of darkness and the hoards in secret places, that you man know that it is I, Yahweh, the God of Israel, who call you by your name.
>
> For the sake of my servant Jacob, and Israel my chosen, I call you by your name, I surname you, though you do not know me." (Is 45:1–4)

For ancient Israel, God was the Lord of history before whose invincible might all earthly kings must finally bow down. It is true that Daniel envisions Israel as being protected by angelic beings who serve God (Dan 12:1). This tradition, however, is as old as Exodus 14:19. As Israel understood history, therefore, God would not need to call upon an angel to establish or represent God's Kingly Reign on earth. When the midrashic associations in Daniel 7 are read in tandem with ancient Israel's traditional theology of kingship, they fully justify the reading given above.

Clearly, Jesus accepted Daniel's teaching about the imminent restoration of God's Kingly Reign over creation. He also believed that the august Son of Adam alluded to midrashically in Daniel 7:13–14 would be sent by God at the end-time to preside over the Final Judgment and the New Creation:

> And I tell you, whoever acknowledges me before others, the Son of Man also will acknowledge before the angels of God. But he who denies me before others will be denied before the angels of God. (Lk 12:8)

Questions for Review and Discussion

1. What is eschatology and when did the ancient Jews begin to believe in "eschatological" salvation?

2. What did the ancient Jews mean by "salvation" before they learned to think eschatologically?

3. What did the ancient Jews think would happen to a person after death before they learned to hope for eschatological salvation?

4. What is the name of the first book of apocalyptic theology? When, where, and by whom was it written?

5. What special set of historical circumstances prompted an ancient Jewish prophet to create apocalyptic theology?

6. What is the historical relation between apocalyptic theology and eschatological hope in ancient Israel?

7. What is a symbol and why must we use symbols if we wish to speak intelligibly about transempirical realities?

8. What is the difference between understanding something literally and understanding it symbolically?

9. Should the apocalyptic language which speaks of God ending the world, raising the dead, and judging the living and the dead be understood literally or symbolically? Explain your answer.

10. What is ancient Jewish midrash?

11. What problem did midrash help to solve in the Book of Daniel?

12. Why should we expect to find midrash in the Gospels?

Chapter Nine

The Risen Jesus as God's Endorsement of Israel's Eschatological Hope

1.

A critical and balanced reading of the Gospels indicates that Jesus accepted the message about God's end-time Kingdom introduced to ancient Israel by the Book of Daniel. Moreover, he experienced a call from God to be a herald of God's approaching Kingdom. For a time Jesus had been a disciple of John the Baptizer who had also preached an end-time message for God. After John was imprisoned by Herod Antipas, Jesus took up John's prophetic mantle and continued to preach his own understanding of John's end-time message. (For a thorough and convincing analysis of the eschatological nature of Jesus' Kingdom message see *Jesus of Nazareth* by Jürgen Becker.)

Jesus believed that his mission was to prepare Israel for the imminent arrival of the Son of Man (Son of Adam) who would preside over the Final Judgment and reign everlastingly as the august representative of God's Kingly Reign over the New Creation:

Lk 12:8–9

> And I tell you, every one who acknowledges me before men, the Son of Man also will acknowledge before the angels of God; but he who denies me before men will be denied before the angels of God.

Mk 8:38

> For whoever is ashamed of me and my words . . . of him will the Son of Man also be ashamed when he comes . . . with the holy angels.

Accordingly, Jesus chose twelve of his disciples to accompany him regularly and assist him symbolically in proclaiming the nearness of God's end-time Kingdom. Jesus chose the Twelve to signify prophetically that he had come to call the "twelve tribes" of Israel to faith and repentance so they would be ready to enter God's approaching Kingdom.

The restoration of the twelve tribes of Israel (Mt 10:6–7) was expected historically when God's Reign was fully established on earth (Is 49:5–6; Jer 31:1; Ezek 31:10; 37:19–22; 47:13–14; Sir 36:11). After the emergence of apocalyptic eschatology, many devout Jews expected the "ingathering" of the twelve tribes to follow the end-time Judgment (Dan 12:2–3; Sir 36:11; 48:10; Ps Sol 17:44,50; Psalms of Solomon is an extrabiblical work found among the Pseudepigrapha):

> And he appointed twelve, to be with him, and he sent them out to preach and have authority to cast out demons: Simon whom he surnamed Peter; James the son of Zebedee and John the brother of James, whom he surnamed Bo-anerges, that is, sons of thunder; Andrew, and Philip, and Bartholomew, and Matthew, and Thomas, and James the son of Alpheus, and Thaddaeus, and Simon the Cananaean, and Judas Iscariot, who betrayed him. (Mk 3:14–19; see also Mt 10: 1–4; Lk 6:12–16)

Some have asserted that the statements about the Twelve in the Gospels are theological creations by which the early church sought to justify her existence as the New Covenant people of God. It is historically certain, however, that Jesus himself chose the Twelve, for Jesus' choice of Judas Iscariot as "one of the Twelve" proved to be a serious embarrassment to the apostolic church. The Jews, understandably, asked how Jesus could have made such a bad choice if he truly was the greatest of God's prophets and God's Messiah.

The church defended Jesus' tragic choice by teaching that his betrayal by Judas was foreordained midrashically in the Scriptures as part of God's secret Messianic purpose (cp. Ps 49:1 and Mk 14:20–21; also Zec 11:12–13 and Mt 27:3–4). Jesus' choice of Judas, the church explained, was something Jesus understood as divinely mandated in the written word of God:

> For the Son of man goes as it is written of him, but woe to that man by whom the Son of Man is betrayed! (Mk 14:21)

The Joyful Supper celebrated regularly by Jesus with his disciples was intended as anticipatory participation in the Great Supper that comes with God's Kingdom. Moreover, Jesus taught that Abraham, Isaac, and Jacob would be guests of honor at this Supper which will celebrate the final ingathering of their faithful descendants:

> I tell you, many will come from east and west and sit at table with Abraham, Isaac, and Jacob in the kingdom of heaven. (Mt 8:11)

The promise of table fellowship in God's Kingdom is presupposed by the ugly attempt of James and John to secure seats of honor at Jesus' right and left hand (Mk 10:35–40). Mark's account of this incident has certainly been expanded theologically by Mark and the early church (Mk 10:38–39), but neither Mark nor the church would have invented the underlying substance of such an unflattering story about two of the Twelve. The early church remembered the incident because (1) it truly happened, and (2) it was the context necessary for understanding Jesus' admonition about the importance of "service" in his Kingdom-anticipating community.

Moreover, the same promise of table fellowship in God's Kingdom is implied by the eschatological saying of Jesus to the Twelve which very likely followed his cup-saying at the Last Supper:

> Truly I say to you, I shall not drink again of the fruit of the vine until that day when I drink it new in the Kingdom of God. (Mk 14:25)

It was his anticipation of being separated from his disciples by impending betrayal and death that prompted Jesus to say sadly that he would not drink wine again until he drank it at the Great Supper in God's coming Kingdom.

The substance of Jesus' saying in Mark 14:25 is probably authentic because it indicates that Jesus expected to be raised at the General Resurrection when the Kingdom of God arrived as a collective phenomenon. This means that Jesus did not anticipate that he would be raised individually by God before the world's end. (The ancient Jewish Scriptures never speak of the resurrection of an individual.) It also means that Jesus was just as surprised as his disciples to learn that God had "raised" him before the Kingdom of God arrived.

In reality, Jesus saw the Twelve again, not at the Great Supper that arrives with God's end-time Kingdom, but when he appeared to them in Galilee while they were at table (Lk 24:41–42; Acts 10:41; Jn 21:13–14; Ps Mk 16:14). It was their stunning encounter with the Risen (1 Cor 15:5) and Spirit-mediating (Jn 20:21–22) Jesus which led the Twelve to realize that Jesus was encouraging them to return to the proclamation of his Kingdom message and the celebration of his Kingdom-anticipating Supper with new revelatory certainty (Acts 10:39–41). If the early church had created Mark 14:25 for theological reasons, it would not contain the telltale discrepancy just noted.

2.

Before we discuss Jesus' prophetic words and deeds, we should reflect briefly on the circumstances that probably contributed to his mission. Mark's Gospel indicates that Jesus practiced the carpenter's trade before he received his prophetic call (Mk 6:3). Jesus, therefore, was very likely working as a carpenter when he learned about the prophetic activity of John the Baptizer:

Mk 1:4–5

> John the Baptizer appeared in the wilderness, preaching

> a baptism for the forgiveness of sins. And there went out to him all the country of Judea, and all the people of Jerusalem, and they were baptized by him in the river Jordan, confessing their sins.

> Mt 3:4, 7, 11–12
>
> Now John . . . said to them . . . "I baptize you with water for repentance, but he who is coming after me is mightier than I, whose sandals I am not worthy to carry; he will baptize you with the Holy Spirit and with fire. His winnowing fork is in his hand, and he will clear his threshing floor and gather his wheat into the granary, but the chaff he will burn with unquenchable fire."

John's appearance would have roused excitement among many devout Jews because public prophecy had lain dormant for several centuries (in large part because the priest-scribes had earlier taught that prophetism ceased after the death of Ezra). It is likely that Jesus also experienced the excitement caused by John's mission. For the Gospels tell us that he traveled to Judea to hear John preach, and that he received John's baptism:

> In those days Jesus came from Nazareth and was baptized by John in the Jordan. (Mk 1:9)

The authentic words and deeds of Jesus suggest that he was a deeply religious Jew who had habitually experienced God's Presence and Love well before he received John's baptism. When Jesus began his own prophetic mission a short time later, he was serenely and unshakably certain that God is gracious and forgiving Love. He was also utterly confident that God wanted him to proclaim the offer of God's love and forgiveness to all, even notorious sinners, in return for their faith, trust, and sincere decision to turn away from destructive behavior, sin.

Some of Jesus' Jewish contemporaries criticized him harshly and rejected his message because of his efforts to assure social outcasts that they, too, were invited to the Great Supper in God's coming Kingdom. When faced with such criticism, Jesus serenely continued to carry his message to the lost sheep of the twelve tribes of Israel. It was Jesus' practice of allowing people of ill repute to join his disciples at his Kingdom-anticipating Supper, even before their conversion, that especially offended his critics.

Jesus' behavior implies that long-standing communion with God was the source of the unshakable certainty that underlay both his promise of God's forgiveness and his mission of healing. To confidently believe that God would forgive and heal others through his mission presupposes a well-established relationship with God—a relationship which had generated profound faith and trust. It is also reasonable to conclude that God healed people through Jesus not only to encourage people to accept Jesus' Kingdom message as divinely authorized but also to encourage Jesus to continue his frequently misunderstood and bitterly criticized mission to the ostracized.

It seems very likely, therefore, that the manifest ability of Jesus to surmount the hostility of those who rejected his Kingdom message presupposes an extraordinary and habitual experience of God's reassuring Presence. The Gospels suggest that Jesus regularly communed with God's indwelling Presence:

> And in the morning, a great while before it was day, he rose and went out to a lonely place, and there he prayed. (Mk 1:35)

So certain was Jesus of his profound experience of God's Presence that he confidently assumed he could ignore narrow interpretations of the law of Moses which were incompatible with his experience of God's unconditional love. The Gospels indicate that Jesus faithfully observed the written law of Moses. But whenever "oral" traditions meant to interpret or supplement the law were unreasonable or interfered with kindness and love, Jesus rejected them. When Jesus was accused of disrespect for God's law by those who were narrowly traditional or harshly legalistic, he remained unperturbed and appealed to the common sense of his critics:

> Now he was teaching in one of the synagogues on the Sabbath. And there was a woman who had had a spirit of infirmity for eighteen years; she was bent over and could not fully straighten herself. And when Jesus saw her, he said to her, "Woman, you are freed from your infirmity." And he laid his hands upon her, and immediately she was made straight, and she praised God.

> But the ruler of the synagogue, indignant because Jesus had healed on the Sabbath, said to the people, "There are six days on which work ought to be done; come on those days and be healed, and not on the Sabbath day."
>
> Then the Lord answered him, . . . "Does not each of you on the Sabbath untie his ox and his ass from the manger, and lead it away to water it? And ought not this daughter of Abraham whom Satan bound for eighteen years, be loosed from this bond on the Sabbath day?" (Lk 13:10–16)

It seems probable that Luke has theologically embellished this story. Nevertheless, its underlying substance is historical, and it accurately reflects Jesus' attitude toward his legalistic critics.

3.

It was probably Jesus' habitual experience of God's indwelling Presence that motivated him to go listen to John the Baptizer's prophetic message. We may surmise that when Jesus heard John's words about the coming end-time Judgment, God caused divine love to well up mightily within Jesus, thereby confirming the eschatological substance of John's message. Jesus, accordingly, would have experienced John's words as divinely inspired because they were Spirit-mediating. Consequently, Jesus "knew" that John was truly God's prophet and that God endorsed (the essential substance of) John's message. Prompted by God's gracious Self-gift, therefore, Jesus received John's baptism and became John's disciple.

Jesus probably remained John's disciple until John was seized by Herod Antipas and imprisoned (Mk 1:14). When John's mission was abruptly halted by his arrest, Jesus very likely anticipated that someone would step forward and continue proclaiming John's end-time message for God. When no one did so, the idea that he should continue John's mission must have occurred to Jesus.

We may reasonably conclude that Jesus prayed over this matter, and that when he did, he experienced divine encouragement (in the form of the silent language of God's love) welling up within him. After prayer and reflection, Jesus probably understood that his extraordinary experience of God's Self-communication was God's affirmation of the idea that he should continue John's mission to Israel. When Jesus decided to do so, God further reinforced that decision by healing people with astonishing frequency through Jesus' word, sometimes accompanied by his touch.

We are told by Matthew (and Luke in 7:19–20) that when John learned from prison of Jesus' prophetic activity, he sent some of his disciples to question Jesus:

> Now when John learned in prison about the deeds of the Messiah, he sent word by his disciples and said to him, "Are you he who is to come, or should we look for another?" (Mt 11:2–3)

It is, of course, Matthew who has inserted the title Messiah into this otherwise reliable memory; the title represents the church's post-Easter theological understanding of Jesus and is absent in Luke's account of the same incident (Lk 7:18). In reality, Jesus was not proclaimed as God's Messiah until after he had begun appearing as the Risen Lord of life and death.

The story of the delegation sent to Jesus by the imprisoned Baptizer is probably reliable because, among other things, it correctly remembers that John did not really understand who Jesus was. This doubtlessly correct memory, however, flies in the face of Matthew's theologically expanded account of Jesus' baptism by John in which John clearly knows who Jesus is:

> Then Jesus came from Galilee to the Jordan to John, to be baptized by him. John would have prevented him, saying, "I need to be baptized by you, and do you come to me?" But Jesus answered him, "Let it be so now; for thus it is fitting for us to fulfill all righteousness." Then he consented. (Mt 3:13–15)

Sending disciples to question Jesus about his mission also contradicts the highly theological baptismal account in the fourth Gospel:

> And John bore witness, "I saw the Spirit descend from heaven, and it remained on him. I myself did not know him; but he who sent me to baptize with water said to

> me, 'He on whom you see the Spirit descend and remain, this is he who baptizes with the Holy Spirit.' And I have seen and have borne witness that this is the Son of God." (Jn 1:32–34)

If the Baptizer had literally received such revelatory information about Jesus, he would have known who Jesus was and would not have had to inquire through emissaries.

When the Baptizer was told by his disciples that Jesus was preaching an eschatological message essentially like his own, and that God was confirming the message with miraculous signs, he was probably perplexed. Jesus clearly seemed to be someone who enjoyed God's approval or God would not have miraculously healed people through him. And yet Jesus was not the eschatological figure that John seems to have anticipated:

> I baptize you with water for repentance, but he who is coming after me is mightier than I, whose sandals I am not worthy to carry; he will baptize you with the Holy Spirit and with fire. His winnowing fork is in his hand, and he will clear his threshing floor and gather his wheat into the granary, but the chaff he will burn with unquenchable fire. (Mt 3:11–12)

John evidently expected the advent of a majestic figure who would preside at a fiery end-time Judgment. Since the coming one spoken of by John is wearing sandals, he is probably not God but an exalted human who is God's end-time representative. John's description of this coming one in the passage cited here is probably reliable. Because the early church believed that Jesus was the one of whom John spoke, she, had she created the description, would probably have described John's ambiguous "coming one" with one of the titles she had decided to bestow on the Risen Jesus (Son of Man, Son of God, or Messiah).

The early church (c. A.D. 30-70), however, probably did modify John's description of the baptism to be administered by the coming one. Matthew and Luke, following the Sayings Source (instead of Mk 1:8), relate that the coming one will baptize "with the Holy Spirit and with fire" (Mt 3:11c; Lk 3:16c). Their additional reference to fire is probably original, whereas mention of the Holy Spirit is probably secondary and theological. The mention of the Spirit was probably added (or substituted in the case of Mark) as a more accurate description of the Spirit-conferring Baptism of Jesus. (The Sayings Source was a collection of Jesus' sayings used by Matthew and Luke in their Gospels.)

By adding "the Spirit" to the Baptizer's description of the coming one's baptism, the author of the Sayings Source intended that the coming one spoken of by the Baptizer would be recognized as the Spirit-mediating Jesus. In addition, there are several literary indications that the coming one's baptism (or cleansing) was originally to be accomplished "with fire." First, baptism "with fire" contrasts and balances more logically and symmetrically "with water" in the Baptizer's total description of the coming one. Second, a fiery baptism or cleansing accords better with the coming one's role as end-time Judge, his "winnowing fan," and his burning of the separated chaff "with unquenchable fire."

Who did John think this mysterious "coming one" would be? We cannot say with certainty. But a possible candidate is the mysterious eschatological figure described as "coming" with the clouds of heaven in the Book of Daniel. This exalted human is invested by God with authority to preside over the expected end-time Reign of God:

> I saw in the night visions, and behold coming with the clouds of heaven was one like a son of man; he came to the ancient of days and was presented before him.
>
> And to him was given dominion and glory and kingdom, that all peoples, nations, and languages should serve him; his dominion is an everlasting dominion which shall not pass away, and his kingdom one which shall not be destroyed. (Dan 7:13–14)

This passage in Daniel is the source of the end-time speculation which eventually produced the explicit title Son of Man (the Son of Adam or New Adam who will be King of the New Creation). But Daniel's midrashic allusion to an exalted one who is like a son of Adam (see Gen 1:26, Ps 8:3–8, and Ps 80:170) is deliberately imprecise and mysterious; it has not yet become the eschatological title "Son of Man." Nevertheless, since the mysterious figure spoken of in Daniel bears a family resemblance to the mysterious coming one spoken of by the Baptizer, the end-time prophecy in Daniel 7 is quite possibly the direct or indirect source of John's end-time expectation.

It was evidently because Jesus did not exhibit the traits of the fiery and exalted end-time Judge expected by John that John sent his disciples to Jesus seeking clarification:

> And Jesus answered them, "Go and tell John what you hear and see: the blind receive their sight and the lame walk, lepers are cleansed and the deaf hear, and the dead are raised up, and the poor have Good News preached to them. And blessed is he who takes no offense at me." (Mt 11:2–6)

The substance of Jesus' response to John's disciples is probably reliable even though it was very likely amplified by the early church. It is reasonable to suspect that Jesus' original reply lacked the catalogue of confirming signs which it now includes. If John's emissaries had observed such signs prior to their question (as Jesus' response indicates), there would have been no need for Jesus to list them. Moreover, the catalogue sounds like a "midrashic" review of the signs which occurred throughout Jesus' entire public ministry. This list of signs was probably appended to Jesus' original response to remind the church that Jesus' astonishing end-time ministry of healing was foreshadowed in the Book of Isaiah:

> **Is 61:1**
>
> The Spirit of the Lord is upon me, because the Lord has anointed me to bring Good News to the poor; he has sent me to bind up the brokenhearted, to proclaim liberty to the captives, and the opening of the prison to those who are bound.

> **Is 35:5–6a**
>
> Then the eyes of the blind shall be opened, and the ears of the deaf unstopped; then shall the lame man leap like a hart, and the tongue of the dumb shall sing for joy.

> **Is 29:18–19**
>
> In that day the deaf shall hear the words of a book, and out of their gloom and darkness the eyes of the blind

> shall see. The meek shall obtain fresh joy from the Lord, and the poor among men shall exult in the Holy One of Israel.

Is 26:19

> Your dead shall live, their bodies shall rise. O dwellers in the dust, awake and sing for joy.

It is not likely that Jesus appealed midrashically to the Scriptures to justify himself and his mission. Instead, it was the apostolic church who carefully searched the Scriptures and habitually appealed to their authority to justify her faith in Jesus' vigorously contested Messiahship. Jesus himself appealed directly to his successful combat with the powers of darkness to vindicate himself and his Kingdom message:

> But if it is by the finger of God that I cast out demons, then the kingdom of God has come upon you. (Lk 11:20)

Therefore, Jesus' original response to the question put by John's disciples was probably as follows:

> And Jesus answered them, "Go and tell John what you hear and see. And blessed is he who takes no offense at me." (Mt 11:2–6)

Jesus' answer implies that John should be able to recognize that the end-time message proclaimed by Jesus is in essential agreement with John's own message. In addition, the exorcisms and miraculous healings which God is manifesting through Jesus are divine authorization of Jesus' decision to continue John's mission. Therefore, those who accept Jesus and his message will be blessed when God's Kingdom, which has already begun to arrive through Jesus' words and deeds, finally comes in the fullness of its healing and saving power.

Although Jesus continued the Baptizer's end-time mission, he modified John's message to accord with his own extraordinary experience of God's Presence and Love. Jesus did not emphasize God's fiery wrath and the terrifying Judgment to come. Instead, he preferred to speak of God's tender concern for all the strayed sheep of the house of Israel. Jesus assured us that God is waiting to welcome us into the arms of God's gracious love and gather us into God's coming Kingdom (Lk 15:3–10).

God, Jesus declared, is like a father who loves unconditionally, and who waits patiently for the repentance of his children when they go astray (Lk 15:11–32). God loves us, Jesus taught, even when we experience ourselves as unlovable; God accepts us even when we experience ourselves as unacceptable; and God forgives us even when we experience ourselves as unforgivable by human standards (Lk 15:19). It is never too late, Jesus announced, to return to God and to ask for God's forgiveness (Mt 20:1–15).

During his public ministry, Jesus did not identify himself as the Son of Man despite the fact that the Gospels frequently imply he did. In several of his substantially authentic sayings, Jesus distinguished clearly between himself and the coming Son of Man. For he spoke of himself in the first person and the present tense, whereas he spoke of the Son of Man in the third person and the future tense:

Lk 12:8–9

> And I tell you, every one who acknowledges me before men, the Son of Man also will acknowledge before the angels of God; but he who denies me before men will be denied before the angels of God.

Mk 8:38

> For whoever is ashamed of me and my words . . . of him will the Son of Man be ashamed when he comes . . . with the holy angels.

Once the early church (c. A.D. 30-70) identified the Risen Jesus with the Son of Man, she inserted the title into remembered statements of Jesus which clearly referred to himself. The church assumed that Jesus knew he was the Son of Man and added the title to his sayings for theological reasons. Although the earthly Jesus probably did not think that he was the mysterious Son of Man destined to come at the end-time, he nevertheless understood his own prophetic message as inseparably related to the Final Judgment over which he expected the Son of Man to preside. It was not until after his resurrection that Jesus learned that God had elected him to become the exalted and mysterious Son of Man.

A critical reading of the Gospels also indicates that Jesus did not think of himself as God's *Messiah* during his earthly mission. (In the post-Exilic period, the Messiah was almost always understood to be a descendant of King David who would be sent by God to bring definitive salvation to Israel and the nations.) He did not know that he had been chosen by God to be Israel's promised Messiah until he had passed through death into Risen Life. Learning to understand and accept this limitation on the earthly Jesus' knowledge is comparable to a "Copernican Revolution" in our reading of the Gospels. Once we grasp the reasons for this critical postponement of Jesus' Messianic consciousness, a host of mistaken assumptions and groundless problems is eliminated, and elegant simplicity emerges from daunting complexity. We are then free to understand Jesus and God's saving purpose at work in him with new clarity, economy, and consistency.

Some people are understandably upset by the idea that Jesus did not know he was the Son of Man or God's Messiah before his resurrection. If we find ourselves among them (and the author of this book once did), we should ask ourselves what difference it truly makes if Jesus did not learn about his exalted Messianic destiny until after he had fulfilled its unexpected requirements with faith and trust in God.

Does accepting this view of Jesus' knowledge truly make the Risen Jesus any less acceptable as the conclusive revelatory sign through whom God assures humans of Eternal Life? On the contrary, it is easier to identify with Jesus as a divinely provided example of faith and trust in God if we assume that he did not have definite foreknowledge about the future events in his life and their glorious outcome. Uncertainty about the future and the need for faith and trust in God's providential goodness are essential characteristics of the human condition, and Jesus was truly human.

God knew from the outset that the best way to give humans definitive assurance about the answers to our ultimate questions was through a human being who was truly one of us and a full participant in the "problem" of human existence. The Christian message tells us that the human being God chose to work through was Jesus of Nazareth. God sent the tragically crucified and Risen Jesus to us as God's guarantee that we can defeat all the destructive forces which threaten our finite existence and can attain Eternal Life and Joy.

In order to become God's conclusive sign of salvation for humankind, Jesus had to submit to the painful and ambiguous conditions of existence with faith and trust in God's goodness. Jesus keenly experienced the tragedy, injustice, and cruelty of life, and the repugnance of premature and undeserved death. But he did not allow these discouraging evils to overwhelm and defeat him with hate-filled bitterness, self-pity, or despair. Rather, through the power of his faith in God's providential love and goodness, Jesus won the victory of the Resurrection and becamc God's confirmation that all other humans can do the same.

Through the Risen and Spirit-mediating Jesus, God has "shown" us that (despite its preliminary ambiguity) ours is truly a sublime destiny. We have also been shown "the Way" to live authentically in order to attain that destiny. God calls us to follow Jesus (Mk 8:34) by living lives of faith, trust, and love which serves (Jn 13:12–15; 15:12; Mt 25:31–46). If we do so, we also will be able to defeat the "powers of darkness" (the personal, social, and physical evils in life which can tempt us to despair).

The Risen and Spirit-mediating Jesus is the great negator of the "terror of history." He is God's conclusive sign that destructive alienation and insane cruelty can be overcome through our faith in God's offer of reconciling love and healing forgiveness. The tragedy and absurdity which can suddenly engulf our lives can be transcended through our faith in God's promise of Ultimate Justice and Eternal Life and Joy. God intends our faith in Jesus to reassure us that good finally triumphs over evil, life over death, and joy over tragic suffering. (For a contemporary explanation of the appearances of the Risen Jesus and the appearance narratives in the Gospels see *Exploring the Resurrection of Jesus* in this series.)

5.

It is true that on several occasions Jesus is depicted in the Gospels as claiming to be (or implying that he is) God's promised Messiah:

Mk 14:61–62

Again the high priest asked him, "Are you the Messiah, the son of the Blessed One?" And Jesus said, "I am."

Jn 4:25–26

> The [Samaritan] woman said, "I know that Messiah is coming (he who is called Christ); when he comes, he will show us all things." Jesus said to her, "I who speak with you am he."

Jn 18:33, 36–7

> Pilate entered the praetorium again and called Jesus and said to him, "Are you the King of the Jews?" . . . Jesus answered, "My kingship is not of this world; if my kingship were of this world, my servants would fight, that I might not be handed over to the Jews; but my kingship is not from the world."

These instances, however, probably represent the early church's (c. A.D. 30-70) theological interpretations of Jesus worked out in the light of her "Resurrection" faith. These interpretations were retrojected onto her memory of Jesus' words and deeds and were meant to express her sincere belief that Jesus knew from the start of his mission that he was God's Messiah. Without doubt, the ancient church assumed, God must have revealed God's secret Messianic purpose to Jesus beforehand:

> Surely the Lord God does nothing, without revealing his secret to his servants the prophets. (Amos 3:7)

The few occasions when Jesus is described as accepting the title Messiah must be carefully weighed against other occasions when he reacted to it differently. When Peter gave Jesus the title Messiah at Caesarea Philippi, Jesus, in the original form of the story, probably rejected the title vigorously (go directly from Mk 8:27–29 to 33). It was very likely Mark, the evangelist, who later expanded the story with his *Messianic Secret theology* (Mk 8:30–32). He did so to render the story compatible with the church's belief that Jesus had been informed by God of his secret Messianic destiny before his death and resurrection. (For a full explanation of Mark's Messianic Secret theology see *Exploring the Messianic Secret in Mark's Gospel* in this series.)

In addition, Mark, Matthew, and Luke are probably correct when they relate that Jesus laconically refused to discuss the title Messiah when questioned about it by the Roman prefect Pontius Pilate:

Mk 15:2

And Pilate asked him, "Are you the king of the Jews?" And he answered him, "You have said so." [*su legeis* = the words are yours (not mine)]

Mt 27:11

And the governor asked him, "Are you the king of the Jews?" Jesus said to him, "You have said so." [*su legeis*]

Lk 23:3

And Pilate asked him, "Are you the king of the Jews?" And he answered him, "You have said so." [*su legeis*]

In effect, Jesus refused to discuss the title Messiah (or king). He probably did so because he considered the title theologically mistaken and in no way related to his proclamation of God's coming Kingdom. To Pilate, however, Jesus' noncommittal response would have seemed suspiciously ambiguous, and it was almost certainly this perception of Pilate's which sealed Jesus' fate. Since Jesus did not *explicitly* deny that he was the "king" of the Jews, Pilate would have suspected him of possibly harboring political aspirations. Jesus, he decided, would have to be executed as a potential threat to Roman authority.

This interpretation is supported by the sign Pilate placed on Jesus' cross to notify and warn the public of Jesus' crime: "The king of the Jews" (Mk 15:26; see also Mt 27:37; Lk 23:38; Jn 19:19). If the church had created the words on the sign for a theological purpose, she would have used the title "Messiah" instead of the Roman equivalent, "king."

Atypically, the Gospel of John relates that Jesus claimed the title king or Messiah before Pilate in a qualified (nonmilitary or spiritual) sense. But John probably does so in pursuit of his characteristic "theological" goals, and even he preserves the substance of Jesus original reply:

> Pilate entered the praetorium again and called Jesus, and said to him, "Are you the king of the Jews?" . . . And Jesus answered, "My kingship is not of this world; if my kingship were of this world, my servants would fight, that I might not be handed over to the Jews." Pilate said

> to him, "So you are a king?" Jesus answered, "You say [*su legeis*] that I am a king." (Jn 18:33, 36–37)

It is easy to see why John would have created Jesus' positive (but qualified) response to Pilate as part of the Johannine interpretation of Jesus' exalted messiahship. But it is very difficult to conceive that Mark, Matthew, and Luke would have created Jesus' noncommittal response for any theological purpose.

In actuality, Jesus probably rejected the title Messiah as theologically unacceptable because of its traditional association with military violence and bloodshed. He did not think that God's coming Reign would be established by military conquest. Rather, its arrival would be accomplished by the irresistible power of God (as indicated in Dan 2:44; 7:23–27). That power, Jesus believed, would be entrusted to the exalted Son of Man.

Contemporary scholarship concludes that Mark's Messianic Secret theology contains a fundamental insight which is correct and profoundly significant for Christian faith. But it also contains an assumption which is historically conditioned and mistaken.

Mark's correct insight was that God truly had destined Jesus for a mysterious and exalted messiahship which was contrary to ancient Jewish expectations. Also correct was his related insight that God's hidden purpose could only be understood after Jesus' death and resurrection. Mark was mistaken, however, when he assumed that Jesus, from the time of his baptism, knew all about God's secret Messianic purpose. In actuality, the only one who understood God's secret Messianic purpose throughout Jesus' public ministry was God.

Because of Jesus' total commitment to the will of God (Mk 12:30), Jesus was certainly open throughout his prophetic ministry to whatever additional office God would eventually call him. A critical reading of the Gospels suggests, however, that Jesus did not learn the Messianic Secret till the time of his resurrection. (The manner in which the Risen Jesus probably learned of his secret Messianic office will be discussed in the final chapter's answer to question twelve.)

We should not fault Mark for having unwittingly woven mistaken assumptions into his inspired interpretation of the history of Jesus. Mark honestly did the best job of interpreting the data that he was capable of at his time in history. As for God's view of this matter, God knew that the future, with its inevitable increase in knowledge, would teach us to winnow Mark's mistaken assumptions from his correct insights. God also knew that Christians with mature faith would then see that Jesus remains God's definitive assurance of salvation to the world even if Jesus did not learn this until he entered Risen Life.

6.

When the Risen and Spirit-mediating Jesus began appearing to and commissioning his disciples, they were stunned into recognition of his revelatory significance for Israel and the nations. The unending process of remembering, interpreting, and witnessing to the Risen Jesus was then launched in history. Suddenly, the disciples were confronted with an enormous task: The Risen Jesus had called them to be his witnesses, but what form should their testimony take?

Jesus' disciples were already familiar with the apocalyptic belief that God would "raise" the dead at the end-time. The resurrection of the dead had been an essential part of Jesus' Kingdom message (Mk 14:25). The disciples, therefore, reached instinctively for the symbolic idea of resurrection and announced that God had "raised" Jesus as Good News to the world. (When speaking of Jesus' resurrection, Mark, Matthew, and Luke always state that God raised Jesus. Paul uses the same language, except for 1 Thess 4:14. Translators frequently obscure this fact to satisfy the popular assumption, fostered by the interchange of divine and human attributes in the fourth Gospel and the Nicene Creed, that Jesus raised himself.)

The astonishing appearances of the Risen Jesus were experienced by his disciples as confirmation of his message about the nearness of God's end-time Kingdom. They concluded, therefore, that since the end-time events had mysteriously begun to unfold with the Resurrection of Jesus, the whole world would quickly come to an end and all the dead would be raised and judged with the living.

Jesus' disciples remembered that he had spoken of the exalted Son of Man as the one appointed by God to preside over the end-time (Lk 12:8; Mk 8:38). They then correctly realized that the Risen Jesus had been revealed to them as that mysterious Son of Man. But they incorrectly assumed that Jesus would quickly return in glory to judge the living and the dead. Accordingly, the title Son of Man was the first regal title conferred on the Risen Jesus by the church. Luke tells us that around three years after Jesus' resurrection, it was still the title for Jesus used by Stephen as he witnessed to a hostile crowd of Jews in Jerusalem:

> Now when they heard these things they were enraged . . . and he said, "Behold, I see the heavens opened, and the Son of Man standing at the right hand of God." (Acts 7:54a, 56)

Initially, the disciples did not consider giving the title Messiah to Jesus. For they remembered that Jesus had vigorously rejected the title at Caesarea Philippi (Mk 8:27–29, 33) and had refused to discuss it at his interrogation by Pontius Pilate (Mk 15:2). Furthermore, the ignominious outcome of Jesus' mission was so painfully contrary to Jewish Messianic expectations that to think of him as Messiah seemed impossible.

Nevertheless, as the disciples had more time to reflect on Jesus' tragic fate and its glorious outcome, they began to consider the possibility and even the necessity of giving him the title Messiah. They were historically encouraged to do so for a variety of reasons:

1. Many devout Jews, because of their faith in the words of God's prophets, still expected a Davidic Messiah to be instrumental in bringing definitive salvation to Israel (and, through her, to the nations). This hope had been given a variety of expressions, but it more commonly took either of the two following forms:
    a. some form of two-stage apocalyptic hope for an ideal and invincible Davidic king who would preside over the conclusion of history and the establishment of God's Everlasting Reign over the New Creation;
    b. the traditional expectation of an ideal Davidic king who would conquer the nations and inaugurate the Golden Age within history.

(The nonmilitary eschatology in the Book of Daniel which Jesus seems to have embraced had probably, by his time, been largely replaced by the militarism of the two-stage apocalypses.)

2. These same devout Jews would have insisted that the many prophetic promises of a Davidic Messiah had to be fulfilled.

These promises began with the pledge of a permanent dynasty which Nathan the prophet, acting as God's spokesman, had made to David:

2 Sam 7:13–14, 16

When your days are fulfilled and you lie down with your fathers, I will raise up your offspring after you, who shall come forth from your body . . . and I will establish the throne of his kingdom forever. . . . And your house and your kingdom shall be made sure for ever before me; your throne shall be established for ever.

Because of Nathan's prophecy to David, many of the prophets during the period of the Exile and thereafter continued to promise that God would raise up a descendant of David to be God's instrument in restoring David's kingdom and in bringing conclusive salvation to Israel:

Ps 89:3

You have said, "I have made a covenant with my chosen one, I have sworn to David my servant: 'I will establish your descendants, and build your throne for all generations.'"

Ps 89:34–37

I will not violate my covenant, or alter the word that went forth from my lips. Once for all I have sworn by my holiness; I will not lie to David. His line shall endure for ever, his throne as long as the sun before me. Like the moon it shall be established forever; it shall stand firm while the skies endure.

Is 11:1

There shall come forth a shoot from the stump of Jesse [David's father], and a Branch shall grow out of his roots.

Jer 23:5

Behold, the days are coming, says the Lord, when I will raise up for David a righteous Branch, and he shall reign

> as king and deal wisely, and shall execute justice and righteousness in the land.

Jer 33:20

> Thus says the Lord, "If you can break my covenant with the day and my covenant with the night, so that day and the night will not come at the appointed time, then also my covenant with David my servant may be broken, so that he shall not have a son to reign on his throne."

Ezek 34:23–24

> And I shall set over them one shepherd, my servant David, and he shall feed them; he shall feed them and be their shepherd. And I, the Lord, will be their God, and my servant David shall be prince among them; I, the Lord, have spoken.

Hos 3:5

> Afterward the children of Israel shall return and seek the Lord their God and David their king; and they shall come in fear to the Lord and to his goodness in the latter days.

Amos 9:11

> In that day, I will raise up the booth of David that is fallen and repair its breaches, and raise up its ruins, and rebuild it as in the days of old.

Zec 12:8–9

> On that day the Lord shall put a shield about the inhabitants of Jerusalem so that the feeblest among them on that day shall be like David, and David shall be like God, like the angel of the Lord, at their head. And on that day I will seek to destroy all the nations that come against Jerusalem.

3. Jesus' disciples believed that he was descended from David. This meant that, despite his jarring history, Jesus possessed the basic Messianic requirement. There is no way of proving that Jesus

was descended from King David. The fact remains, however, that the apostolic church believed that he was:

Rom 1:1, 3

Paul, a servant of Jesus Christ, called to be an apostle, set apart for the gospel of God . . . concerning his Son, who was descended from David according to the flesh.

Acts 13:22–23

And . . . he raised up David to be their king; of whom he testified and said, "I have found in David the son of Jesse a man after my own heart, who will do all my will." Of this man's posterity God has brought to Israel a Savior, Jesus, as he promised.

1 Tim 2:8

Remember Jesus Christ, risen from the dead, descended from David, as preached in my gospel.

Rev 22:16 (see also 5:5)

I Jesus have sent my angel to you with this testimony for the churches. I am the root and the offspring of David, the bright morning star.

4. It is quite possible that two-stage apocalyptic teaching had already begun to assign Messianic titles to the end-time king called the Son of Man (1 Enoch 48:10; 52:4; 2 Esdras 7:28; 13:3–4; 51–52). If it had, then that development made it possible to reconcile traditional Messianic hope with the new end-time expectation introduced in the Book of Daniel.

5. The exalted end-time king (and Kingdom) promised in Daniel 7:13–14 (and 2:44) could be understood midrashically as a hidden foreshadowing of God's "secret" Messianic purpose accomplished in a spiritual manner through the exalted Jesus. This interpretation also explained why Jesus was raised individually before the General Resurrection.

6. Jesus had sternly rebuked Peter at Caesarea Philippi for assigning him the title Messiah (Mk 8:27–29, 33). Yet, Jesus'

noncommittal response to the title when he was questioned by Pontius Pilate allowed the disciples to wonder: Did Jesus perhaps know that God secretly intended him to be an unexpected spiritual Messiah instead of a military Messiah?

> The charge against him read, "The king of the Jews." (Mk 15:27)

Added to the above considerations was the gradual recognition that although Jesus had not invincibly led Israel in military conquest of the nations and imposed God's law on them, he had nevertheless won a much greater victory over the "powers of darkness." This spiritual victory, the disciples realized, was God's assurance to Israel and the nations that they, too, through the power of faith and trust, could defeat death and all the other evils encountered in history. The attainability of Eternal Life and Joy in God's victorious end-time Kingdom had been divinely guaranteed in advance through the Risen and Spirit-mediating Jesus.

All of these considerations finally led the majority of Jesus' disciples to understand that it was profoundly fitting to proclaim Jesus as God's "Messiah." They realized that they had almost completely redefined the title. But they assumed that this redefinition was a necessary corrective called for by the sacred history of Jesus which had culminated in his Spirit-mediating appearances as Risen Lord.

(Not all the disciples of the Risen Jesus agreed that he should be given the title Messiah. Those disciples, for example, who belonged to the community that produced the Sayings Source [also called the Q sayings] refused to do so. They preferred to understand Jesus as the exalted Son of Man. Jesus is never called Messiah in the Sayings material. The leaders of the community that compiled the Sayings Source probably remembered that Jesus had rejected the title Messiah. For that reason, therefore, they would not accept the title's redefinition by Jesus' other disciples. It was probably for that reason that Mark refused to use the Sayings Source in his Gospel. Mark wrote his Gospel specifically to defend the secret nature of Jesus' spiritual messiahship. He would not, therefore, have wished to encourage the theological views of the community that embraced the Sayings Source.)

We may be sure that the redefinition of the title Messiah by Jewish Christians was vigorously contested by the Jews. Jewish objections, in turn, required the Jewish Christians to search the Scriptures for midrashic proof texts. The authority of Scripture was needed to support the Jewish Christian claim that God's "secret" Messianic purpose had all along been quite different from Israel's literally conceived military Messianism. The more important of these proof texts were woven into the sacred history of Jesus to aid in understanding and defending Jewish Christian faith in his disputed messiahship.

The Jews, no doubt, demanded to know why God would have concealed the true nature of the Messiah's mission. The church replied (in a culturally conditioned and apologetic fashion) that God had done so in order to prevent Satan, the prince of darkness, from comprehending and interfering with God's hidden Messianic purpose. The Messiah's secret mission was to destroy Satan's power over creation by undergoing an atoning death mysteriously presaged in the Scriptures:

> "Let us condemn him to a shameful death, for according to what he says, he will be protected."
>
> Thus they reasoned, but they were led astray, for their wickedness blinded them, and they did not know the secret purposes of God. (Wis 2:20–22)

The Messiah's death, in turn, made possible the victory of his resurrection which is God's assurance to humankind of liberation from sin and death.

Through the unexpected triumph of Jesus' resurrection the satanic powers that bring darkness and death into the world have been defeated in principle:

> Baptism . . . now saves you . . . through the Resurrection of Jesus Messiah, who has gone into heaven and is at the right hand of God, with angels, authorities, and powers subject to him. (1 Pet 3:22)

The subjugation of the demonic powers will be concluded when Jesus returns in glory to defeat death forever and inaugurate the New Creation:

> Then comes the end, when he delivers the Kingdom to God the Father after destroying every rule and every authority and power.(1 Cor 15:24–25)

The apostle Paul expressed the early church's faith in Jesus' "secretly" achieved victory over the powers of darkness when he declared:

> But we impart a secret and hidden wisdom of God, which God decreed before the ages for our glorification. None of the rulers of this age understood this; for if they had, they would not have crucified the Lord of glory. (1 Cor 2:7–8)

7.

The Christian assertion of Jesus' messiahship, however, involves a great paradox, for the majority of the Jews have obviously never acknowledged Jesus as Israel's promised Messiah. Why was Jesus rejected by the Jewish nation as a whole? The answer to this question is complex, but the basic reason, as we have already observed, is that Jesus was not the kind of Messiah anticipated by the Jews. How did this discrepancy between Jewish expectations and God's purpose arise historically? The following answer is that of a believing Christian. A believing Jew would obviously provide a different answer.

By repeatedly revealing the gift of divine Presence and Love to ancient Israel's prophets, God encouraged the prophets to infer and teach that God intended to bless Israel in the future with definitive salvation. The prophets correctly understood that a "promise" of sublime blessing to come was implicit in their privileged experience of God's repeated Self-communication. Consequently, they assured Israel that when her response to God's steadfast Love became acceptable, God would empower David's heir to conquer all the nations and teach them to submit to God's law.

This hope was expressed in the royal psalm sung on the day when David's successor was anointed and installed on David's throne. The king thus anointed was believed to have become the privileged representative of God's Kingly Reign on earth. (The anointed Son of David is speaking throughout the psalm we are about to read. The psalm was probably written during the brief period of glory when David's son Solomon ruled over his empire):

> Why do the nations conspire, and the peoples plot in vain? The kings of the earth . . . take council together against the Yahweh and his anointed [representative] saying, "Let us burst their bonds asunder and cast their cords from us."
>
> He who sits in heaven laughs; Yahweh has them in derision. Then he will speak to them in his wrath, and terrify them in his fury, saying, "I have set my king on Zion, my holy hill."
>
> I will tell of the decree of Yahweh: He said to me, "You are my son, today I have begotten you. Ask of me, and I will make the nations your heritage, and the ends of the earth your possession. You shall break them with a rod of iron, and dash them in pieces like a potters vessel."
>
> Now therefore, O kings, be wise; be warned, O rulers of the earth. Serve Yahweh with fear, with trembling kiss his feet, lest he be angry, and you perish in the way. (Ps 2:1–11)

Under the influence of the royal Davidic ideology, the prophets in the kingdom of Judah began to teach that when the ideal Son of David finally came and extended God's Reign over all the nations, the Golden Age would arrive. The Golden Age was to be a time of unprecedented longevity, fertility, and security. There would then be no more injustice or warfare on earth, and all the nations would come to know and serve the God of Israel:

> It shall come to pass in the latter days that the mountain of the house of the Lord shall be established as the highest of the mountains, and shall be raised above the hills; and all the nations shall flow to it, and many people shall come and say, "Come, let us go up to the mountain of the Lord, to the house of the God of Jacob; that he may teach us his ways and that we may walk in his paths."

> For out of Zion shall go forth the law, and the word of the Lord from Jerusalem. He shall judge between the nations, and shall decide for many peoples; and they shall beat their swords into plowshares, and their spears into pruning hooks; nation shall not lift up sword against nation, neither shall they learn war any more. (Is 2:2–4; see also Mic 4:1–4)

We find another early expression of this hope in Isaiah 9:2–7. Isaiah's lyrical prophecy was probably occasioned by the birth of King Ahaz's son and heir, Hezekiah. This royal heir was born after a period of crisis which threatened David's dynasty with extinction. Isaiah clearly hoped that the child Hezekiah would become the righteous king who would establish the Golden Age:

> **Is 9:2–3**
>
> The people who walked in darkness have seen a great light; those who dwelt in a land of deep darkness, on them has light shined. You have multiplied the nation, you have increased its joy. They rejoice before you as with joy at the harvest, as men rejoice when they divide the spoil.
>
> **Is 9:5–7**
>
> For every boot of the tramping warrior in battle tumult and every garment rolled in blood will be burned as fuel for the fire. For to us a child is born, to us a son is given; and the government will be upon his shoulder, and his name shall be called "Wonderful Counselor, Mighty God, Everlasting Father, Prince of Peace."
>
> Of the increase of his government and of peace there will be no end, and upon the throne of David, and over his kingdom, to establish it and to uphold it with justice and with righteousness from this time forth and for evermore. The zeal of the Lord of hosts will do this.

In a related oracle, a post-Exilic disciple of Isaiah became even more exuberant in describing the Golden Age. The Golden Age, he declared, would return the original innocence and freedom from violence that characterized the Garden of Eden before the Fall. Everything would then be restored except immortality:

> The wolf shall dwell with the lamb, and the leopard shall lie down with the kid, and the calf and the lion and the fatling together, and a little child shall lead them, The cow and the bear shall feed; their young shall lie down together; and the lion shall eat straw like the ox.
>
> The sucking child shall play over the hole of the asp, and the weaned child shall put his hand in the adder's den. They shall not hurt or destroy in all my holy mountain; for the earth shall be full of the knowledge of the Lord as the waters cover the sea. (Is 11:6–9)

God never intended that the promise of future "salvation" implicit in God's revelatory Self-communications would be attained by military conquest. It was the prophets who assumed, in a culturally and historically conditioned fashion, that a final state of peace and justice for humankind could only be attained through military imposition of God's law on all the nations.

The post-Exilic prophets assumed, therefore, that since God had promised David an unending dynasty (2 Sam 7:11–15), God would surely raise up a Davidic Warrior-Messiah as the instrument through whom Israel's kingdom would be restored and universal justice would be imposed on earth. By such means, the prophets concluded, God would restore God's Kingly Reign over the Kingdom of creation disrupted by Adam of old.

Initially, Israel thought the salvation God had promised her would come within history in the form of the Golden Age. Only later, after the Book of Daniel had been written, did she learn to hope for Everlasting Life in the New Creation. The Book of Daniel did not suggest that either an heir of David or a military conquest would contribute to the arrival of the New Creation. Nor did it state that the king of the end-time alluded to as the Son of Adam (Dan 7:13–14) would be a leader of earthly armies.

Many of the Jews, however, did not abandon their traditional hope for a manifestly regal and victorious Messiah from David's line. After the crisis caused by the Syrian persecution in 168 B.C.

had passed, they combined the traditional Messianic hope for the Golden Age with the new eschatological hope introduced in the Book of Daniel. This combined hope is expressed in the "two-stage" apocalypses which appeared after the Book of Daniel. It is also voiced in the eschatological teaching of some of the rabbis preserved in the Talmud.

By way of illustration, one of these apocalypses, 2 Esdras, teaches that God's Messiah will come and win a decisive victory over all the nations; he will then reign gloriously for 400 years (probably to compensate for the 400 years of oppression in Egypt). All who have shared in the Messiah's victory will enjoy miraculous prosperity and longevity (7:28). This abbreviated Golden Age will conclude with the end of the world; it will be followed by the resurrection of the dead, the General Judgment (7:31–35) and, finally, the New Creation (7:75). In the Talmud, some of the rabbis refer to these two consecutive stages of expected salvation as (1) "the days of the Messiah" and (2) "the world to come."

Because of such combinations of traditional and eschatological hope, many of the Jews at the time of Jesus believed the Messiah would come as a military leader who would triumphantly establish the Reign of God on earth as a preamble to the New Creation. This blend of nationalistic and eschatological hope is understandable when considered in the light of ancient Israel's history. However, it fell woefully short of the spiritual salvation which God had envisioned for humans from the outset.

8.

When God raised Jesus as the Good News from God to Israel and the nations, a number of concurrent circumstances providentially expedited the success of the apostolic witnessing:

1. Roman law and order brought unprecedented freedom from the dangers of warfare, piracy, and banditry. This freedom enabled the apostles and disciples of Jesus to travel with relative safety by land and sea from the eastern to the western side of the Roman Empire.

2. The Greek language (which had been spread by Alexander the Great in the final third of the fourth century B.C.) was spoken

in all of the cities and large towns of the Roman Empire and well beyond. The apostles, therefore, could be understood in all of the larger communities of the empire (and far beyond) to which they carried the Good News. (This circumstance explains why the New Testament was written in Greek.)

3. In every city in the empire to which the apostles came, there was usually a community of monotheistic Jews who gathered every Sabbath to study the law of Moses and the writings of the prophets. Gentiles who admired Jewish monotheism were allowed to become fully observant converts (proselytes), or to sit in the rear of the synagogue as worshipers (God-fearers) during the service.

(Before the Romans destroyed the Jerusalem temple in A.D. 70, the synagogue ordinarily gathered in a large room of a private residence. There are many written references to synagogues before the destruction of the second temple. But there is very little uncontested evidence for the existence of a building used exclusively for the synagogue service [and related community functions] until the middle of the second century A.D. The ancient Jewish practice of gathering for worship in the houses of community members explains why the earliest Christians, who were Jews, established house-churches.)

4. Belief in the resurrection of the dead was introduced to the Jews in the Book of Daniel c. 165 B.C. (see Dan 12:2). Since the Book of Daniel was read and explained at the Sabbath gatherings in Palestine and the Diaspora (all the territory outside of Palestine where Jews had settled), its end-time teaching about the resurrection of the dead had become part of the theological tradition of the synagogues scattered throughout the empire and beyond.

As the apostles journeyed throughout the ancient world to proclaim the Good News, they always found the location of the Jewish synagogue in any given city. When the Sabbath arrived, they attended the synagogue service and, after the readings from the law and the prophets, they would seek an opportunity to speak to the assembled community. Since the ancient synagogue service was basically egalitarian in spirit, their request was usually granted.

The apostles would then proclaim that the salvation promised by the law and the prophets had finally arrived. The Risen Jesus, they announced, is God's conclusive assurance that Israel and the nations can be saved from tragedy, absurdity, and death, and can attain Eternal Life. The Jews and worshiping Gentiles who believed the testimony of the apostles then became the beginning of the Christian faith community in that region. In the Acts of the Apostles, we find a summarized account of how the apostles customarily carried out their task:

Acts 13:13–15

> Now Paul and his company . . . came to Antioch in Pisidia. And on the Sabbath day they went into the synagogue and sat down. After the reading of the law and the prophets, the rulers of the synagogue sent to them, saying, "Brethren, if you have any word of exhortation for the people, say it."

Acts 13:16–33

> So Paul stood up, and motioning with his hand said, "Men of Israel, and you that fear God, listen. The God of this people Israel . . . raised up David to be their king. . . . Of this man's posterity God has brought to Israel a Savior, Jesus, as he promised . . . God raised him from the dead, and . . . he appeared to those . . . who are now his witnesses to the people. And we bring you the Good News that what God promised to the fathers, this he has fulfilled to us their children by raising Jesus from the dead."

Acts 13:43

> And when the meeting of the synagogue broke up, many Jews and devout converts to Judaism followed Paul and Barnabas, who spoke to them and urged them to continue in the grace of God.

In his Letter to the Romans, Paul the apostle explains that the process by which individuals are called to faith in the Risen Jesus through the apostolic testimony actually involves two distinct yet intimately related stages of "witnessing." The first and preliminary stage is the apostolic witnessing itself delivered externally in history. (This stage is continued by the church's mission of preaching the Good News):

> But how are men to call upon him in whom they have not believed? And how are they to believe in him of whom they have never heard? And how are they to believe without a preacher? And how can men preach unless they are sent? As it is written, "How beautiful are the feet of those who preach Good News." . . . So faith comes from what is heard, and what is heard comes by the preaching of Christ. (Rom 10:14–15, 17)

The second and conclusive stage of witnessing is the internal testimony of God in which God "confirms" the truth of the external apostolic proclamation by pouring the experienceable gift of God's reassuring love (the Holy Spirit) into our hearts:

> And hope does not disappoint us, because God's love has been poured into our hearts through the Holy Spirit which has been given to us. (Rom 5:5)

We finally decide to believe in the Good News delivered by the apostles because of our experience of the inner witnessing of God's own Spirit (the transcendent peace, joy, and love that accompany, encourage, and corroborate a faith-filled hearing of God's word):

> When we cry "Abba! Father!" it is the Spirit himself bearing witness with our spirit that we are the children of God. (Rom 8:15–16)

The gift of God's Spirit, Paul tells us, is given to us as a foretaste and "guarantee" (*arrabona*) of the joy and love which await us in Eternal Life:

> But it is God who . . . has . . . given us his Spirit in our hearts as a guarantee. (2 Cor 1:21–22)

Paul understands that the preliminary preaching of the Good News which prepares us for God's inner witnessing and the resulting gift of "confirmed" faith is an essential part of God's revelatory purpose in history. For God's confirming testimony is nonverbal and would be ambiguous without the external apostolic witnessing which precedes and supplies it with essentially correct historical meaning. Paul emphasizes, accordingly, that the apostolic witnessing, although secondary and instrumental, is nevertheless essential to God's conclusive revelation of God's saving purpose for humankind.

God's wisdom fully comprehends that nothing can be consciously grasped by an inquiring mind without the mediation of a clarifying word. To insure that God's definitive Self-disclosure would be intelligible, God inspired the apostles (through the Risen Jesus and the gift of the Spirit) to bring into being a privileged constellation of words called the "apostolic proclamation."

The substance of this historically privileged proclamation has been preserved in the New Testament. The inspired words and sacred symbols of the New Testament insure that throughout the remainder of history there will always be a faith community able to grasp and proclaim the meaning of God's conclusive Self-communication. Through the Risen Jesus and the foretaste of the Spirit, God is assuring us that we can reach Eternal Life and participate in the Joy of God's Eternal Self-exploration.

Questions for Review and Discussion

1. Why did Jesus choose twelve of his disciples to assist him regularly with his prophetic mission?

2. Why can we be reasonably certain that Jesus himself actually did choose the Twelve?

3. How did God "inform" Jesus that the Baptizer was indeed God's prophet?

4. After the Baptizer was imprisoned, why did he send his disciples to ask Jesus about Jesus' identity and mission?

5. When did Jesus probably discover that God had elected him to be the exalted Son of Man and God's Messiah?

What reasons can be adduced in defense of the answer you gave?

6. What correct insight and what mistaken assumption are present in Mark's Messianic Secret theology?

7. Why did Jesus probably refuse to discuss the title Messiah when he was questioned by Pontius Pilate?

8. Why were Jesus' disciples initially unwilling to think of him as God's Messiah, and what are some of the probable considerations which eventually changed their minds?

9. Why did the early church think that God had kept God's true Messianic purpose a secret until Jesus' resurrection?

10. Why did the majority of the Jews reject the claims of the Jewish Christians about the spiritual messiahship of Jesus?

11. What prophetic experiences and historical developments seem to have led to the Jewish expectation of a manifestly royal and invincible military Messiah?

12. Why did God send a spiritual Messiah so ostensibly contrary to Israel's expectations?

13. What four historical developments providentially expedited the success of the apostolic witnessing to the Resurrection of Jesus?

14. According to Paul the apostle, what is the second form of witnessing which always accompanies and confirms the apostolic witnessing?

Chapter Ten

Remaining Questions

The answers to the following questions presuppose that the reader has read the preceding nine chapters. If the reader has not done so, the answers will not be fully intelligible.

1. **If the explanations of the Bible given in this book are basically correct, does that mean the church has been reading the Bible incorrectly for centuries?**

The church's literal reading of the Bible in past centuries was not incorrect but, rather, less correct in some respects. A literal reading of Scripture is not devoid of truth. The general meaning of the inspired biblical text is usually accessible to any sincere reader or hearer even when the text is understood literally. Prior to the Enlightenment (c. A.D. 1650-1800), a literal reading of the Bible ordinarily caused no serious problems.

A literal reading of the ancient Scriptures, however, is unwittingly burdened with a number of naive assumptions from the past that are joined together with enduring truths about God. When the increasing knowledge of later ages detects and criticizes these naive assumptions, their nonliteral (and nonessential) nature should be readily granted, and they should be explained accordingly.

But all too often the conservative tendencies of religious people prompt them to cling defensively to the comforting certainties of the past, and they resist necessary change. This mistaken resistance causes the timeless religious truth in the sacred Scriptures to be compromised, and their valid meaning is rendered suspect in the eyes of the increasingly educated public.

The unwillingness of some conservatives to relinquish the outmoded and nonessential religious ideas of the past is the result of their mistaken identification of past interpretations of God (and the world) with the reality of God. They sincerely fear that if they deny outmoded biblical assumptions about God, they will be denying God, and they understandably reject that possibility as intolerable.

In such a situation, the absolute authority of God is mistakenly conferred upon merely relative human expressions about God (and the God-human relationship). This mistaken transfer results in the subtle and insidious form of idolatry called *bibliolatry* (idolatrous worship of the Bible). Any time we equate something finite and created with God, and assign God's dignity to it, we are guilty of idolatry and are breaking the first and most important of the Ten Commandments.

Those who are guilty of bibliolatry usually assume that God has dictated all the words in the Bible, and that these words should be identified with God and given divine or absolute authority. Contemporary scholarship, however, emphatically rejects such a view of revelation as oversimplified and mythological.

God does not dictate words to the prophets; rather, God communicates an experience of God's own Presence and Love. (Most adult Christians "know" from experience that God's Self-communication is undeniably real but nonverbal.) Under the impact of God's Self-communication, the prophets are enabled to see how to use language in creative new ways to teach about the reality of God and the God-human relationship. The Bible, therefore, does contain words "given" to us by God. But God gave us these words indirectly by inspiring a free and intelligent human to speak words in God's service.

Even though it is true that the words spoken by the prophets and the evangelists are divinely inspired, it is also true that they are culturally conditioned and historically limited. When expressing their inspired insights into the mystery of God and the God-human relationship, the inspired authors of the Bible included a number of assumptions and teaching devices present in their tradition. These assumptions and conventions were thought to be true or necessary at that time, but later ages, because of increased experience, will find many of them mistaken or no longer adequate without qualification.

When the words which God inspired the biblical authors to write are identified with God and are given the absolute authority that belongs to God alone, those words soon become the enemy of the spiritual progress which God is continually encouraging throughout history. All of the words in the Bible are inspired (they were written by an author who was moved by an experience of God to teach in God's service), but only those inspired words that speak with enduring validity about God and the God-human relationship are truly the "word of God."

2. Why do Christians continue to read the ancient Jewish Scriptures?

We do so for several reasons. To begin with, the ancient Jewish Scriptures contain the history of Israel's divinely encouraged journey from polytheism through henotheism to exclusive monotheism. The record of this journey is profoundly significant in its own right, for it helps us to understand the origin and development of many of our present ideas about God and the God-human relationship. Moreover, the religious symbols in the Bible have entered into the very fabric of our Western culture. We cannot understand the history and meaning of Western painting, sculpture, architecture, music, drama, literature, law, theology, and even philosophy, unless we are acquainted with the sacred stories and symbols in the Bible.

More importantly, Christian faith sees the Risen and Spirit-mediating Jesus as the culmination of God's Self-disclosure in ancient Israel and all of history. The Risen Jesus is God's definitive answer to humankind's ultimate questions. He is God's assurance that we humans can truly transcend tragedy, injustice, and repugnant death, and can participate in God's Eternal Discovery and Joy. If we truly wish to understand Jesus and the Good News from God which was revealed to the world through him, we must understand the sacred tradition which prepared for him and still renders him intelligible. Jesus claimed to be a conclusive prophet for the God who is spoken of throughout the ancient Jewish Scriptures.

Furthermore, Jesus and the first Christians were Jews. These Jewish Christians drew repeatedly on the ancient Jewish Scriptures to provide their interpretation of Jesus' definitive revelatory significance for the world. We cannot understand the Gospels unless we understand why their authors wrote about Jesus as they did and where they obtained the ideas they employed to defend their faith in him. It was for reasons such as these that St. Jerome, the greatest of the ancient Christian biblical scholars (A.D. 342-420), asserted that whoever is ignorant of the Old Testament is ignorant of Christ.

3. Does the interpretation of the Gospels presented in this book deny genuine Christian faith in Jesus?

To enter into dialog with the interpretation of the Gospels presented in this book will actually strengthen and deepen one's faith-understanding of Jesus. Our faith in Jesus as God's Good News to the world will be more meaningful and secure if we learn that it is essentially compatible with a scientific world view. Whenever unquestioned assumptions of a legendary or mythological kind are operating unconsciously in our faith-understanding, our faith is in some sense vulnerable. For if we were to experience a convincing refutation of these unquestioned assumptions, there is a possibility that our faith experience might be abandoned along with our outmoded faith-understanding.

This danger is especially present if those criticizing our understanding of our faith experience are atheists, agnostics, or ill-informed believers. Such persons will offer nothing new, positive, and reasonable to replace a discredited understanding of our faith. It is beneficial, therefore, to enter into dialog with Christians whose faith-understanding agrees with the essentials of the apostolic witnessing and is integrated with a scientific worldview. If such Christians convince us that some aspect of our faith-understanding is outmoded, they usually do so while advancing a new understanding which can successfully replace the old one.

Even conservative Christians who reject the critical interpretations of the Gospels expressed in this book will come away from it with a more secure faith-understanding. For unconsciously, if not consciously, they will be reassured by the knowledge that Christians who think critically and scientifically share the essentials of their own faith. If ever their customary faith-understanding ceases to suffice, they will know that there exists a set of answers to critical questions which is essentially compatible with the reasonable demands of contemporary science.

4. **Do contemporary biblical scholars believe that God was truly present and acting during the Exodus event, and that God miraculously caused all the wonders recounted in the Book of Exodus?**

Contemporary biblical scholars agree that God was indeed present and acting during the Exodus event. But they believe that God manifested God's Self internally in the minds and hearts of religiously concerned Hebrews in a way that reassured and encouraged them when they experienced the discouraging and even terrifying events in their history. God's experienced Presence reassured and encouraged the Hebrews during their struggle for deliverance from oppression in Egypt and during their sometimes frightening journey through the harsh desert.

God knew that the Hebrews would unconsciously project their vivid experience of God's Presence onto the external happenings of the Exodus event. Whenever these happenings seemed conducive to their unexpected escape or their survival in the desert, they naively assumed that God was intervening directly in the physical realm on their behalf. They then hyperbolized their interpretations of these events to call attention to their understanding of God's action on their behalf. God accommodated God's Self to their historically limited knowledge in order to encourage them to recognize two fundamental and closely related truths: (1) God is always present to those who believe and trust in God, and (2) God watches over them with providential Love and Care.

God also knew that in time humans would learn that God does not intervene in historical events in ways that contradict the laws of nature. God can and does cause miraculous occurrences in history. But when genuine miracles occur, they never contradict the laws of nature. On such occasions, (1) God works through human freedom which has opened itself to God, and (2) God then activates some paranormal possibility that is normally latent and inactive within human nature. Such supernatural activity on God's part does not contradict the laws of nature. Rather, it accelerates capacities present in nature in a manner which lies outside the range of the normal. When God intervenes miraculously in nature, God intensifies the rate at which natural results would normally occur, even if paranormal in kind. For one who has faith, such divine influence results in a supernatural sign event which points to God's saving Presence.

However, when the priest-historians who wrote the Book of Exodus describe an event in a manner which seems miraculous, we should not assume that the event actually was miraculous. If a recounted event contradicts the laws of nature, we should understand it as a form of hyperbolized folk poetry. Even if it does not necessarily contradict natural laws, we should still proceed with great caution, for an unusual or unexpected natural occurrence has possibly been interpreted mythologically. Such matters have to be judged carefully on a case-by-case basis.

Contemporary scholarship prefers the view that probably all the marvels recounted in the Book of Exodus have natural explanations which were not understood at that time. The truly supernatural element operating throughout the Exodus event was the subtle experience of God's Presence and Love conferred regularly on those Hebrews who had genuine faith in God.

The ancient Israelites were inspired by God to write a sacred history which vividly illustrated their experience of God's reassuring Presence in all the dangers through which they passed. This extraordinary history recounts that when they were overtaken by the tragedy and terror which periodically erupt in history, their faith in God enabled them to rise above their discouragement and their temptation to despair. Because of their reassuring experience of God's Presence during times of crisis, they were able to endure as a people and continue making their unique contribution to history as the first nation of exclusive monotheists.

God intended the religious lessons vividly enshrined in the Exodus event to help us understand that God is also present in the events of our personal history. God is always ready to strengthen, reassure, and guide us through the pain and tragedy which occur in our lives because of chance and misused freedom. If we learn to trust in God's providential care as ancient Israel did, we also can find the strength to live courageously and rise above our discouragement and temptation to despair.

When scientific method developed during the Enlightenment, it ushered in a period of religious ambiguity and skepticism during which even believing historians have become reluctant to speak about God for fear of sounding naive or mythological. Well in advance of this foreseeable development, God inspired the Israelites to write an interpretation of their historical experience that unhesitatingly employed arresting symbolism to point to God's saving Presence in the events of their lives.

God worked through the first nation of monotheists to provide succeeding ages with a sacred history which vividly testifies to the reality of God's Presence in our lives and hearts. God's comforting and reassuring Presence also journeys with us as we suffer the painful and ambiguous events which periodically threaten our existence. Reading the Exodus event with faith helps us understand that God intends to bring us safely to the promised land of unending participation in the adventure of God's Creative Discovery and Joy. This sublime promise is already implicit in our capacity for unlimited self-transcendence. But it is especially implicit in the encouraging foretaste of God's Love which is given to us from time to time as we sojourn in this life on our way to the true promised land of Eternal Life.

5. Did not Ezekiel 37:1–14 and Isaiah 26:19 teach about the resurrection of the dead before Daniel 12:2–3?

When Ezekiel 37:1 –14 speaks of God raising the dead, it is not teaching that God intends to raise individual Israelites from physical death to Everlasting Life as does Daniel 12:2 –3. Instead, it is using the idea of resurrection as a "metaphor" for the political restoration of the Israelite people after the Exile to Babylon in 587 B.C.:

> Then he said to me, "Son of man, these bones are the whole house of Israel. Behold they say, 'Our bones are dried up, and our hope is lost; we are clean cut off.' Therefore prophesy, and say to them, Thus says Yahweh God: Behold, I will open your graves, and raise you from your graves, O my people; and I will bring you home into the land of Israel. . . . " (Ezek 37:11 –12)

On the other hand, eschatological belief in the resurrection of the dead is truly being taught in Isaiah 26:19:

> Your dead shall live, their bodies shall rise. O dwellers in the dust, awake and sing for joy! For your dew is the dew of light, and on the land of the shades you wilt let it fall.

This verse, however, was placed in the writings of Isaiah by an anonymous apocalyptic teacher after the Book of Daniel was written. This anonymous prophet considered himself to be a disciple of Isaiah, and is sometimes referred to as "apocalyptic Isaiah."

6. **Do contemporary biblical scholars believe that Jesus truly expelled demons from people?**

All the strands of tradition gathered into the four Gospels affirm that Jesus enjoyed extraordinary success at healing people in God's name. Granted that Mark is prone to folk hyperbole, he is probably an essentially reliable witness when he reports that Jesus was renowned for having healed many people from various physical and psychological infirmities:

> And they brought to him all who were sick or possessed with demons. . . . And he healed many who were sick with various diseases, and cast out many demons. (Mk 2:32a, 34a)

Even those who rejected Jesus' prophetic authority could not deny his astonishing ability to free people from demonic torment. They maintained, however, that Jesus derived his power over demons from one of the rulers of the demons who assisted Jesus in order to lead the multitudes astray:

> And the scribes who came down from Jerusalem said, "He is possessed by Beelzebul, and by the prince of demons he casts out the demons."(Mk 3:22)

The apostolic church would never have invented such an ugly accusation; she only preserved it for the sake of Jesus' canny response:

> How can Satan cast out Satan? If a Kingdom is divided against itself it cannot stand. . . . And if Satan has risen up against himself and is divided, he cannot stand, but is coming to an end. (Mk 3:23b –24, 26)

This authentic saying of Jesus recalls another in which Jesus expressed his understanding of his power to perform exorcisms:

> But if it is by the finger of God that I cast out demons, then the kingdom of God has come upon you. (Lk 11:20)

The hostile charge brought against Jesus by his critics and his response to that charge remind us that in Jesus' day, illness, physical and psychological, was explained mythologically not scientifically. Jesus and his contemporaries, because of their historically limited knowledge, would have assumed that all mental illness and many physical infirmities were caused by demons (fallen angels). We should recall, for example, the "loathsome sores" which "Satan" inflicted on Job's body:

> So Satan went forth from the presence of Yahweh and afflicted Job with loathsome sores from the sole of his foot to the crown of his head. (Job 2:7)

In continuity with this mythological tradition, one of the stories in Mark's Gospel relates that Jesus healed an autistic boy who was thought to be afflicted by an evil spirit. However, when the boy's father describes his son's symptoms, it is apparent that the boy was probably suffering from epilepsy:

> Teacher, I brought my son to you, for he has a dumb spirit; and wherever it seizes him, it dashes him down; and he foams and grinds his teeth and becomes rigid. . . . And it has often cast him into the fire and into the water to destroy him. But if you can do anything, please have pity on us and help us.(Mk 9:17b –18a)

This story's sacred power to instruct our faith is not undone by the realization that the boy's problem was physiological not demonic. For no matter what explanation is employed, the boy, his parents, and their community were faced with a frightening problem. The boy's predicament, therefore, vividly exemplifies the terror of history from which God sent Jesus to free our minds and hearts. By healing the boy through Jesus, God was assuring us that the threatening evils in life which discourage us and tempt us to despair have no lasting power to harm us. God's saving power can finally heal us from all evil, regardless of whether that evil is explained mythologically or scientifically.

7. Did Jesus truly heal people of their physical and psychological infirmities?

We have already learned in the answer to question four that moderate scholarship believes genuine miracles occur. God truly healed people through Jesus to endorse Jesus' promise of God's Love and Forgiveness to all who believe and turn away from sin. This conclusion is reasonable because God continues to heal people miraculously in our day through their faith in Jesus. But moderate scholarship does not think genuine miracles ever violate the laws of nature.

A modern thinker recoils at the suggestion that God would interfere with or contradict nature's laws. Our God-given power of reason tells us that it is wrong for us to act illogically, contradictorily, or uneconomically. We conclude, therefore, that God does not act in such ways.

If God were to interfere with the laws of nature, that would mean that God was acting illogically and contradictorily by destroying the very laws which God is everywhere creating and upholding. Critical reason suggests, therefore, that if miraculous healings genuinely occur, they do not violate the laws of nature. There is probably a way to understand miraculous healings which is fundamentally in harmony with nature.

Any credible explanation of the miraculous should also take into account the "law of parsimony." This law states that hypothetical entities should never be multiplied beyond necessity. In other words, we should always prefer the explanation which allows us to assume the existence of fewer hypothetical entities rather than more. For if we humans can see that we should always act with economy and avoid waste or contradiction, it follows that God always acts with economy and logical consistency.

Accordingly, the miraculous healings wrought by God through Jesus should not be understood as unnatural but as "paranormal" in kind. Paranormal occurrences are those which fall outside the expected range of the "normal." They predictably seem strange and uncanny to us. Nevertheless, such occurrences still fall within the range of the "natural," albeit rarely and elusively. When a genuine miracle occurs, God activates and accelerates some latent paranormal potentiality which is not ordinarily operative in our experience. This divinely activated occurrence, however, does not contradict natural laws. Rather, it transcends their customary range and accelerates their natural rate of occurrence.

It seems likely that when God produced a miraculous healing through Jesus, God acted through (1) Jesus' willingness to serve as God's mediating instrument, and (2) the free request or hope of the person healed through Jesus. The divine influence mediated through Jesus activated and accelerated some latent therapeutic potentiality in the healed person's own nature. God's freely invited intervention resulted in a remission of the healed person's symptoms. And this extraordinary remission was correctly experienced as an act of God wrought through God's prophet, Jesus:

> Fear seized them all; and they glorified God, saying, "A great prophet has arisen among us!"and "God has visited his people!" (Lk 7:16)

Furthermore, by accelerating the remission of pathology, physical or mental, God would not have contradicted any laws of nature. For natural processes themselves can reverse physical or mental pathology. God's power, accordingly, can supernaturally engage and accelerate the healed person's own natural capacity to be healed under optimum conditions.

This contemporary understanding of a miracle clearly differs from the traditional view which assumes a divine contradiction of nature. Traditional insistence that a miracle is something which contradicts the laws of nature, and which only God, therefore, could have caused, is a form of folk hyperbole. This hyperbole unconsciously intends to insure that God is acknowledged as the cause of a miraculous sign. Those who advocate the traditional definition, however, are unnecessarily overstating their case.

Given the mythological naivete of the past, defending the possibility of miraculous healings will seem unacceptable to some in our skeptical age. Naivete, however, is not the exclusive prerogative of the uneducated. It is true that it would be wrong to return to the oversimplified explanations of the past. But it would also be wrong to presume that we can tie God's hands. Divine action which respects and works through freedom is not the same as interference. If we humans are able to creatively influence and accelerate natural processes, so can God if human freedom opens itself to God with faith and trust.

8. Were the ruler's daughter, the widow's son, and Lazarus truly dead when Jesus raised them?

Contemporary standards of reason tell us that it would contradict the laws of nature (and, therefore, be contrary to the creative purpose of God) for someone who had truly died to be brought back to life. Contemporary scholarship concludes, therefore, that anyone thought by the early church to have been "raised from the dead" by Jesus was not truly dead. Instead, such a person was probably in a coma judged to be dead by the prescientific standards of the ancient world. We know that on various occasions throughout history people have been buried when they were thought to be dead but were actually still alive in an unconscious state with drastically diminished vital signs.

Even if someone healed by Jesus was thought to be dead, but was actually still alive, the saving significance intended by God when God healed that person through Jesus remains essentially the same. God was signifying through such an event that no matter what the evils are that threaten us in life, including death, God's gracious love can ultimately save us from all such evils if we believe and trust in God's goodness as God taught us to do through Jesus.

9. Did Jesus truly "appear" to his apostles as Risen Lord after his tragic death?

Paul the apostle assures us that the Risen Jesus "appeared" to him (1 Cor 15:8) and to the other apostles (1 Cor 15:5–7) as a revelatory sign who could be "seen" (1 Cor 9:1). Yet Paul's understanding of Risen Life implies that when Jesus appeared to him Jesus had a "spiritual" body not a physical one (1 Cor 15:44–46, 50; Phil 3:21). Paul insisted that Jesus appeared to him and the other apostles as "somebody" whom they could see, but Paul realized that a physical body cannot appear and disappear the way the Risen Jesus did.

Moreover, a physical body can be observed by anyone in the area (if there is sufficient light). But the Risen Jesus was not ordinarily visible and was "seen" by only a few privileged witnesses on rare revelatory occasions. For these reasons, it seemed clear to Paul that the Risen Jesus now has a "spiritual" body not a "physical" one.

The question then arises, if the Risen Jesus no longer has a physical body on which physical light can shine, how could he be "seen" by the apostles as appearing? No one can answer this question with full certainly, but the following hypothesis seems reasonable and probable:

The Risen Jesus was probably able to communicate an awareness of his "personal presence" to his disciples in a paranormal *and* divinely graced way that triggered the release of his physical "appearance" from their memories and projected it onto their extraordinary experience of his invisible presence. The resulting revelatory "vision" of Jesus (accompanied by the revelatory communication of God's Holy Spirit) enabled the apostles to "see" the Risen Jesus "appearing" to them as God's assurance that we humans can truly defeat death and reach Eternal Life.

To repeat, the brief and astonishing experience of Jesus appearing "externally" was accompanied "internally" by a revelatory communication of God's Spirit (the divine Self-communication as Love). This simultaneous "inner experience" assured the apostles that God was there and that God's life-creating Love was the power which had enabled Jesus to transcend death and appear to them as God's Good News to the world (Jn 20:22; Rom 5:5).

We may be reasonably certain that the "Risen" Jesus did not literally "eat" with his disciples. Nor did he speak with them at length or join them as they journeyed. The "theological" narratives in which Jesus is described as doing these things are much later than the original reports of the brief revelatory "appearances" (1 Cor 15:3–8: 9:1) and are meant either to explain the sublime import of the "appearances" or to defend their reality against hostile attacks (Lk 24:36 –51).

These revelatory "appearances" of the Risen Jesus violated neither logic nor the laws of nature. They were not unnatural but paranormal in kind. (The paranormal occurs outside the expected range of the normal but is still within the realm of natural possibilities latent in nature.) The resulting revelatory "appearance," we should note, was not purely subjective. It was truly extramental in the sense that it was triggered by a mysterious but real encounter with the Risen Jesus who was truly present "outside" the experiencing subject. (For a contemporary explanation of Jesus' "appearances" and the later "resurrection narratives" based on them, see *Exploring the Resurrection of Jesus* in this series.)

10. Was Jesus the first human to enter Eternal Life?

Jesus was the first human to pass through death and to appear as a definitive sign from God that humans can reach Eternal Life. However, Jesus was probably not the first human to go through the event of death into God's Eternal Life of Discovery and Joy.

Contemporary scholarship concludes that all humans, since the beginning, who have tried to follow their conscience and live a responsible life (as they understood it) have probably been enabled by God to evolve through death into Eternal Life. But humans who were still living within history before God raised Jesus were either unaware or uncertain of this. Consequently, they were fearful of what might lie beyond death. It was precisely to free humans from such fear and uncertainty that God empowered the Risen Jesus to appear to his disciples and to begin mediating the foretaste of the Holy Spirit (the experience of God's reassuring and implicitly forgiving Presence and Love).

The Genesis creation and fall stories taught the ancient Hebrews that humans had originally been immortal but had lost Everlasting Life through moral failure. Eventually, however, God encouraged the author of the Book of Daniel to teach the Jews that they could "regain," at the end of history, the Unending Life which they believed Adam and Eve had lost for humankind at the beginning.

When the Jews began to believe (c. 165 B.C.) that they could regain immortality at the end of history, they assumed that the righteous dead were waiting in the upper part of Sheol (the place where the righteous dead were detained) for the end of the world, the Final Judgment, and entry into the New Creation. And since the earliest Christians were Jews, they held the same view. The early church concluded, therefore, that the righteous dead would have to wait in upper Sheol until Jesus returned at the end of history to judge the living and the dead. After the Final Judgment, all the righteous dead, they believed, would be taken by Jesus into the New Creation (see 1 Thess 4:13–17).

Contemporary scholarship, however, no longer accepts the mythological assumptions about human destiny that guided the thinking of the ancient Jews and early Christians. There is no good reason to believe that humans who have tried to live responsible lives will be kept in a mythological place of detention or state of incompletion until the end of the world.

The highly respected theologian Karl Rahner (1904-1984) reminds us (*Theological Investigations,* v. 4) that the only final human state beyond death about which God has revealed something definite to us is the victorious passage of the Risen Jesus into God's Eternal Life. All the other teaching in the New Testament about final states represents inspired but historically limited speculation. We have not only a right but a duty to revise such precritical speculation (and also critical speculation) when advances in knowledge require it.

11. If God never dictates words to anyone, how did the Risen Jesus learn that he had been chosen to be God's secret Messiah?

We cannot know with certainty how Jesus learned that he is God's Messiah, but the following inferred explanation seems reasonable: When the Risen Jesus evolved through death into Risen Life, he immediately understood that his Risen Life sublimely confirmed the substance of his Kingdom message. He desired, therefore, to communicate with his disciples to assure them of his participation in God's Eternal Life. He also wanted to encourage them to continue proclaiming his Kingdom message in God's service. And since Jesus' desire was in full accord with God's own revelatory purpose, God encouraged Jesus (nonverbally) to communicate with his disciples. Initially, however, the Risen Jesus probably had no awareness of being God's Messiah. Rather, he called his apostles to witness to his Risen Life as confirmation of his Kingdom message, not his messiahship.

When the disciples experienced the Spirit-mediating appearances of the Risen Jesus, they concluded that God had revealed him to them as the mysterious and exalted Son of Man of whom Jesus had spoken. "Son of Man," therefore, was the first regal title conferred on Jesus by his disciples. The history of Jesus was so incompatible with the traditional meaning of the title Messiah that, at first, his disciples thought it impossible even to consider assigning that title to him. Accordingly, they began their witnessing to the Risen Jesus by proclaiming him as the exalted Son of Man who would soon return in glory as Judge of the end-time and King of the New Creation.

The Jews, to be sure, rejected this eschatological claim by reminding the Jewish Christians of the many prophetic promises of a Davidic Messiah. They demanded to know how the claims made for Jesus by his disciples could be reconciled with the words of God's prophets without denying them. Such a challenge forced Jesus' disciples to reconsider their original assumptions in the light of the Jewish Scriptures.

Fairly soon they realized that the spiritual victory of Jesus' Spirit-releasing resurrection and his descent from David indicated that Jesus, albeit jarringly and unexpectedly, truly is God's Messiah. They also understood that God had all along intended to send a spiritual Messiah to Israel. The disciples then redefined the title with Messianic Secret theology and proclaimed that the title belonged to the Risen Jesus. It was probably at this time that Jesus learned what his disciples had discovered about his hidden role in God's Messianic purpose. He then grasped that, in addition to being a conclusive guarantee from God of Eternal Life in God's coming Kingdom, he was also the one through whom God had fulfilled the Messianic promises made to David and Israel.

When he arrived at Eternal Life, the Risen Jesus would have had no real incentive to rethink and almost totally redefine the title Messiah. Because of its traditional connotations of military violence, Jesus had rejected the title as incompatible with his understanding of the coming restoration of God's Reign over creation. It was Jesus' disciples who, in their debates with the Jews, were confronted with the need to redefine the title and reconcile the word of God with the history of Jesus. Nothing is as conducive to rethinking presuppositions as vigorous opposition.

Contemporary parapsychology informs us that when two persons share a strong family tie or deep love bond, it sometimes happens that one of them can be vividly aware of what is happening to the other, even when great distance is involved. A paranormal spiritual power latent in our nature becomes activated on such occasions and makes possible the extraordinary state of consciousness then experienced. It is reasonable to assume that in Risen Life our paranormal spiritual capacities are intensified and perfected rather than diminished.

The Risen Jesus shared a deep love bond with his disciples, and this personal bond probably enabled him to know with paranormal spiritual power what they had concluded about his mysterious Messianic dignity. The existence of such paranormal spiritual power is presupposed by traditional Christian belief in the "communion of saints." This traditional belief avers that the conscious fellowship that exists between us and our loved ones on earth continues even if they reach Eternal Life before us. They continue in Eternal Life to love and encourage us. The Risen Jesus, therefore, continued to love and encourage his disciples and, in his paranormal awareness of them, he learned of their decision to identify and proclaim him as God's secret Messiah. He probably also discerned from his constant experience of God's Self-communication that God fully endorsed this development.

12. Since the electrical impulses required for consciousness are derived from the material body, how do Christians answer the objection that there can be no consciousness after the dissolution of the body at death?

It is true that the electrical impulses required for spiritual (rational, self-transcending) consciousness are derived from the material body. But we have learned from twentieth-century physics (beginning with Albert Einstein) that matter and energy are convertible ($E = mc^2$). Energy, therefore, is an ultra-subtle and invisible form of matter, and matter is a concentrated and visible form of energy. We have also been taught by the Life philosophers (e.g., Emile Bergson, Pierre Teilhard de Chardin) that human spirit (the power of unlimited self-transcendence) is the most complex form of energy released by the evolutionary process.

This insight suggests that our spiritual center (traditionally called the spiritual soul), which can anticipate transcending our physical body's dissolution, is actually a subtle form of matter. This subtle form of matter can be thought of as the "spiritual body" which is the subtle precipitate of our physical body's dissolution. As such, it is the subtle material source of the subtle electrical impulses required for transformed consciousness beyond death. Given this monistic interpretation of human spirit, there is no compelling reason why human consciousness cannot transcend death. And there are impressive indications in our self-transcending design that it probably does. (Scientific monism assumes that everything in the universe is a form of energy.)

13. Does belief in Eternal Life and unending consciousness after death contradict the law of entropy which says that all things in the universe will eventually run out of the undissipated energy necessary for work (or continued activity)?

In the physical dimension, energy always tends toward maximum *entropy* or heat death. (Entropy is the decline in ordered or undissipated energy available to do work in any physical system). There are indications in our experience, however, that the law of entropy is transcended (is no longer operative) in the dimension of spirit.

We have already observed that spiritual energy is the most complex form of energy released by the evolutionary process. (Spirit is the power of unlimited self-transcendence; the power to engage in creative discovery and attainment with mathematical infinity.) Our self-transcending design implies that human spirit has been programmed to lock into everlasting *permanence* when it emerges from the evolutionary process. This conclusion cannot be experimentally verified but it can be experientially verified when we reflect on our astonishing ability to think about unending permanence, infinity (mathematical and metaphysical), eternity, and immortality.

Human spirit possesses the power to think about everlasting permanence even though nothing in our universe is everlastingly permanent. The ability to think about such permanence was probably programmed into our spiritual design to enable us to creatively anticipate our death-transcending destiny. This recognition allows us to conclude with good reason that the spiritual body which transcends physical dissolution also transcends the law of entropy. The spiritual energy which makes conscious activity possible beyond death is no longer bound by physical laws. Spiritual energy is permanently recycled instead of being degraded and does not arrive at maximum entropy or heat death.

14. Why is it reasonable to hope for immortality beyond the dissolution of our physical bodies?

Design implies destiny. The design of any being's nature indicates the goals it can or cannot attain in the universal order of things. If a man, for example, wishes to be a parent, the very design of his body tells him he is destined to be a father not a mother. He can beget a child, but he can never bear it in the womb or nurse it at the breast. For a man to aspire to be a mother is utterly unrealistic because such a parental destiny is obviously contrary to his design. Experience tells us that what is true of our physical dimension (our "without") is probably also true of our spiritual dimension (our "within").

When we reflect on the design of our spiritual dimension, we realize that we are self-transcending beings who can think with mathematical infinity about surpassing any limits by which we presently find ourselves bound. If transcending some limit is essentially compatible with our design (would not violate our nature), and would be creatively beneficial for ourselves and others (is in harmony with our design's creative intent), it is reasonable to assume that we should aspire to do so. This assumption underlies the progress achieved by humans throughout history.

All the limits we have successfully transcended in history were transcended during the physical span of our existence. Death, however, is the limit which must be transcended at the conclusion of our physical sojourn. There is no convincing evidence that the power to transcend limits, which we have enjoyed during life, will abandon us at death. The total range of our experience suggests otherwise.

If we look carefully into the implications of our spiritual design, we can discern a number of indications that ours is probably a death-transcending destiny. To begin with, we can think about infinity, eternity, and immortality. The fact that we (who are recycled stardust) have been programmed to think such astonishing thoughts implies that they are probably elements in our destiny. Furthermore, we can think about everlasting permanence and aspire to such a permanent destiny beyond death even though nothing in our universe is everlastingly permanent.

The extraordinariness of our spiritual design suggests to us, therefore, that human spirit has been programmed to lock into permanence when it emerges from evolutionary potentiality.

Accordingly, our intuitive knowledge of our design suggests to us that our self-transcending consciousness should go on increasing in knowledge and joy forever, and our "story" should never come to an end. So likely is this implication of our design that many humans have preferred to believe that they might be tormented forever after death rather than accept that their consciousness will be permanently extinguished.

We are the only species that buries its dead because the very structure of our self-transcending consciousness implies that we were designed to transcend death. Ancient belief in the "immortal gods" was a projection of our unconscious awareness of the death-transcending destiny implicit in our design.

Moreover, experience tells us that God would be sadistic if God gave us the power to yearn for unending life only to frustrate and deny us by consigning us to permanent nonbeing in some form. Such a purpose on God's part would allow injustice and tragedy to finally prevail over history's countless victims and would render life absurd. Our God-given power of reason tells us that it is hideously wrong to treat others sadistically. Reason also tells us, therefore, that God would never treat us in such a way.

The promise of a merely "objective" immortality in God's eternal memory of our temporary existence does not truly satisfy the requirements of our self-transcending design. Nor would such a sop allay the sense of cruel betrayal we would justifiably experience if it were somehow to become evident to us that God intends to withhold the ultimate fulfillment which God has given us the ability (therefore, encouragement) to yearn for (and which God certainly has the power to grant).

The chief objection raised against the possibility of subjective immortality is that no mental activity is possible without a material body as the source of the electrical impulses required for consciousness. Since it is evident that our physical bodies undergo dissolution at death, this objection concludes that our spiritual consciousness, lacking a material instrument, must then be extinguished. But we have seen in the answers to the two preceding questions that there are good reasons for concluding otherwise.

15. How should Christians answer the claim that the appearances of the Risen Jesus reported by Paul and the other apostles were nothing more than hallucinations?

Hallucinations are the subjective perceiving of sensory phenomena which are not objectively present even though they are judged by the perceiver to be so. These purely subjective experiences can be caused by (1) psychotic states marked by hallucinations, (2) mind-altering drugs, (3) extreme sensory deprivation, or (4) pathological longing for someone deceased or physically distant from the hallucinator.

It should be admitted without hesitation that hallucinations and the appearances of the Risen Jesus have something in common. They both involve the unconscious projection of an image which originates in the memory of the experiencer. However, we saw above that the appearances of the Risen Jesus were triggered paranormally by the nonsubjective or extramental communication of his personal presence.

The resulting "appearances" of the Risen Jesus were simultaneously accompanied by a communication of God's Spirit (the divine Self-communication as Love, Peace, and Joy) which assured the apostles that the "appearing" One was a conclusive revelatory sign from God. Hallucinations, on the other hand, are induced by pathology, drugs, or sensory deprivation.

Among the causes of hallucinations, pathological longing for someone deceased seems to be the only one possibly applicable to the apostles' claims to have seen the Risen Jesus. But while it is certain that Jesus' disciples would have grieved over his death, it does not seem likely that large numbers of them would have been susceptible to pathological longing for his continued presence. Most, if not all, of them had families and friends who would have compensated for Jesus' absence.

Far more significantly, however, the appearance reported by Paul is indirect evidence that the appearances were probably not hallucinations. Everything indicates that Paul had never known the earthly Jesus. Paul was not, therefore, grieving or yearning pathologically for Jesus' continued presence. On the contrary, Paul had to make a number of painful reversals of religious, professional, and social commitment because of his unexpected encounter with the Risen Jesus.

But in the last analysis, it is not because of any compelling philosophical or historical arguments that Christians believe the Risen Jesus truly appeared to the apostles and began mediating the "foretaste" of God's Spirit. We believe the apostolic witnessing to the

Spirit-mediating appearances of the Risen Jesus because we also experience the confirming foretaste of God's Spirit being communicated to us when we hear this Good News effectively proclaimed or read it with faith and reverence.

16. Did God truly require Jesus to suffer and die as vicarious atonement for the sins of all humans before it was possible for humans to receive God's forgiveness and Eternal Life?

The New Testament states or implies in a number of places that Jesus understood his death as substitutional payment for the sins of all other humans (Rom 4:25; 5:19; 1 Cor 6:20; Mk 10:45; 14:24; Jn 1:29; Heb 9:11–12, 15, 24–26). Nevertheless, there are good reasons for concluding that this view of Jesus' death was foreign to the thinking of Jesus himself. Instead, it represents an interpretation of Jesus' tragic death that was created by the early church (A.D. 30-70) for *apologetic* reasons. (Apologetics is teaching designed to defend religious beliefs from attack.)

It is difficult for Christians living at our time in history to appreciate the enormous apologetic task which faced the early church two thousand years ago. As members of a predominantly Christian culture, we have become accustomed to the idea that God's Messiah was a politically insignificant human being with no military or political power whatsoever. More importantly, we are no longer troubled by the fact that Jesus was rejected by the majority of the Jews and suffered a shameful death at the hands of the Romans. It is difficult for us to appreciate that the first Christians were forced to view this matter far differently.

To the apostolic church, it was painfully clear that Jesus was a shockingly unexpected kind of Messiah. He was not the regal and invincible military conqueror of traditional Jewish expectations. The Jewish majority vigorously reminded the Jewish Christian minority that the ignominious fate of Jesus was utterly contrary to the Messianic ideal which Jews had been taught by their prophets and scribes.

The Jewish Christians had to defend their faith claims about the "spiritual" messiahship of Jesus by creating an apologetic interpretation of his tragic history which was reconcilable with the Jewish Scriptures. To accomplish this task, they searched the Scriptures for midrashic texts which seemed to indicate that God's

Messiah was mysteriously destined to suffer and be rejected. Accordingly, whenever a suffering righteous man was found in the Scriptures, his tragic lot, if in any way similar, was seen as foreshadowing that of Jesus.

Teachers in the apostolic church soon discovered the idea of vicarious (substitutional) atonement in the fourth of the four "suffering servant poems" in the Book of Isaiah (53:13–53:12). This poem describes the rejection and sufferings of a mysterious figure referred to as God's righteous servant (Is 53:11). The sufferings of God's servant are explicitly interpreted in the fourth poem as substitutional atonement for the sins of Israel (53:1–12). The servant's faithful endurance is also seen as instrumental in bringing salvation to the nations (49:5–6).

Scholars disagree about the identity of the servant who suffers in Isaiah 52:13–53:12. Some think the servant is an individual; others think the servant is Israel or an idealized group within Israel. The author of this book is convinced by the view that the "servant" is probably a metaphor for a "group" of devout Israelites among the exiles in Babylon. (A Babylonian context is inferred because the prophet who is encouraging this group has learned that Cyrus the Persian is marching to take Babylon and concludes that God will use Cyrus to free the Israelites from captivity; see Is 45:1–4; 44:27. Regardless of the servant's identity, contemporary scholarship agrees that Second Isaiah was not providing previews of Jesus' tragic fate five hundred years later.)

The group designated as God's "servant" is struggling against harsh opposition to fulfill faithfully the requirements of God's law (Is 53:11) and is encouraging other Israelites to do the same (Is 49:5). The servant's mission to Israel continues (Is 53:10–12) even after a member of the group (possibly its leader) has suffered death (Is 53:9) at the hands of either angry Babylonian officials or hostile Jews (probably the former). Such an ongoing mission indicates that God's "servant" is not an individual but a group. This group is presented in the servant poems as the "ideal" Israel. Second Isaiah certainly admired and probably belonged to this group.

Their experience of harsh opposition (Is 50:6; 53:7–8), however, has discouraged this devout group and has led some of them to fear that God does not favor their mission (Is 53:2–3). They are nevertheless assured by Second Isaiah that their sufferings are not a sign of divine disfavor. Rather, God is allowing them to atone substitutionally for the sins of their nation (Is 53:4–12). And if they persevere in their courageous efforts to be faithful to God's law, they will be instrumental in Israel's restoration (Is 49:5; 53:11) and the eventual conversion of the nations (Is 42:4; 49:6) to the worship of the one true God (Is 44:6; 45:5–6).

Jewish Christian teachers in the early church eagerly appropriated Isaiah's suffering "servant" figure and the idea of "vicarious atonement" to defend their faith in a suffering and rejected Messiah. These teachers believed that Jesus' tragic fate was foreshadowed in the sufferings of God's servant and was part of God's secret Messianic purpose. Consequently, they wove allusions to the servant and his substitutional sufferings into their apologetic interpretation of Jesus' rejection and death.

The authentic parables and sayings of Jesus, however, contain no suggestion that Jesus thought he had to suffer vicariously for the sins of the Jews and all others before God would forgive them. Instead, Jesus assured those who believed in his Kingdom message (Mk 2:5–7), even notorious sinners (Lk 7:47–49; 19:1–10), that their sins were forgiven from the moment they responded with faith and conversion. Jesus did not tell sinners, "Your sins will be forgiven after I die and satisfy the demands of God's justice." Rather, he assured them in the present tense, "Your sins are forgiven" (because God is graciously loving and merciful toward all, even disgraced prodigals; Luke 15:11–32).

Traditional exegetes may object that there are several gospel sayings of Jesus in which Jesus speaks as though he knows that he, like Isaiah's suffering servant, must vicariously atone for the sins of others. The sayings which are usually adduced are Mark 10:45 ("The Son of Man also came not to be served but to serve, and to give his life as a ransom for many.") and Mark 14:24 ("This is my blood of the covenant, which is poured out for many").

Less conservative exegetes respond, however, that both of these sayings have probably been expanded theologically to provide an apologetic rationale for the hideous and disgraceful death suffered by Jesus. These exegetes defend their view by reminding us that there are earlier forms of the sayings in Mark 10:45 and Mark 14:24 in which the language suggesting that Jesus must pay for our sins (Mark's "ransom" theology) is absent.

Luke 22:26 is clearly an earlier form of Mark 10:45. We know it is earlier because Jesus refers to himself without using the title Son of Man ("I am in the midst of you as one who serves"), and because Mark's ransom theology has not been added to the saying. We may be confident that the early church did not shorten but, rather, expanded Jesus' sayings over the decades.

In addition, about fifteen years before Mark wrote his Gospel, Paul the apostle (in 1 Cor 11:25) also quoted Jesus' cup-saying at the Last Supper ("This cup is the new covenant in my blood"). There is, however, no reference to Mark's vicarious atonement theology in Paul's much earlier version of the saying. This indicates that the words in Mark's version which regard Jesus' death as atonement for others were probably added to an earlier form of the saying for apologetic reasons.

Moreover, the traditional vicarious atonement interpretation of Jesus' death presupposes that God would not have loved and forgiven humankind until Jesus satisfied God's offended justice by paying for our sins. However, if God had sent Jesus to atone substitutionally for our sins, that would mean that it was love for us that moved God to send Jesus to suffer and die for us. But that would further imply that God already loved us before God sent Jesus to die for us, which logically cancels the necessity of sending Jesus to die for us so that we could be forgiven and loved.

These (and other) observations lead contemporary Christian theologians and exegetes to the conclusion that God did not require the sufferings and death of Jesus as payment for our sins. That way of explaining Jesus' death was a later and secondary (nonessential) interpretation of his tragic history which met an urgent (but historically limited) apologetic need of the apostolic church.

Does this conclusion mean that it was not necessary for Jesus to die in order to assure us of salvation? Our answer must be a dialectical one which includes both "no" and "yes." God did not require Jesus to accept tragic and unjust death as substitutional payment for our sins. But God did encourage Jesus to accept his tragic and unjust death with a "yes" of faith and trust so that God could bring "Resurrection" out of that death. The appearances of the Risen Jesus to his disciples were intended by God as revelatory signs to Israel and the whole world that all who have faith and trust in God's creative goodness, as Jesus did, can defeat tragedy and death along with Jesus.

Jesus' acceptance of his death with faith and trust in God's creative wisdom and goodness was an essential part of God's saving purpose for the world. In that sense, therefore, Jesus' death was necessary and full of "saving power":

> Death is swallowed up in victory. O death, where is your victory? O death, where is your sting? But thanks be to God, who gives us the victory through our Lord Jesus Christ. (1 Cor 15:54–55, 57)

17. Will Jesus literally come on the clouds of heaven at the end of history to judge the living and the dead?

In the view of contemporary Christian scholarship, the eschatological symbolism in the New Testament which speaks of the second coming of Jesus as final Judge should be taken very seriously but not literally. Second-coming symbolism correctly intends to remind us that all of our lives (and all of human history) are moving inexorably toward a solemn conclusion.

This conclusion will necessarily include a mysterious Ultimate Justice which will right all wrongs and finally correct all the injustice committed throughout history. The symbols of Christian eschatology are also meant to assure us that Ultimate Fulfillment is truly attainable by all who open themselves to that promised gift with faith and trust in God.

But the state of Final Justice and Fulfillment which this symbolism intends to assure us of can be achieved without requiring Jesus to literally return with an army of angels at the end of history. When the last human to complete the maturation process and evolve through death into Eternal Life has done so, that person will be with Jesus and all other humans who have reached that sublime goal. The final state of fulfillment for humans promised by eschatological symbolism will then have been achieved. And it is the attainability of this Ultimate Justice and Final Joy beyond the terror of history which is essentially being promised by the second-coming symbolism in the New Testament.

These insights lead us to conclude that when the very last human to reach Eternal Life at the end of history does so, and is gathered into God's love along with Jesus and all of God's saints, the essential equivalent of what eschatological symbolism has taught us to expect at the second coming will have been achieved. In effect, the second coming of Jesus to gather all of God's faith-filled children into Eternal Life will then have taken place.

Therefore, when contemporary Christians anticipate the second coming of Jesus at his Supper, we are not anticipating his literal return on the clouds of heaven. Instead, we are reminded by such eschatological symbolism that all of our lives are subject to God's Ultimate Justice, and that we can attain Ultimate Fulfillment along with the Risen Jesus if we guide our lives by truth, justice, and love which serves (see Mt 25:31–46).

18. Since the apostles believed and taught that the world would end in their lifetime, does the world's continuing existence indicate that the eschatological teaching in the New Testament is mistaken?

The eschatological teaching in the New Testament which warns that the world will end in the lifetime of the apostles (Mk 1:14–15; 9:1: Mt 10:23; 1 Thess 4:15–17; 1 Cor 15:51–52) is not essentially mistaken. On the contrary, this teaching remains permanently true in a profoundly meaningful way for the entire Christian faith community. The sense in which this teaching is true, however, presupposes a willingness to understand its language in a nonliteral way. It is obvious that the entire world did not end in the lifetime of the apostles. And yet, the *individual* world of every person who heard the apostolic message did come to an end.

Jesus and his apostles were evidently inspired by God to accept the eschatological hope expressed in the Book of Daniel and the preaching of John the Baptizer. God encouraged them to proclaim a message of eschatological hope and warning to the world even though God knew that their understanding of the "timing" involved would suffer from their historically limited assumptions. Jesus himself refused to predict the time of the end (Mk 13:32). Yet one gets the impression that he believed the Kingdom would arrive in the lifetime of his contemporaries (Mk 1:14).

The apostles understood that the essential substance of Jesus' end-time teaching was confirmed when God "raised" Jesus from the dead and empowered him to begin mediating the foretaste of God's Spirit. When the Risen Jesus began appearing to his apostles, they concluded that the world was already beginning to end because the resurrection of the dead had already begun with Jesus' appearances.

Accordingly, they thought the Risen Jesus would quickly return in glory to conclude history and gather the righteous into God's Kingdom. They mistakenly announced, therefore, that the whole world would literally end in their lifetime.

However, despite their mistaken assumptions about the time when the whole world will end, the end-time teaching of Jesus and his apostles remains an essential and profoundly true part of God's saving purpose in history. For God knew that when Jesus did not return in the lifetime of the apostles, the church would have to reconsider the apostolic announcement of the world's impending end. She would then be forced to realize (with the help of Ps 90:4) that eschatological language should be construed in a nonliteral manner:

> **Ps 90:4**
>
> For a thousand years in your sight are but as yesterday when it is past, or as a watch in the night.
>
> **2 Pet 3:3–5**
>
> First of all you must understand this, that scoffers will come in the last days with scoffing, following their own passions and saying, "Where is the promise of his coming? For ever since the fathers fell asleep, all things have continued as they were from the beginning of creation."
>
> **2 Pet 3:8–9**
>
> But do not ignore this one fact, beloved, that with the Lord one day is as a thousand years, and a thousand years as one day. The Lord is not slow about his promise as some count slowness, but is forbearing toward you, not wishing that any should perish, but that all should reach repentance.
>
> But the day of the Lord will come like a thief, and then the heavens will pass away with a loud noise, and the elements will be dissolved with fire, and the earth and the works that are upon it will be burned up.

The nonliteral mode of understanding eschatological symbolism remains valid for every generation of faithful Christians till the end of time. For while it is true that the entire world did not end in the lifetime of the apostles, we noted above that the individual world of every person in the apostolic age did come to an end. Likewise, the individual world of every member of the present age is rapidly moving toward its conclusion, irrespective of whether we will still be alive when the whole world ends. God's word, therefore, contains a divinely intended warning that our allotted time in this world is short and that, all too soon, we will have to give an account of our stewardship.

Accordingly, the Kingdom of God and the Final Judgment which precedes it are always drawing near. Each successive generation must prepare to submit to God's Final Judgment in order to enter God's always-approaching Kingdom. For this reason the Christian tradition teaches that there is a "particular judgment" which precedes the General Judgment. And we have already seen, in the answer to the preceding question, that the General Judgment is a powerful eschatological symbol for the unfailing triumph of God's Justice and Goodness at the end of human history:

> Then I saw thrones, and seated on them were those to whom judgment had been committed. Also I saw the souls of those who had been beheaded for their testimony to Jesus and for the word of God. . . . They came to life and reigned with Christ a thousand years. . . . This is the first resurrection. Blessed and holy is he who shares in the first resurrection! Over such the second death has no power. (Rev 20:4–6)

19. Traditional Christian theology has taught that the earthly Jesus knew everything that God knows. But this book has implied in a number of places that he did not. How should we understand the difference?

Traditional Christian theology sincerely assumed that Jesus knew everything that God knows for several "precritical" reasons. (1) The fourth Gospel says that the word of God became incarnate in Jesus (Jn 1:1–5,14), and in that Gospel the divine "Word" is a sacred symbol for God's Knowledge and Wisdom. Early Christian theology (A.D. 100-600) decided, therefore, that because the divine Word had joined itself to Jesus, Jesus, while on earth, must have had privileged access to God's knowledge. (2) Furthermore, Jesus is presented in the Gospels as possessing foreknowledge of future events (Jerusalem's destruction, Judas' betrayal, Peter's denial, and his own death and resurrection); accordingly, it was assumed that he must have been privy to God's knowledge of the future.

Contemporary Christian theology, however, makes a clear distinction between the human knowledge of Jesus and the divine Word (God revealing) present in him. Jesus enjoyed extraordinary experience of God and the God-human relationship, but his knowledge about everything else was ordinary. (For example, Jesus, like everyone else in his society, probably assumed that epilepsy was caused by evil spirits; Mk 9:14–27.) When the reality of "God's Word" (God's revelatory presence) united with the "flesh" (the human nature) of Jesus, the nature and knowledge of God remained distinct from the reality of Jesus' finite and created human nature. United does not mean identical.

Moreover, many contemporary theologians would agree with the process philosophers that God's foreknowledge of free human actions is relative not absolute. This view asserts that God has a highly probable statistical foreknowledge of our free future actions, but not absolute foreknowledge. If God possessed absolute foreknowledge of our future actions, then our actions would be absolutely predetermined and we would not truly be free. (Traditional theologians, of course, would not agree with the process philosophers and theologians about this matter.)

Also, when we reflect on Jesus' foreknowledge of the future, we should do so with the help of *Ockham's razor* (the law of parsimony = we should always prefer a simpler to a more complicated hypothesis). Ockham's razor enables us to shave away the precritical assumptions present in past interpretations of Jesus' predictions. If we do not assume that Jesus knew everything that God knows because of the presence of God's Word in him, we are free to look for a simpler, more economical explanation of his predictions:

1. Jesus could see that the political fanatics in his society were determined to instigate a revolt against Rome. He also realized that the might of Rome would crush such a revolt and destroy Jerusalem in the process. Jeremiah the prophet had earlier been able to foresee the similar consequences of Judah's revolt against

Babylonia. We should remind ourselves that Jesus was probably not the only one who could foresee the likelihood of coming disaster.

2. Jesus was probably forewarned by some sympathetic person who had learned that one of the Twelve planned to betray him. This person might have been the "beloved disciple" mentioned in the fourth Gospel. This disciple was possibly related to the high priest, for he was able to take Peter with him into the secured courtyard of the high priest's residence (Jn 18:15–16). We need not conclude that Jesus learned about his betrayal directly from God, even though the folk mentality and conservative tradition still encourage us to do so.

3. Peter's denial was something Jesus could foresee as probable because of his knowledge of Peter's personality. Jesus realized that when his enemies actually came to seize him in the garden after the Last Supper, Peter would probably be just as frightened and confused as the other disciples and would flee to avoid capture and possible death. Additional details learned "after the fact" (*vaticinia post eventum*) were joined to Jesus' original prediction by the early church (Peter's "three denials" before a cock's crow reminded Peter of Jesus' prediction).

4. Jesus' predictions of his death and resurrection will be explained in the answer to the following question.

20. Did Jesus literally speak the three predictions of his death and resurrection which we find in Mark 8:31, 9:31, 10:33–34?

Jesus probably did predict his death and his resurrection. But it is very likely that he predicted each of these events in separate sayings, not in one saying. The three predictions we find in Mark are later folk combinations and expansions of Jesus' original predictions. It was probably Mark who decided to combine the originally separate sayings and who expanded and multiplied the combined form of the sayings in order to teach his Messianic Secret theology.

We find in Luke 13:31–33 the substance of a genuine prediction made by Jesus about his coming death. We know that the underlying substance of this saying is probably authentic because it speaks of death instead of resurrection as something which Jesus expected in three figurative days. Because the empty tomb was discovered on the "third day" (and because Hos 6:2 seemed to foreshadow Jesus' resurrection on that day), the early Greek-speaking church soon decided that Jesus' remembered reference to three days (which implied a "third day") should be understood as predicting his resurrection. (Note that the creed Paul quoted in Cor 15:3–5 contains a midrashic reference to the "third day" in Hos 6:2):

Lk 13:31–33

> At that very hour some Pharisees came, and said to him, "Get away from here, for Herod wants to kill you." And he said to them, "Go and tell that fox, 'Behold, I cast out demons and perform cures today and tomorrow, and the third day I finish my course. Nevertheless I must go on my way today and tomorrow and the day following, for it cannot be that a prophet should perish away from Jerusalem.'"

Hos 6:2

> After two days he will revive us; on the third day he will raise us up that we may live before him.

1 Cor 15:4

> He was raised on the third day in accordance with the Scriptures.

In the authentic substance of Jesus' saying (which Luke has theologically modified), Jesus probably employed two Aramaic idioms. The first speaks of a dangerous or ambiguous event in the not too distant future as coming in three figurative days (see Gen 22:4; Ex 19:11; Hos 6:2). This traditional Aramaic (and Hebrew) idiom was probably derived from observing the three days of darkness which conclude each lunar cycle. (The ancients watched the sky at night, not television.)

The second idiom ("to go on one's way") is an Aramaic euphemism for death. Jesus probably anticipated that when he went to Jerusalem to deliver the challenge of his prophetic message and to rebuke the chief priests for the unfair trafficking they allowed in the temple precincts, his action would very likely lead to his rejection and death. (The fate of his predecessor, John the Baptizer, would not have been far from his thoughts.)

Jesus is also remembered in Mark 14:25 as having predicted his resurrection at the Last Supper:

> Truly, I say to you, I shall not drink again of the fruit of the vine until that day when I drink it new in the kingdom of God. (Mk 14:24–25)

When Jesus came to the Last Supper, he was troubled because he had been warned that one of the Twelve had agreed to betray him. Jesus probably anticipated, therefore, that events which would lead to his death had been set in motion, and he would never again break bread or drink wine with his disciples on earth. However, because of his habitual experience of God's Presence and Love, Jesus was confident that he would soon be raised at the General Resurrection when the Kingdom of God arrived. He assured his disciples that he would then be with them again and would drink wine with them at the Great Supper in the New Creation.

We know that Jesus' prediction of his resurrection in Mark 14:25 is probably authentic because it indicates that Jesus expected to be raised at the General Resurrection when the Kingdom of God arrived as a collective phenomenon. This means that Jesus did not anticipate that he would be raised individually by God before the world ended. In reality, Jesus saw the Twelve again not at the General Resurrection but when he appeared to them in Galilee (Mk 16:7; Mt 28:16; Jn 21:1), probably while they were at table (Lk 24:41–42; Acts 10:40; Jn 21:12 –13; Ps Mk 16:14). If the early church had created Mark 14:25 for theological reasons, it would not contain this discrepancy.

It seems likely that Mark is the one who took Jesus' separate predictions of death and resurrection and joined them into one saying. When Mark combined the predictions for use in his Messianic Secret theology, he then added the "Son of Man" title and one additional prediction. At this stage, the saying became Mark 9:31. (Mk 9:31 is the least embellished of the three Markan predictions; it adds only the prediction of betrayal to Jesus' original predictions of death and resurrection):

> "The Son of man will be delivered into the hands of men, and they will kill him; and when he is killed, after three days he will rise." (Mk 9:31)

Mark produced two additional versions of this saying by adding more details from the passion of Jesus (which Mark assumed Jesus had foreseen):

> And he began to teach them that the Son of Man must suffer many things, and be rejected by the elders and the chief priests and the scribes, and be killed, and after three days rise again. (Mk 8:31)

The most embellished form of the combined saying was placed on Jesus' lips in Mark 10:33–34, just before Jesus arrived at Jerusalem to fulfill his secret destiny. This form of the saying amounts to a brief summary of the Passion which (Mark believed) Jesus knew would precede his resurrection as the exalted "Son of Man":

> "Behold we are going up to Jerusalem; and the Son of man will be delivered to the chief priests and the scribes, and they will condemn him to death, and deliver him to the Gentiles; and they will mock him, and spit upon him, and scourge him, and kill him; and after three days he will rise." (Mk 10:33–34)

The Markan version of Jesus' predictions of death and resurrection still understood that Jesus had actually anticipated "death" on the third of three figurative days. For that reason Mark always has Jesus say that the Son of Man will rise "after" three days. But Matthew and Luke later changed Mark's "after" three days to "on" the third day (Mt 16:21; 17:22–23; 20:18–19; Lk 9:22; 18:31–33). It is evident that by the time they wrote their Gospels the original meaning of Jesus' idiomatic reference to death in three figurative days had become blurred. Matthew and Luke understood the three days of Jesus' metaphor literally and related them to Jesus' resurrection "on the third day."

Questions for Review and Discussion

1. If the explanations of the Bible given in this book are basically correct, does that mean the church has been reading the Bible incorrectly for centuries?

2. Why do Christians continue to read the ancient Jewish Scriptures?

3. Does the contemporary interpretation of the Gospels presented in this book deny genuine Christian faith in Jesus?

4. Do contemporary biblical scholars believe that God was truly present and acting during the Exodus event, and that God miraculously caused all the wonders recounted in the Book of Exodus?

5. Did not Ezekiel 37:1–14 and Isaiah 26:19 teach about the resurrection of the dead well before Daniel 12:2–3?

6. Do contemporary biblical scholars believe that Jesus truly expelled demons from people?

7. Did Jesus truly heal people of their physical infirmities?

8. Were the ruler's daughter (Mk 5:36–43), the widow's son (Lk 7:11–17), and Lazarus (Jn 11:1–44) truly dead when Jesus raised them?

9. Did Jesus truly appear to his apostles as Risen Lord after his tragic death?

10. Was Jesus the first human to enter Eternal Life?

11. If God never dictates words to anyone, how did the Risen Jesus learn that he had been chosen to be God's Secret Messiah?

12. Since the electrical impulses required for consciousness

are derived from the material body, how do Christians answer the objection that there can be no consciousness after the dissolution of the body at death?

13. Does belief in Eternal Life and unending consciousness after death contradict the law of entropy, which says that all things in the universe will eventually run out of the undissipated energy necessary for work (or continued activity)?

14. Why is it reasonable to hope for immortality beyond the dissolution of our physical bodies?

15. How should Christians answer the claim that the appearances of the Risen Jesus reported by Paul and the other apostles were nothing more than hallucinations?

16. Did God truly require Jesus to suffer and die as vicarious atonement for the sins of all humans before it was possible for humans to receive God's forgiveness and Eternal Life?

17. Will Jesus literally come on the clouds of heaven at the end of history to judge the living and the dead?

18. Since the apostles believed and taught that the world would end in their lifetime, does the world's continuing existence indicate that the eschatological teaching in the New Testament is mistaken?